VEGAS P.I.

VEGAS P.I.

Lake Headley
WITH
William Hoffman

THUNDER'S MOUTH PRESS
NEW YORK

Published by
Thunder's Mouth Press
632 Broadway, 7th Floor
New York, NY 10012

Library of Congress Cataloging-in-Publication Data
Headley, Lake.
    Vegas P.I. / Lake Headley, with Bill Hoffman. — 1st ed.
    p. cm.
    ISBN 1-56025-057-7 : $22.95
    1. Headley, Lake. 2. Private investigators—United
States—Biography. I. Hoffman, Bill. II. Title.
HV8083.H43A3   1993
363.2′89′092—dc20
    [B]   92-45664
                                                               CIP

Portions of chapters 10, 14, and 15 condensed from *Loud and Clear,*
© 1990 by Lake Headley and William Hoffman; Henry Holt and
Company, Inc. and *The Court-Martial of Clayton Lonetree,* © 1989
by Lake Headley and William Hoffman; Henry Holt and Company,
Inc. Reprinted with permission.

Distributed by Publishers Group West
4065 Hollis Street
Emeryville, CA 94608
(800) 788-3123

To Bill Hoffman. I want it that way and so would my father. Without Bill's talent and persistence none of Dad's stories would have been written.

—L.H. III

To my good friend Eric Protter who introduced me to Lake and never stopped urging us to write this book.

—W.H.

TABLE OF CONTENTS

FOREWORD

This book is about the life and times of my best friend. From infancy our lives were inextricably entwined as we each moved about the country from our beginnings in a small rural community in northern Indiana.

The chronicles of Lake Headley, I hope, will allow the reader to capture the essence of a man who devoted a life to righting wrongs—injustices heaped upon those who were not in a position to defend themselves.

Lake has been described as "the best p.i. in the world." Maybe so, but he was a lot more than that. He didn't stop at investigation. If a cause grew weak, he often assumed the burden of the cause itself.

Lake was a selfless person who showed no fear of physical harm; nor did he cower before political persecution. Somehow he was impervious to such human frailties, though he was not without transgression (some we enjoyed together).

When advised by a series of doctors that the end was near because he was afflicted, probably, with the disease that took the life of Lou Gehrig, Lake thought that it was unlikely because he was such a terrible schoolboy baseball player; and that he was.

Lake was both a radically free man and yet responsible. He was a rebel with a cause—always someone else's cause. To so live was costly and not very rewarding financially.

Anyone who could come to the active defense of the oppressed Native Americans at Wounded Knee and then the Symbionese Liberation Army when neither cause was then acceptable to society cannot be viewed as a shrinking violet. Yet Lake was kind and courteous when the world allowed him to act that way.

I speak as the only person who has known Lake from mutual infancy when we fought over teething rings. We grew up together and continued on a crossing for sixty years. Over the years nothing changed about his character and integrity. He started absolutely straight and unswervingly committed, many times at his personal peril, and remained unbendingly true to his causes.

He was the only person I have ever known or am likely to know who was absolutely reliable. In his mind he came last. I would like this book to tell the world that today he comes first.

George P. Vlassis

ACKNOWLEDGMENTS

Special thanks are extended to Nick and Becky Behnen, two of my father's closest friends. They were always there when he needed anything. Nick's daily visits during my dad's fatal illness were appreciated more than Nick can ever know.

Thanks to Anthony, Rod, Tammy, Matthew, and Mark, who gave Dad and me the strength to hang in there; Terri Lee Headley; Victoria Cerenich; Margie Sterling; Elaine Levi; and J.R. Davis.

My father's dear friends Mike and Sandy Stuhff also visited almost daily—Dad always loved to work cases with Mike. Thanks also to George Vlassis, my father's oldest friend, and his wife Nancy; Bill and Paulette Rittenberg; Jon and Glynna Robinson; Gilbert and Kathy Sims; and Michael Deppman.

There are other people who touched his life deeply: Sheriff Ralph Lamb; Judge Harry Claiborne; Billy Dean Smith; Jeanne Davis; Benny Binion; Donald Freed; Jerry Kelly; William Kunstler; Ben Barrington; Max Dunlap; and Jim Robison.

I know Dad loved Bill Helmer at *Playboy* magazine, and others at that publication who trusted his ability to do jobs no one else could, or had the guts to do. Also thanks to the many members of NORML and the ACLU.

Thanks to Judy Hoffman, Bill's alter ego, who spent many years with my father—in person, on the phone, sifting through mountains of paper—to make Dad's investigations into real stories.

Tony the Greek, thanks for the biggest story my father ever had the chance to do.

Last, but not least, to Uncle Carter, Carter Camp, and his brothers Buck and Craig, and all the brave members of AIM who taught us that to fight and be willing to die for what we believe in is the only way to live.

                —L.H. III

I want to thank my friends Jerry Shields, Charles Ced, and Andy Stapp—maybe the best thing I did for them was to introduce them to Lake. Also, my children, William III, Joe, Terri, and John, were affected by getting to know our friend, and they contributed many memories to this story.

Lea, Ethan, and Micah Lewis, as always, deserve thanks. So do John and Anita Reeves, Jim Gosdin, Bill Stack, Julio Escalante, Lisa Schaffer, my grandchildren, Kasha and James Patrick, Birdie Segrest, and Rudy and Betty Ced.

Two different and very reliable sources have called our publisher, Neil Ortenberg, a "national treasure," and I concur.

Most of the people acknowledged by Lake III would have been on this list had he not named them first. I think, however, that it wouldn't hurt to mention attorney Mike Stuhff a second time. Mike embodies many of the qualities that made Lake unforgettable.

Finally, thanks to Marion Cole and attorney David Lubell. Marion delivered some of the best news Lake or I ever received, and Lubell stood tall for us when we needed a friend.

                —W.H.

INTRODUCTION

I met Lake in 1979 in San Diego where I lived at the time. He was working on the Don Bolles murder case and stopped by, at the suggestion of editor Eric Protter, to discuss our collaborating on his autobiography. Indeed, we began work almost immediately, and some of the early chapters of *Vegas P.I.* were written back then.

However, soon thereafter Lake and his future wife, Terri Lee, got burned horribly in an arson fire, likely set by the same forces that murdered Bolles and wanted to stop Lake's investigation. What they succeeded in doing was stopping the book—for a while.

Off and on through the 1980s we'd start up again, but something always intervened: usually someone in deep trouble whom Lake had to "rescue." He almost always succeeded.

We did manage to write three books together: *Loud and Clear,* about the Bolles murder (the *New York Times* called it "a primer on how to conduct a murder investigation"); *The Court-Martial of Clayton Lonetree,* a book Lake hoped would free the wrongly convicted Native American; and *Contract Killer,* about the notorious underworld murderer Donald "Tony the Greek" Frankos.

The book he really wanted published was this one. He was the least vain person I ever met, yet like most of us he wanted his story told. "For my kids," he said. He meant it, but I never saw the project that way. I saw it as a blueprint—if a person wants one—of how to live a worthwhile life.

"If he was so great, why wasn't he rich?" I've been asked by many. While I can dismiss these people as dense and wrong-headed, the question tells us something about how far too many of us think.

Lake possessed four qualities, in abundance, that made him what Vince Bugliosi said: "the greatest p.i. in the world." The qualities were honesty, bravery, persistence, and a bone-deep love of the underdog.

I never knew Lake to lie, even once. I know of no time he ever exhibited fear, though often his life was in danger. If he felt "the angels" were on his side, he never gave up. And the poorer the victim, the more hopeless the case, the more eager he was to help. He *could* have been rich—what wealthy defendant wouldn't have wanted Lake on his side?—but he knew the rich could take care of themselves.

Why was Lake what he was? I think the incident described in the first chapter affected him profoundly, and he never forgave himself. After he really got his ducks in a row—and I believe it happened at Wounded Knee—he was something to behold.

We worked on this book until the day he died. Three days after his death I received a letter from him, probably the last he ever wrote, telling me how much he looked forward to our getting together in a few weeks.

That was good.

What meant much more was the way he signed off. He told me he loved me.

William Hoffman

VEGAS P.I.

1

DEATH ON
BLUE DIAMOND ROAD

I opened the door and stepped out of the brutal, mind-searing, 110-degree Las Vegas heat into a cool, dim interior.

I coughed, and heard the irritated voice of my partner, Zeke Lenahan*—or Detective Cyril D. Lenahan, Narcotics Detail, Clark County Sheriff's Department, Las Vegas, Nevada.

"What are you doing here so early?" Lenahan asked. "We don't go on till eight tonight."

"Can't help it," I said. "The lieutenant called. He insists that we see him at four. It's about . . ."

It was about a junkie and robbery suspect named Lathrop, and I'd almost said something I shouldn't. "Anyway, you know Griffin. When he wants to see us, we gotta go."

Lieutenant Robert Rutter Griffin—he hated that middle name, which is why I often used it—was night commander of the sheriff's department. From 8:00 P.M. until the day shift came in, he ran the whole show.

Zeke Lenahan and I were one of several teams of detectives

---

*Where a name is followed by an asterisk, the name and other identifying details have been changed.

working directly under Griffin's supervision. Griffin's men were something of an elite, and although the lieutenant had a richly deserved reputation as a harsh taskmaster, every detective in the bureau wanted to be assigned to his shift. To work for Griffin meant handling all the important cases, especially homicides, which is what being a police officer is all about. Just as firemen would rather battle large, dangerous blazes than get assigned to hosing down off-duty equipment, so do police officers prefer robbery/homicide over writing parking tickets. Of course, there is the occasional exception, the individual who seeks out and clutches the easiest job and then goes to sleep for twenty years dreaming about a pension.

Anyway, Bob Griffin was justifiably proud of his long record of successful homicide investigations; we all were. Thus, when Griffin barked, which occurred frequently, everyone jumped, including Lake Headley and Zeke Lenahan—especially Headley and Lenahan.

Sheriff Ralph Lamb was proud of us too. He said so every time he suspended us for an infraction, which also was frequent. Our philosophy: "Get those assholes in jail and we'll worry about the other shit later."

This was 1961 and two police forces guarded Las Vegas: the Las Vegas Police Department and the Clark County Sheriff's Department. Each employed about 250 men and divided the county into two sections. Roughly, the LVPD was responsible for Greater Las Vegas and we, the sheriff's department, handled the Strip and the remainder of Clark County. Later these two forces merged into the Metropolitan Police Department under Sheriff Ralph Lamb, but in 1961 there existed considerable rivalry between us. It was this competition that promoted the gung ho attitude personified by Bob Griffin.

Zeke had been talking to Judy, a pretty, brown-eyed young hooker recruited by Zeke and me as an informant. She gave us information and we fixed it for her to turn tricks on the

Strip, unmolested by us or any other detectives in the sheriff's department. This allowed her to work freely on the Strip, which meant she made $900 to $1,500 a week, tax free. It wasn't bad money for a twenty-one-year-old prostitute from Anson, Texas, and as long as she stuck to turning tricks and didn't roll anyone, get in any beefs, or become involved with the FBI, we could keep her safe from the law—us. In exchange, she needed to keep a steady stream of valuable information flowing our way. If she got heat from one of the casinos, we visited the joint, talked to the boss, and cooled things off.

So far Judy had lived up to her end of the bargain, and then some. She ranked as a good, reliable informant, particularly in the area of narcotics, which was our specialty. Zeke and I were the narcotics detail. In fact, we were the *first* narcotics detail in the history of the sheriff's department. Previously, drug cases got handled as they arose, by whatever detectives happened to be available, and enforcement was spotty at best. In 1959 the entire Clark County Sheriff's Department made less than a dozen drug arrests. The next year, with eager beavers Headley and Lenahan comprising the narcotics detail (I was in charge), there were ninety-one arrests.

"Come on, Zeke," I pleaded. "Or Griffin will have his ass over the dashboard all night. You know how he hates to wait, and you know what being late for his workout at the gym does to his personality."

"Okay."

In the car, with the windows closed, air conditioner on high, I passed the time thinking about Judy and other informants. An informant must be close to people who break the law in order to obtain information important to the police, FBI, DEA, or whatever agency or combination of agencies the informant is working for. The reward for this sort of thing varies greatly from snitch to snitch and frequently from case to case, but the enticement for ratting usually fits into one of two categories: money and/or favors from the police. The first speaks for itself. So much good information brings so much money, and good information is information that results in arrests, convictions, and jail sentences. Long jail sentences.

The feds have the most money for informants. Local police go begging, but they do have a certain advantage in the ever-frantic scramble for informants, and that is the threat of arrest. Local police have greater latitude than the feds in their ability to arrest with little or no probable cause. The feds almost always need an arrest warrant, which is not the case with the locals.

Obtaining an arrest warrant involves the courts. A judge is needed to sign the warrant—after probable cause has been shown that a crime has been committed, usually a felony. The feds have to stay within this framework, whereas local police can arrest on "suspicion" or for "investigation." Police can and do regularly book "suspects" on the open charge of "investigation robbery." The person is often held up to seventy-two hours, then let go with an RNC—released no charge, in the vernacular of the squad room.

This forces the "suspect" to (1) endure the booking and release procedures, fingerprinting and photographing, and the generally demeaning experience of being shuttled in and out of jail; to say nothing of (2) the considerable irritation and expense of locating an attorney and a bail bondsman to begin turning the wheels of justice toward some kind of reasonable conclusion; plus (3) seventy-two hours in a filthy, miserable cell with helpless halfwits who are too confused or broke to do any of the preceding. It is all very uncomfortable.

This is what happened to Judy, and is almost invariably how it comes down. Zeke and I arrested her a few times and then informed her that if she cooperated the harassment would end. She was reminded that we had initiated the arrests and we could end them—if she furnished good information. "A detective is only as good as his informants" remains the truest adage in police work. Give me one knowledgeable snitch and you can keep the computers.

Accepting the offer we made to take the heat off transported Judy into a shadowy, ugly twilight. As her information produced increasing arrests, her associates would inevitably learn of her activity. Different results can spring from this revelation, including sudden and violent death. At the least, Judy could look forward to scorn and rejection not only from her friends, but from the police as well.

Judy traded in secrets, activities someone wanted hidden, but the irony was that the police almost all had something they were hiding: bribery, girlfriends their wives are unaware of, a drinking problem . . . something; they are hiding a gambling addiction, or bad credit, from their superior . . . something; they use drugs, or deal them . . . always there is something.

Everyone has a secret that can only surface if there is an informant. Police know this better than anyone, and they deeply resent the necessary contact they must maintain with snitches (a snitch might do *them* in) to function successfully. They do it, but they hate it, and they hide their hatred and playact what they want the snitch to believe is a warm, close relationship. That is why the ulcer is an occupational hazard of police work, as is the divorce.

Zeke was quiet on the first part of the ride downtown. He was always quiet, but more so today than usual.

Zeke was twenty-two to my thirty, a kid-brother type to me and the rest of the department. He stood my height, five foot eleven, and was clean-cut, blond-haired, and slender. The son of a lifetime policeman, he started to work at the sheriff's department before he was old enough to be a regular deputy. Zeke was handsome, young, brave—a good man, friend, and partner. Quiet, too, like I said.

"Lake," he said softly, "we're in a bad spot. We're gonna have to kill Lathrop." Zeke was serious as hell.

"We've been through that shit," I said, "ever since Judy turned snitch last month. I don't want to hear it any more."

"It bothers me. It bothers me a lot."

"But it don't change, partner. It don't change. The choice is Lathrop's, not ours. I promised you I'd give him a chance to surrender, and I'll sure do that no matter what the rest of those crazy bastards say. I'll be the one in the right spot to do that, and I will, but if he won't give up, all I can do is leave him lay."

"I know that," Zeke said. "And I believe you'll do what you say, like you always do, but it's *him,* don't you fucking see? Judy talked to Lathrop last night. She asked him what if he got caught."

"I can imagine what he said."

"He showed her an air-force survival gun. I guess that's what it was from the way she described it—wire stock, 410 over 22 Hornet, nasty motherfucker up close."

"And?"

"He said he didn't want to kill people. That he'd use the gun to blow off their feet. He's crazy, Lake, really crazy, and that's no bullshit. Judy says she knows for sure he fired into a house in North Vegas with a woman and kid inside just to scare the old man over a dope deal. And he shot that guy in that drug heist, sure as hell. You posing as a sucker, carrying all that bread, is fucking dangerous."

That was quite a speech coming from Zeke, and I knew he was right. Lathrop was a monster who, despite his disclaimer to Judy, enjoyed shooting people. Couple that with a $100-a-day morphine habit and it wasn't difficult to see the picture.

Still, I saw no way of turning back. I had agreed to pose as an executive returning home fat with the day's receipts from a prosperous insurance business. "Afraid of banks" was the information we'd channeled to Lathrop through Judy, and using her we were even able to orchestrate the moment when the robbery would take place. We'd had meetings with Sheriff Lamb and with two ranking LVPD officers. The plan was set and that was that. All the same, my feet ached and were cold.

"If it will make you feel better," I said, "tell Judy to set up a meet with Lathrop at her place and I'll have Griffin okay a bug installation. If she's cool, maybe we can get him on tape repeating what he said. I'll have that going for me if I have to waste him. The part about shooting off feet."

Although this room bug was legal (having Judy's permission would make it so), I had been responsible for many that were not. That is for sure. Once I wanted a room bug installed but the sheriff's department lacked the necessary sophisticated equipment. I went to a friend, a Las Vegas FBI agent named Bill, and he agreed—somewhat reluctantly—to help. At the time the FBI denied it even had the capability to bug, but Bill was a professional, albeit a cautious one: in short, he was more afraid of being caught than I was—it would cost him his job, while I'd merely receive an "infraction," which sometimes counted as much as a commendation.

Bill and I worked it out. I had to make the initial entrance into the apartment, with a key easily obtained from the building manager, and Bill followed when I determined the place held no surprises. While Bill installed a miniature transmitter in the apartment's air conditioner, my partner and I maintained a lookout. Anyone arriving at that apartment, for *any* reason, would have been arrested for "investigation robbery," or *something,* long before he got a glimpse of Bill.

I talked with Bill later as we sat in his car waiting for voices to come over his receiver from that room bug.

"I appreciate your doing this," I said. "I know your ass is out a mile. Does the bureau send you to school to learn this skill?"

"Yes," he said, after some hesitation. It was something he normally would not have admitted. Confidences build quickly in the boring hours of a lengthy stakeout.

"What's the name of the school?"

"It doesn't have a name. It's not in the FBI directory. You're selected and sent, and then told to forget you've been there."

"Well, I appreciate what you've done."

"The guy in the apartment won't appreciate it. I had to knock out his air conditioner because of the noise."

"Good. The idea is to make it hot for the asshole."

"Zeke," I said, when we arrived at the door marked "Lt. Robert R. Griffin, Night Commander," "put on your tie. You know how fussy he is."

"Griffin don't wear no fucking tie in this heat."

"Griffin's the lieutenant," I sighed, and Zeke flipped me the finger while adjusting a neat knot. Then we went inside.

Robert R. Griffin, former Stanford fullback and offensive guard, six foot one, 220 pounds, black hair, black eyes, thirty-three years old, and in better shape than anyone. He was a weight lifter and physical-fitness fanatic who worked out seven times a week, every week. He had a thirty-two-inch waist and a temper. I often wondered how he managed to control that temper enough to play through the entire 1952 Rose Bowl game, a 40–7 thumping by Illinois. On the Stanford team with Griffin was the outstanding quarterback Gary Kerkorian, later of the Pittsburgh Steelers and Baltimore Colts, and Hall-of-Famer Bill McColl. Bob Griffin was a man of contradictions.

"Where the fuck have you two been?" Griffin asked.

"Well . . ." I began.

"You know damn well I've got to go to the gym and work out or I'll feel like shit the rest of the night. My sinus is killing me and you keep me waiting with my finger in my ass. Where have you been?"

I could have told him to shove it, that we were off duty until eight, but then again I could have turned in my badge. "Sorry," I said, "but we got hung up with our informant. She's shaky about the Lathrop deal. We stopped by to calm her down."

Griffin suddenly turned serious and very concerned. I had never doubted that he genuinely cared for his men. "Lake," he said, "Bruce Lathrop is a certified, dangerous nut. If he tries to take you out, and he will, don't fuck with the asshole, blow him away. If you don't promise you'll do that, then this thing is dead. I'll abort it right now, this fucking minute."

Looking back, and I'd look back for the rest of my days, I remember this moment with Griffin, and I know I could have bowed out. Instead I looked at Zeke, who was staring into space. He had already told me what he thought. I eyed Bob Griffin and said, "I promise."

"Okay," he said, leaning back in his chair. "Now, about the car you'll use . . ."

I didn't really listen. I wondered why, when people talked about this sort of thing, they substituted slang for what they really meant: killing. Hence, you always snuffed, offed, laid out, iced, wasted, erased, neutralized, dispatched, dumped, dusted, eliminated, chilled, did in—anything but actually killing someone. I'd noticed an almost universal reluctance, shared by cops and bad guys alike, to use the word "kill." No one says, "Kill the sonofabitch." Even the Mafia employed "hit" and "whack" instead of "kill."

Griffin had finished with us and I brought up the subject of the bug for Judy's room. Zeke added the part about Lathrop shooting someone's feet off. He told the story simply, calmly, without emotion. A chilly kid for just twenty-two. That's a good quality for sure in a police officer.

"Move off your asses and arrange it," Griffin said. "A tape recording would be a big help. There's always a lot of fucking heat after a shootout."

"We're on our way," I said.

"Make sure the broad gets it right."

As we left, Griffin picked up his phone and asked a switchboard operator to connect him with the identification division to arrange for the bug.

"Griffin's a nut," I said, when we were in the plainclothes car on our way back to Judy's room.

"Why," Zeke asked, "do you say that about a solid, stable fellow like Bob?"

We often joked about Griffin this way. The truth was, at the time, we both respected him, even liked him—almost. Griffin saw to it that no one really liked him.

Zeke knocked on Judy's door with the tips of his fingers, a universal knocking technique employed to inform the person inside that everything is all right. Nothing shakes up a hustler like a loud, booming, full-fisted knock. It sounds too much like the cops.

Inside I noticed that the room had changed little since our earlier visit. Judy had been smoking a joint, judging from the smell that hung in the dark little room.

"You stoned already?" Zeke asked, a note of annoyance in his voice.

"Yes, I'm stoned already. What I do, I do just as well stoned as straight."

"Tell her about the bug," I said. I wanted to get it on, get the thing done. I had a terrible hangover. Besides, we had been working on this caper for a month and I was tired of Judy,

Lathrop, the heist, everything connected with the case. I decided I needed a drink.

"Let's get a drink," I said.

"Feeling shaky?" Zeke asked. Now he was annoyed with both of us. Zeke drank, but not the way I did.

We went to LaVista on Paradise Road, an interesting little spot we knew would be temporarily deserted by the late crowd of pimps, prostitutes, dope peddlers, and burglars who comprised the bulk of its clientele. We sat in a booth and ordered three Bloody Marys.

"Here's what's going to happen," I said, hopping right to it. "While we're enjoying our drinks, the ID bureau will be installing a bug in your pad. Then . . ."

"A *what?*"

"Be quiet and listen. We want you to call Lathrop and invite him over to your place. *Don't* go to his place. Tell him you're waiting for a trick to call and can't leave the room, you might miss the call, or some shit like that."

I took a swallow of vodka and waited to see if she was receiving.

"If he goes for it," I said, "and he should, then . . ."

"He will." I didn't like the tone of her voice.

"Once he's at your place, I want you to rehash the whole deal, right from the top. Get him to talk about blowing someone's feet off."

This is known as covering your tracks before you make them. I finished the Bloody Mary and ordered another.

"Relax," said Judy. "You worry too much."

"Well, honey, Griffin's on our asses to get Lathrop on tape, in case anything goes wrong."

This is known as Blaming the Lieutenant, but I figured that was a function lieutenants served.

"I have one question," Judy said. Zeke winced, placed his head in his hands, nodded sadly and knowingly. He had seen this before and wasn't eager to witness a painful rerun. Neither was I, but it constituted part of the job, so I drank half of the second Bloody Mary and pretended a curiosity that did not exist. Snitches always have one question, and it is always the same. I imagine it's their way of protesting what they are doing, or perhaps it's an attempt to establish an independence they cannot possess.

"What's your question?" I asked.

"What if I refuse?" she said.

I had to evince surprise, disappointment, shock, anger, none of them honest emotions. First I pounded the table so hard the half-asleep bartender, twenty feet away, took notice. Then I stared hard at Judy. She was a pleasant, attractive, frightened young woman, her young life already headed in a deadened direction.

"What the fuck is that supposed to mean?" I growled, my voice full of menace.

She had to go ahead. "Just that," she said. "What if I say no?"

I cursed myself for what I was about to do. "Okay," I said. "You asked, so I'll tell you. If you say no, then I'm gonna make a thing out of your case. A big thing. I'm going to bust you every time I see you on the Strip, and that's a promise. I'll see that every deputy in the sheriff's office does the same. That's a promise too. And it isn't all. I'll heat you up with the city P.D., all the security guards in all the joints, and everywhere you try to work they'll call me and I'll bust you. Bellmen. Bartenders. Every fucking person you need to turn tricks will call me. I'll stay on your ass, and I'll slam your ass in the joint. And when you get out, I'll see that you go back. Judy, there ain't no fucking way you can say no."

"I just wanted to know my options," she said. Her hands were shaking and she'd gone pale.

"There ain't no fucking options."

We rode back to the motel in silence. Judy was thinking about our talk in LaVista; but what the hell, I consoled myself, I'd only told her the truth.

There were things on my mind too. Nagging doubts about the Lathrop caper. Once I had even voiced those doubts to Griffin, and what I got in return was an admonition to do my civic duty: the community needed an example. Too many robberies had been taking place lately in Las Vegas. Put one of those junkie heisters away and let everyone know we meant business—"make those assholes take notice" was the way Griffin put it. Thus, we pressed on with the Lathrop deal, on to what seemed to me an inevitable and inescapable conclusion.

Killing someone had to be what made me nervous. Certainly, I didn't fear performing dirty tricks. I had become proficient in unauthorized wiretaps, illegal room bugs, burglaries, kidnappings, assaults, and beatings—all tasks I had willingly performed.

I say I became proficient, but that's an understatement. I was very good. Good at all of it. I suppose I qualified as a natural: the son of a small-town Indiana police chief, I had never wanted to be anything but a cop.

Las Vegas in 1961, as wide open as a town could be, represented the perfect spot for a zealous, ambitious young police officer. If I wanted a search warrant and lacked "probable cause" to obtain one, I burglarized the suspect's home, got a firsthand glance at the evidence, then went before a justice of the peace saying that "a usually reliable informant, who has in the past provided information that's proven accurate," stated that he saw heroin (or whatever) at the location in question. Obviously, the "informant" would fear for his life should his identity be revealed. I always obtained my search warrant.

Two days after my talk with Judy in LaVista—the Thursday before *the* Friday—Zeke and I sat in the plainclothes car and listened to what we imagined was one of Bruce Lathrop's last conversations on earth.

"Hi, baby." Lathrop's voice came through the monitor loud and clear. "I got here as quick as I could. I could have walked faster than traffic was moving."

"It's okay," we heard Judy say. "I'm waiting for a john to call. He's usually late, but he's a hundred-dollar john so I ride it."

"Pretty soon you can stop," Lathrop said. "I've been cutting down on my shit. Got it down to half a spoon three times a day. Before long we'll be able to ball."

"I hope so," said Judy. "You know I ain't got an old man to take care of me, and doing it with johns don't make it at all. Most of them are fat, ugly old men, and stinking drunk besides."

"Scary," Zeke mumbled. He must have been reading my mind.

"Yes," I said. The scary part was hearing her run it down just like we had rehearsed, and the sincerity in her voice.

"What do you hear about *my* john?" Lathrop was saying. "The insurance guy. Can I still take him off tomorrow?"

"That's the day. My girlfriend who works in his office says he's got big cash payments coming in tomorrow. Like I told you, he always takes the money home with him, out to the house—the place I showed you—on Blue Diamond Road."

"He's in for a big surprise," Lathrop said.

No, I thought, *you* are.

"Will you be alone?" Judy asked.

"Art will drive. I'll do the heisting. We keep it simple and nothing goes wrong."

Judy was a cunning little hooker. "I'm not sure he'll give it up so easy," she said. "He's a real freak about money."

"Then I'll blow the bastard's feet off. That will slow him down." Lathrop laughed. "Get it, baby? Blow off his feet and slow him down."

So there it was. Right from the horse's mouth. Or horse's ass. Griffin and Lamb would love it. For a moment even I felt better. Those were my feet he talked about blowing away, and why should I care about him?

But my anger passed and the doubts returned. I sensed deep down that something was terribly wrong with this entire arrangement.

Friday afternoon Zeke and I waited for the kickoff. All the meetings were over. Chief of Detectives O'Reilly—a man with curly, iron gray hair—had conducted his usual production number with a joint sheriff's department/city police department meeting. The city had agreed to assist us by following us to the Las Vegas boundary, where a county car would pick us up. The sheriff liked the arrangement because we'd be covered all the way, so that's how it came down. "Finalized," I think they called it.

O'Reilly took me aside after the meeting and delivered a Father Flanagan–style speech that ended with, "Don't fuck with this man, Lake. Waste him. And don't worry about the publicity. It'll do us good to let these felons know they can't get away with this shit in Las Vegas."

It was 5:15 P.M. when Zeke and I began our journey in the new Cadillac that had been borrowed for the gig: all white, two-door, a real beauty. Zeke crouched on the floor on the passenger side, out of sight, cradling a twelve-gauge shotgun loaded with buckshot.

I did the driving. I headed for the Strip, where we would turn south and aim for Blue Diamond Road, take a right, and travel the mile or so to the house we'd borrowed for the purpose. That is where we had programmed Lathrop, through

Judy, to do his job, and the house had already been surrounded by submachine-gun-toting Bob Griffin and fifteen
deputies under his command. Sergeant Gene Clark perched
on the roof with a telescope-equipped .270 Winchester, a helluva deer rifle. We were set.

After we turned south on the Strip, the city car right behind
us, Zeke asked, "Christ, Lake, how can you be so steady?
Don't this bother you?"

"You've got a tougher job than me, partner. You're curled
up like a sheepdog on the floor. You can't see a thing. At least
I can tell what's coming. You might as well be in the glove-
box."

"That don't explain it."

"All right. I'll tell you my secret. This ain't gonna happen.
Something will fuck it up. Lathrop won't be there. He'll find
an excuse and back down. He'll have a hangnail. His last pair
of shoelaces will break. Something. But it ain't gonna happen."

"That's a lot of horseshit."

At the Stardust, just past the Las Vegas boundary, the city
car pulled off the Strip. Moments earlier an unmarked county
car had slid into the procession. I kept Zeke informed of
developments.

"Drop me off at the Hacienda," he said.

"What the fuck is this? A Yellow Cab?"

"I need to take a piss. You go on ahead. I'll meet you
there."

"This car makes one stop, partner, and you're going to the
end of the line."

I turned right, west, on Blue Diamond Road. The county
car continued straight ahead.

Blue Diamond Road was a narrow two-lane blacktop
flanked on each side by a mix of country and desert. It was
very dark, like a tunnel, more dark I'm sure because of the

perpetual daylight we had just left behind. Turning onto Blue Diamond seemed to mark the point from where there was no turning back.

"Nothing's gonna happen," I said.

"Like hell."

"That's it, partner. On the square."

"Come on, Lake. Cut the shit."

"Speaking of shit, partner, you'd better get yours together. We're here."

I pulled the Cadillac off Blue Diamond Road and into the driveway of the house. The Caddy's lights hit the big building and I saw him, flattened out against the carport wall.

"Zeke, he's here," I said. "Stay down."

"Good luck," Zeke said.

"He's coming out of the carport."

I killed the car lights, with great reluctance, and shut off the motor. I picked up a briefcase stuffed with telephone books to use as a shield—practice runs had proven a bulletproof vest too unwieldy for use behind a steering wheel. I took my .357 Magnum, loaded with six rounds of 200-grain Manstopper ammunition, out of my belt and concealed it behind the briefcase.

Lathrop walked fast and I could see the gun in his hand. It was indeed an air force survival weapon, with separate barrels over and under. One rifle, one shotgun.

"He's on his way," I said.

"I've got to get out," Zeke said. "I'm worthless here."

"Dammit, sit tight!"

I used to laugh secretly at robbery victims. Very few ever described being held up by anyone less in stature than six foot two and 200 pounds, but as the man approached that is how big he looked to me. I was certain it could not be Lathrop, five foot eight and 140; this colossus was not Lathrop! A terrible mistake had been made. But it *had* to be Lathrop, the rational part of my brain told me, and helping to magnify his size was the woman's stocking pulled over his head. Also, that awesome weapon he carried.

Lathrop jerked the door of the Cadillac open with his left hand. He held the gun in his right. "Get out of the car," he said flatly. Nothing more. Just get out of the car. From where he stood he couldn't see Zeke. He saw me, though, saw me good because he put the muzzle of the gun right against my neck where it joins the shoulder. Right on the collar bone and held it there.

I started to do what he said, had just turned on the seat when from the dark field came Griffin's unmistakable voice. "Throw down your gun! Police officers!"

Lathrop's head jerked in the direction of Griffin's command. When his head moved, so did his gun, thank God, because he looked back at me and fired.

The blast lit up the night. It resembled nothing so much as a garden hose spewing a bright stream of orange, blue, and white fire. The main charge exploded just over my right knee and punched a two-inch hole in the Cadillac's corner post. Part of the shot slapped the inside of my right knee.

I rolled out of the car and fired where his chest ought to be. It was, I saw by the flash. The gun kicked and I corrected, fired again, and I could see Lathrop's plaid shirt, even the buttons. I'd been assured that the 200-grain Manstoppers I used would knock down an elephant, but they sure as hell didn't knock Lathrop down. The force of the heavy shells drove him back to the Cadillac's rear bumper and prevented him from firing the rifle portion of his over and under.

Then he whirled and ran staggering across the dark yard toward a waiting car. I laid across the trunk of the Cadillac and fired four more times. I know I hit him but still he didn't go down. At the same instant I heard the deep *thump-thump* of Zeke's double-barrel shotgun.

Now everyone seemed to be firing at the fleeing figure. Inside the house a telephone line had been kept open to facilitate communications to the radio room at the sheriff's department, and the operator, an army veteran, said "It sounds like taking a hill in Korea."

Somehow Lathrop made it over a six-foot fence and into a waiting car that sped off. Four police cars leaped into pursuit from hidden parking areas, their sirens wailing.

They found the vehicle, stuck and abandoned, a half mile away. The driver escaped. Lathrop was dead, face down in the sand, shot twice in the chest and once in the back with my .357, and twice in the left arm from Zeke's shotgun.

And that, for me, was where it began.

2

LEAVING THE FORCE

"What the fuck is happening to me?"

I asked myself the question a thousand times, and anyone else who would listen: Margie, my girlfriend (later, my wife); Zeke, my partner; Wayne Anderson, patrol division watch commander; cocktail waitresses; bartenders, lots of these; I even asked a couple hookers.

"What the fuck is happening to me?"

I knew the problem, but not how to resolve it. The problem was I'd killed a man, murdered him, no matter what the law said, and how do you resolve that? It got so bad the only way I could sleep at night was to drink myself unconscious.

Then, on December 19, 1961, barely two months after the Bruce Lathrop affair, it almost happened again.

Late that afternoon Bob Griffin received a call from an informant. The information could not have been more specific: the suspect, name provided, who lived at, address provided, had purchased a shotgun, make provided, was going to saw it off, reason provided, which was to rob a store, location provided.

"Lake," said Griffin, "this might be a hot one. I want you to ride with me tonight."

Bob Griffin was deadly serious on a stakeout. Zeke and I would have passed time talking about fast cars or an imaginary, elaborate vacation, but with Griffin it was all business. We sat in a plainclothes Dodge in the parking lot of Casa La Paz apartments on Tam Drive in southwest Las Vegas discussing the most likely candidates for the dossiers he had to compile for the Law Enforcement Intelligence Unit (LEIU), a secret nationwide network of police agencies that exchange information on criminal suspects and political activists who travel interstate. I would rather have been talking to Zeke.

The suspect appeared like clockwork, within a minute of when Griffin's informant said he would, carrying what we assumed to be a standard-length (approximately forty-four inches) shotgun wrapped in an Indian blanket. We watched him go into an apartment.

I reached into the backseat and horsed a Thompson submachine gun onto my lap.

"Be careful with that son of a bitch," Griffin said.

We took up preplanned positions in the parking lot. It was unlit and both of us were shielded by cars. We had an unhampered view of the apartment's only exit. We waited.

Waiting is the toughest job a cop has. It can drive him crazy. I was always super keyed-up, hyper, eager for action; yet time passed in nightmarish slow motion. I often felt I'd waited three hours but my watch said five minutes. What I did on long waits, after reviewing every possible scenario and how I needed to react to each, was daydream. I thought about women, the beach, jetting to some exotic corner of the earth. I knew police officers who play mental games, like adding columns of figures in their heads. Others fantasized about being rich and how they would spend their money. Some recited rosary after rosary.

This time the wait lasted only ten minutes. He came out carrying a rolled-up newspaper inside of which was a fourteen-inch-long sawed-off shotgun. He stood just outside the door looking around, illuminated by the lighted window of the apartment next to his.

"Police officers!" Griffin shouted. "Throw down your weapon!"

The suspect turned in the direction of Griffin, twenty feet away but invisible in the darkness. I saw him raise the shotgun, pointed at the ground, an inch or two.

No way was I going to allow a Bruce Lathrop rerun with the bad guy getting off the first shot. I'd been lucky to get away from that one with a torn-up leg and was in no mood, ever, to take unnecessary chances again.

With my thumb I flipped the safety lever of the Thompson to the fire position, leaned across the hood of the car that shielded me, quickly aligned the gun's sights on the suspect's belt buckle (in combat training I'd been taught to aim for the center of the mass, but I aimed low to compensate for the barrel's climb), and squeezed the slack out of the trigger. I braced, anticipating the recoil of the gun against my shoulder. The suspect was half a second away from dying.

Bent over, crouched, running like the powerful fullback he once had been, Griffin came hurtling out of the darkness with a flying tackle that nearly tore the guy in two. I relaxed off the trigger and walked over to learn we had a nineteen-year-old kid with an unloaded shotgun. This wasn't the worst part. Virtually directly behind him, kneeling on a couch, looking raptly out the door, *were six small children.* Had Griffin not done his Batman imitation, some and perhaps all of them would have been killed.

I envisioned a future filled with endless shootings and didn't like what I saw. Other things had been building inside also, like the hypocrisy: we broke the law as often as the people we threw in jail. We rationalized that the end justified the means, but often the means we employed were nothing more than crimes. The TV-inspired image of police—i.e., a crime is committed, detectives investigate, clever Sherlock Holmes–type work snares lawbreaker, court metes out justice—couldn't have been farther from the truth. The more I thought about the teenager and the six children, the more I questioned what I was doing and where I was headed.

The police in Las Vegas more resembled a vigilante committee than a law-enforcement agency. Many of us followed our own lights, uninhibited by encumbering guidelines, which meant much of our time was spent arresting people simply because we didn't like them. Once a fellow cop I'll call Mike* and I were in the Sands when Mike, whose phenomenal ability to match a face with a mug shot became legend up and down the West Coast, spotted someone he thought he recognized. Back to the sheriff's office we went and, sure enough, there he was among the loose pictures, Tony, a minor figure in organized crime with no warrants outstanding.

In less than thirty minutes from the sighting, we called him out of the Sands casino area and identified ourselves as police officers.

"Tony, what you doin' in Vegas?" Mike asked in a no-nonsense tone.

"It's a tourist town, ain't it? I'm a tourist."

"Got anything upstairs you don't want us to see?" Mike pressed.

"No, of course not."

"Good, let's take a look."

"Wait a minute," Tony said. "You got a warrant to search my room?"

"No," I interjected, "not in hand. But if you want to be a hard-on, we can get one while you're being booked for investigation burglary."

Upstairs, we shook his room down, jotted down all his

phone numbers and names, and took an address book and anything that might furnish insight into his activities. Then we arrested him for vagrancy, conveniently overlooking that he had an expensive room in a plush hotel and *$8,000 in cash,* and made certain he was booked into the county jail after midnight, which ensured he couldn't post bail until a justice court opened at 9:00 A.M.

A typical roust arrest, designed to tell a person—Tony R in this case—he would be happier in New York than Las Vegas, that every time he came to Vegas he could expect the same. The problem is that the arrest, made without probable cause, was unconstitutional; but we knew full well there would never be prosecution.

We had completely lost sight of the fact that a police officer's job is not to put people in jail: that is the function of a court. For us the arrest had become the end, the whole, not part of a whole that included a district attorney and a court. We figured our job was done when the assholes, as we called them, were behind bars, *We* decided, based on our own standards, just who the assholes were.

In our opinion, the courts and the district attorney were enemies of the police, bleeding-heart liberals who turned criminals loose faster than we could lock them up. What we perceived as a soft-on-crime atmosphere goaded us to even more frantic efforts to circumvent the judicial system and mete out justice on our own: namely, use the arrest as punishment. To us, the courts were the "fucking" courts and the district attorney was the "fucking" district attorney.

I'm sure, although I was not aware of it at the time, that the Bruce Lathrop killing was what led me to examine the role I played and the function I served. It was becoming increasingly clear to me that Lathrop's death had not been the only imaginable conclusion to the case. Another solution, which would have disarmed him and gotten him off the street, would have been to have arrested him for conspiracy to commit robbery after we had that tape recording of his conversation with Judy.

Conversion for me came not like a thunderclap from on high, but more subtly, like peeling an onion, each incident I reviewed stripping away a layer until only the core—a rotten core—remained.

Had it really been necessary to pull five members of a famous band off the Riviera Lounge stage at the end of a performance and charge them with narcotics violations? Did proper police work involve a toss-up of whether the officer is more drunk than the person he is arresting for intoxication? Should a hooker's arrest depend on whether she balls the officer? What about casinos routinely handing out large tokes (gratuities) to police officers? All of this and much, much more was commonplace and molded mosaics of corruption so pervasive only the blind could fail to recognize. But worst of all, as I well knew, a police officer, without the slightest fear of punishment, could take upon himself the jobs of judge, jury, and executioner.

The arrest of band members off the Riviera Lounge stage sparked national headlines. It was my pinch. I was in charge of it. An informant had told me the entire band was strung out, so Zeke and I kept their motel under surveillance. The stakeout began taking too long, so I said to myself I'd speed it up. I went to a maid, showed identification, and asked for keys. When she hesitated, I reminded her that I could take away her sheriff's card, which meant losing her job. A sheriff's card is required in Las Vegas for anyone working in gambling, liquor, or food and beverage, and employment is unlawful for both employer and employee without it. Incredibly, had the maid refused to give me the keys, her appeal of my decision to take her sheriff's card would have been to the sheriff's department, hardly an ear designed to be sympathetic—"Get out of here, asshole, I'm busy" is how similar appeals had been dismissed. I got the keys.

I entered the rooms when the band was performing. In several rooms I found heroin (a brown or white powder, very bitter, like quinine) plus syringes, and decided immediately to act without pain-in-the-ass arrest warrants that couldn't possibly be obtained until the next day, by which time the evidence might have disappeared into someone's arm. The arrests I intended to make might be illegal but, like I said, that was not a concern. The collar was the thing, not making sure it would stick.

When I called the office and announced what I had found, I was told, "Good work. But what are you waiting for? Bust them."

"I'll need some help, for Christ's sake. I found smack in three rooms. Five suspects are involved. Zeke and I can't collar them all at once, and shake down the rooms too." For this operation to be successful all of the suspects had to be arrested simultaneously; otherwise, after the first arrest, the remaining suspects would destroy the evidence.

Six of us made the arrests just as the band finished its final set of the night. Perhaps twice as many uniforms stood by to transfer the prisoners while we conducted the search of their rooms, a *second* search—of course, I knew right where to look. I.D. took pictures, and we rode to the sheriff's department to book the evidence and write the arrest reports, a routine that kept me at the office till 6:00 A.M.

At 9:00 A.M. I was jolted awake by a telephone call from Frances, Sheriff Ralph Lamb's secretary. The sheriff wanted to see me right away.

"Jesus Christ, Frances," I said. "I worked all night. Can't it wait?"

"Sorry, Lake, but no it can't. The wire services have been calling all morning asking the sheriff about the arrests you made last night. He doesn't know anything about them."

"I'll be right there," I said. I imagined Lamb would be effusive with his praise once I ran down the details of the stellar work we'd performed.

Instead, Ralph Lamb was livid. I no sooner had opened the door to his office than I knew that praise appeared nowhere on his agenda. "Sit down," he said, "and tell me what the fuck happened out there last night."

Seated behind a big oak desk, flanked by the flags of the United States and Nevada, Lamb resembled the rangy, raw-boned cowboy he once had been. Lamb had blond hair, blue eyes, and huge hands, and he still kept himself in shape roping calves on the family spread in northern Nevada.

Lamb had many dislikes; highest on the list were pimps. Once he held one of them against a cement-block wall and told him to get out of Las Vegas. In an eclipse of judgment the pimp told Lamb to fuck himself. The sheriff punched the pimp in the face, drew his fist back, and punched again. But the pimp had already gone down from the first hit, and the second shattered Lamb's fist against the cement wall. "Can't trust those motherfuckers," Lamb later told me. "One of them broke my hand."

Nothing I could say about the arrest of the band members was going to mollify Lamb. But I tried. I told him all of it. He listened intently but didn't enjoy what he heard.

Appointed sheriff in 1960, Lamb won election after election to that office until his defeat in 1978, and despite his gruff demeanor and rough and ready exterior, his eighteen-year tenure could only have been accomplished by a very clever and astute politician.

Politically, what we had done was neither clever nor astute. Already, owners of the Riviera had called Lamb demanding an explanation of the arrests. Their position: they had spent a lot of money hiring the band, and the arrests had not only disrupted the casino's operation but had given it and the entire community a black eye. These Riviera bigshots were people to be heard.

"Jesus Christ, Lake," Lamb said, "why didn't you people come and talk to me about this thing? Maybe I could have gone to [the band leader] and told him to clean up that fucking band of his if he wanted to stay in Vegas."

"Nobody gives a shit about those junkies," Lamb continued, "but [the band leader] runs with U.S. presidents. Wire services and big newspapers have been hounding me all morning. The only thing that's gonna get me off the hook is a confession from at least one of those junkies."

I left Lamb's office and walked the hundred feet to the detective bureau, where I called the jail sergeant and requested that he send one of the band members to me. I chose a specific musician because the previous night he had been in the worst shape of all; the others had been relatively okay, but I knew from the way this man had acted that he had a big monkey, maybe a gorilla, on his back, and after six hours in the slammer the monkey would be scratching for a fix. Also, he had the most needle marks, or tracks, on his arms, a point I was certain of because I'd had Sergeant Lee McCullough of the I.D. bureau photograph each man's arms.

The band member, looking pathetic, was brought into my office. I found it hard to believe that here stood a much-honored musician, winner of many awards, a man at the very top of his profession. He was starting to get sick from the lack of a heroin fix, was still dressed in his tuxedo, and obviously had slept little or not at all. Dirt and sweat ringed his open white silk shirt collar, and from under his jacket came the peculiar, unmistakable stench of a sick junkie. He shook into a chair facing my desk.

"Good morning," I said. "How do you feel?"

"You know how I feel. I'm very sick. I need a doctor."

"You want to see a doctor, and you should. Maybe we can get one up here to give you a shot of something."

"Could you do that? I really am very ill. I need my medication."

"All I have to do is pick up this telephone and I'll have a croaker here in five flat minutes."

I was lying, and it nagged at me that I felt very clever in my lies. Worse, why did I feel no compassion for this man?

"First," I said, "we have a little business to take care of. I want you to sign a statement for me, just a short statement, telling me what happened, what your pinch was all about, who you got the smack from, and how much."

The man flinched. "You mean a confession."

"What's the difference? A statement. A confession. The deal is, I get my statement, you get your medication."

"I don't know . . ."

"Well, it's the only deal in town. You either take it, or I put you back in the slammer, but this time I hang a charge of investigation burglary on your ass. That means seventy-two miserable fucking hours before you get out. How do you think you'll feel then?"

The fellow nodded slowly. His fear of the sickness running through his insides like thick sorghum molasses made his trembling more pronounced, almost uncontrollable. I viewed him with revulsion. The only saving grace was that it bothered me to view him this way.

"If you sign the statement," I said, "I'll call the doctor. What do you say?"

"I'll sign it. I'll do anything you want. But please, arrange for that doctor."

He signed the statement, admitting to possession of heroin and naming his connections. I took him back to the jail. I didn't call a doctor, but I didn't put any more charges on him either. There was no reason. I had the confession.

The band-busting case, whose ending fortunately did not feature the terrible finality attendant to Bruce Lathrop's, was just one of many in which there was no real honor for us. I remember Zeke and I being called to the Stardust Hotel to investigate a complaint that a drunk was soliciting money inside the front door. Normally this was not our job, but we got dispatched because it was the sheriff's policy not to send uniformed officers inside a casino. The sight of a uniformed cop presumably upsets gamblers, and almost everyone in a casino is a gambler.

At the Stardust we found a docile, middle-aged drunk who had collected $1.24 he claimed was going to the Girl Scouts. We were about to tell him to move along when onto the scene burst Chief of Detectives William O'Reilly. Over the police radio in his car he had heard the dispatcher send us to the Stardust, which presented him with the opportunity to be seen in a popular nightspot diligently working long hours and exercising supervision over the detectives under him. In truth, he had spent the night drinking in the Sands and seemed as plastered as the suspect who solicited money for the Girl Scouts.

"Handcuff the son of a bitch," O'Reilly said, after he noticed that a pit boss and assistant casino manager had been drawn to the action. "We'll take him down and book him. I'll ride with you."

On the way to the station, the panhandling drunk made a casual, offhand remark, and O'Reilly turned around in the front seat and punched him in the mouth. I had seen plenty of people get belted, had done some of it myself, but this was particularly appalling: an apparently drunken chief of detectives, with no more dignity than the man in his custody, hitting a handcuffed suspect.

Then there was the question of hookers. There are more hookers in Las Vegas than oranges in Florida, and all of them have one goal uppermost in mind: avoiding arrest. How this got accomplished varied from hooker to hooker, but more often than not involved establishing a sexual relationship with a detective. "I've fucked more whores in the back of police cars," a vice-squad cop told me, "than I have in beds," adding that this permitted him to remain close to his radio.

Despite department policy to the contrary, virtually every detective took tokes, and their size varied according to the officer's rank and assignment. In a real sense we were employees of the casinos, not the Vegas citizenry.

Christmas was a time when Santa Claus really did come. We visited the casinos, ostensibly to wish the employees a Merry Christmas, and the pit boss or casino manager shoved money in our pockets. I hit the jackpot one year: almost $2,500, including a high of $500 from one casino operator. But tokes were not limited to Christmas. To a lesser degree they got handed out year-round.

Thus, after what had almost been my second fatal shooting in two months—the teenager outside that apartment, and the little kids inside—I began to peel the layers of the onion, to probe deeper than the surface to learn where I was headed, and, most important, What the Fuck Was Happening to Me? I knew my five years of service in the sheriff's department had been no shining, inspiring example of high principle, and the belief that I was no more than a mirror reflecting attitudes and practices originating from the top was no justification for my actions. Nonetheless I felt a sense of betrayal. I had possessed at least a smidgen of idealism when I'd joined the department, felt a little perhaps the way crusaders did when they marched with Richard III, wanting to accomplish through positive action some form of good. But my ripple of idealism got inundated by the waves of cynicism, corruption, cruelty, graft, and greed permeating all levels of Las Vegas law enforcement.

I continued talking with everyone I could about my doubts. The conversation that turned the doubts that started with Lathrop into action was held with Zeke and took place one early evening in January, 1962, as we drove to work.

"This job sucks, buddy, you and I both know that," I said. "I can't deal with it any more."

"I know what you mean," Zeke said. "On top of that, I'm not thrilled with the hours or the pay."

"The pay can be improved."

"Yeah." But Zeke didn't mean it. He held to certain principles, and one of them was not accepting tokes. Before starting at the sheriff's department, Zeke had been employed at the Dunes Hotel on the Strip. He'd earned more in a week parking cars than he now made in a month with the department, where his salary was $425, before taxes. Also, parking cars was a lot less hectic and stressful than the detective bureau.

My experience had been similar. Five years earlier I had worked for the Hotel Royal Nevada as a bellman, and I too had grown fond of the $300 to $400 a week the job was good for—*tax free*. There were heavy advantages working on the Strip for a small salary and big tips.

But Zeke and I heard the siren call of police work, and coincidentally answered for the same reason. We each stood in awe of our fathers, who both had been police officers, albeit different types from those with whom we now associated.

"I understand your gripe about the pay," I said, proceeding from there to trying to verbalize what bothered me most: the *nature* of our jobs. We weren't really concerned about protecting potential victims, I said, but in keeping Las Vegas casinos safe so they could continue to reap enormous winnings. A poor area of the city *might* see a cop now and then, while a small army of us waited in case another Girl Scout fund-raiser disrupted some gambling joint's decorum.

"That's it," Zeke said, "and it makes you wonder if it's worthwhile. Even when we do a cop's job, everything gets screwed up. The perps we put in the slammer are back on the street before the ink dries on the arrest reports."

"We both know the problems," I said. "We need a solution."

"I'm thinking of hanging it up," Zeke said, "telling them to stick this five-pointed star up their asses."

Exactly what had been on my mind. I didn't want to let the matter rest. "What would you do if you quit, Zeke? Go back to parking cars?"

"I don't know for sure. I've been talking to my pal Bob, and he says he's been approached by several lawyers—Claiborne, Manzoni, some others—to start a private detective agency. They tell him he wouldn't lack for clients."

"Bob interested in bringing you in?"

"Bob's not interested at all. He wants out of the department, but he intends to get clear away from anything even remotely related to this shit."

Bob was in the detective bureau and came into daily contact with attorneys whose clients were seeking restitution for bad paper they had received. Bob viewed this distasteful assignment as tantamount to running a collection agency, and he was right. He hated the job and all the heat that went with it from casinos that shouldn't have accepted the rubber in the first place. His dissatisfaction was what had prompted the conversations with the lawyers.

"Might not be such a bad idea," I judged. "It can't be worse than what we're doing, and working for ourselves, maybe we'd make some money."

"A nice change."

"What do you think, Zeke? You want to give it a shot?"

"I don't know. I don't have any idea what that line of work involves. I've never been a p.i. and haven't a clue whether I'd like it."

"We're supposed to know something about investigations. It's not like we'd be opening a soda fountain, or a car-repair shop. We're not just walking into something completely cold."

"Let me think about it," Zeke said. "It's something worth thinking about."

"Don't take too long. This job's got me crazy."

On January 10, 1962, Cyril D. Lenahan and Lake W. Headley submitted formal letters of resignation to Ralph Lamb, Sheriff of Clark County, Nevada.

3

THE LAS VEGAS DETECTIVE AGENCY

The Las Vegas Detective Agency, set up slapdash fashion in a single rundown room on Bridger Street across from the rear of the Clark County Courthouse, opened for business on February 1, 1962. Furniture consisted of one telephone, two desks, two chairs (clients would have to stand to state their business), and a very large bottle of Scotch. A much smaller bottle of muscatel had paid for hand lettering the firm's name on the wood-framed, dirt-streaked glass door.

The room itself was narrow, little more than the width of a bowling lane, and not much in the length department either.

"Fucking place is a closet," Zeke said when he first saw it.

"Think of it as intimate," I said.

"I've been in bigger elevators."

"We'll get close to our clients."

"It's filthy, too."

"Kick back, Zeke. Have a drink and wait for the multitudes to bring money."

Although we had no clients and zero operating capital, cause did exist for optimism. There was only one competing private investigator in all of Las Vegas, and no one would have mistaken him for Mike Hammer.

Our tenures with the sheriff's department were a definite plus. We knew everyone on the force, and many of them had promised to steer any action coming their way to us. Police officers frequently receive requests that are beyond their scope, but wouldn't be for a p.i. For example, law enforcement can't grind to a halt to search for a runaway teenager (the entire juvenile detail consisted of Detective Bob Runkel), and with hundreds of runaways coming to Las Vegas annually, the most a distraught parent would get from the police was a cursory effort. "Cursory effort" meant, in its entirety, a records check to determine if any of the dead-body reports on file with the sheriff's department contained the name and/or a description of the juvenile being sought. If a parent wanted further investigation, however, it was a simple matter for a deputy to refer him or her to the Las Vegas Detective Agency.

Another plus for our fledgling enterprise was the assurance that we would have access to sheriff's department records, an invaluable aid. Restricted information, years in the gathering, was ours for the asking. Additionally, our contacts in the department could request data from any other police agency in the country, get it, and turn it over to us.

We even had a promise from Sheriff Ralph Lamb that he would send business to us, despite the fact that he'd expressed dismay over our resignations.

"What do you want to do this for?" he asked, an aggrieved father figure upset that two of his children were leaving the fold.

"Can't make it on the salary," I said. What could I say? That the whole department was crazy and we couldn't handle it any more? That the job required killing more people?

"You could transfer to uniform if you think that would be easier."

"That means even less money," Zeke pointed out. Detectives received $25 a month as a clothing allowance.

"Well, this puts us in a helluva spot. We're already short of men, and you two are old hands."

That's tough, I thought, maybe you'll have to close down.

"I know you'll make a lot of money," Lamb said. "I did when I was a private investigator." He grew pensive. "A lot of times I've wished I'd stayed in that business, so I know how you feel. And speaking of business, you men know you can count on our helping as much as we can."

Griffin's reaction to our resignations was typically unemotional. "I don't blame you," he said. "You're doing the right thing. I'd do it too if I didn't have twelve years invested in this fucking lash-up. There's too much work and too much heat. You should get out of this fucking mess."

"That's what we're doing," Zeke pointed out.

It felt great to be free, on our own, away from the thousand petty bullshit assignments at the sheriff's department. It would be great too, I thought, for my three children—Lake III, age nine; Anthony, seven; and Rod, six. I was separated from my wife, but saw my sons often (now I could see them more), and I for sure didn't think my job as a sheriff's department detective had been a healthy influence on their lives. Children of that age tend to admire their police-officer fathers, but I felt as they grew older their assessment of me would be harsh. An eighteen-year-old reading about how his father killed Bruce Lathrop might have a different perspective from someone age nine.

My father, at one time the youngest police chief in the nation, knew full well what I had been doing at the sheriff's department—and didn't approve. In Goshen, Indiana, population 15,000, where he was police chief, there never had been even a hint that he'd been involved with violence or used his position for extralegal activities. I imagine he had witnessed enough mayhem during the London blitz as a member of General James Doolittle's staff—he earned the Legion of

Merit, our nation's third highest award—and I believe that his war experiences steered him away from violence.

The citizens of Goshen nicknamed my dad Modoc, after an elephant in the Ringling Brothers Circus. My father's strength, legendary in Goshen, usually made physical force unnecessary, and I'm quite sure he never fired his gun. As a boy, Modoc had to forfeit a football scholarship to Notre Dame offered during Knute Rockne's recruitment of the legendary Four Horsemen to work and support his mother and six siblings.

My dad was a quiet, gentle man, a real-life pacifist, and he simply would not have involved himself in the things I did while in the sheriff's department. "I suppose you know what you're doing," he said on several occasions, "but maybe you should back off and think about it for a while."

Anyway, my decision to resign from the Sheriff's Department was a popular one with all the members of my family. My mother, much more outspoken than my dad, had told me, "Lake you're going to get hurt fooling around in that business. I wish you'd get a job like other people and move out of this dangerous work."

My uncle, a police officer in Gary, Indiana—the man who'd arrested Dillinger's Lady in Red, Anna Sage—also applauded my decision to resign. "Good that you're getting out while you still can," he said. "You're young enough to do something else. It sounds like you've been running with a bunch of wild cowboys."

So I leaned back, glass of whiskey in hand, daydreaming about all the time I could now spend taking my kids to movies, ball games, and Lake Mead. I decided to call Lake III and set up a date. My ex-wife answered the telephone.

"I think it's great," she said, "that you've gone into business for yourself. Maybe you can catch up on the child support."

That was definitely a priority. Like many other parents who have not made a roaring success of their lives, I hoped my children would accomplish all the things I had not. I wanted to contribute—financially and spiritually—in a manner that would positively influence their futures.

All we needed were clients. We had our private-investigator licenses, were bonded, and had secured permits to carry guns. Guns would be totally unnecessary for us, and our request for permits indicated that our break with the past was not complete. Like Linus clutching his security blanket, we couldn't bear to go anyplace without guns.

Ralph Lamb kept his promise to steer business in our direction. Ten days after the Las Vegas Detective Agency opened its doors, Lamb's first referral was on the telephone. Zeke looked on anxiously—he had begun to think we were lunatics for striking out on our own—while I did the talking.

"Las Vegas Detectives," I said briskly.

"T.L. Byers* here. I'm calling from Nashville, Tennessee."

"Right, T.L. What can I do for you?"

"Find my wife. I know she's in Las Vegas with him. He's a player, and he's bound to be somewhere on the Strip."

What he asked for was virtually impossible. I knew that because even the sheriff's department fugitive detail and the LVPD working in concert with the FBI usually couldn't find people in Las Vegas. How did he expect a pair of clowns like Zeke and me to succeed? But we needed the business.

"Describe your wife," I said.

He did, and our chances seemed even bleaker.

"Describe the male subject." I was still using police vernacular. I thought it sounded more professional.

He did this, too, and if we hadn't been so desperate I would have told him to save his money.

"Okay, T. L. Great. Now, are they driving a vehicle?"

"I think they flew."

Terrific. "Do you know what airline?" I asked.

"No, I don't. There are several that fly from here."

"What hotel do you think they'll stay at?"

"I don't know."

"Does the subject prefer a certain casino?"

"I don't know."

"Well, T. L., because you've never done business with this firm, we'll need a retainer. Five hundred dollars should get us started."

"Do you think you can find them?"

"We've got good contacts out here. The best."

"I want a full report on their activities. My lawyer will need it for the divorce he's going to file for me. The lawyer was very definite. We need a report."

"We always supply our clients with full written reports, and photographs when possible."

"That's what I want."

"About that retainer . . ."

"How should I send it?" The magic words.

"Western Union money order. Soon as it arrives we'll start looking."

I used the "start looking" phrase quite innocently, but it turned out it has special meaning to many private investigators. A veteran p.i. out of Los Angeles later told me what "start looking" really meant. "Hell, yes, I'll start to look. I'll look all around the office. I'll look in my car. I'll drive down Sunset and look on both sides of the street. I'll look in every bar where I stop to have a drink. When I get home I'll look in my closets and under the bed. I'll look every place I go until the money runs out, and then I'll try to get more. When the client asks what I'm doing, I can honestly say I'm looking."

By and large, this is the modus operandi of most private

investigators: take the money, that's the cry, and little thought is given to the result. Retaining a p.i. can be compared to buying a ticket to a movie. You pay before you see the result, and likely would not have parted with the cash had you known what was coming. Years later, when I received some awards and what I thought was kind but extravagant praise, I really didn't think I deserved it. I believed I was just doing my job, and that if I looked good, it was only in *comparison.* Like many fields, I suppose, there isn't much competition, and therefore a workmanlike job took on the appearance of excellence.

Regardless, I can categorically state that with few exceptions people will be happier, richer, and generally better off if they stay away from private investigators. Until recently most states demanded no requirements whatever from a person wanting to become a licensed p.i., and even today the regulations are laughably lax. In some states all that is needed is the purchase of a business license. The field is wide open for hustlers, con men, adventurers, quick-buck artists, incompetents, and other unsavory characters. The bottom line is that with a modicum of creative initiative the average individual can learn what he or she is paying the p.i. to uncover.

Along the same line, however, often not much can be expected from the regular police. The average cop is a salaried employee who unless motivated by obtaining promotion, doesn't possess overwhelming incentive. For example, when I first started out with the sheriff's department as a detective, a dead-body report came in. Al Jenkins,* a veteran officer nearing retirement and determined to rock no boats, asked me to ride along with him to investigate.

We found the body of an old man who evidently had put a gun to his head and squeezed the trigger. Nearby lay a detailed suicide note that read like so many others I would see: the lonely, sick man had nothing to live for, this was the best way out. Jenkins sent me to canvas the neighborhood to learn if anyone had heard the shot.

A woman next door told me she had known the old man. "I used to go over and make sure he was all right," she said. Then a look of worry creased her face. "I hope I'm not in trouble. I used to sign all his Social Security checks for him. He was blind, you know, and I was just trying to help."

A pillow had been placed over the old man's head before the gun had been fired through it. And that lengthy suicide note from a blind man who couldn't write his own name. I rushed back to Jenkins with what I thought was startling information: a murder had been committed; there was no other way it added up.

"Are you crazy?" Jenkins said. "What we have here is a nice, clean suicide. You listen to me and leave it that way." No further investigation was made.

In any event, the T. L. Byers case was our first, and we determined to do it up right. All we had was the name of the couple—Robert Robinson* and Sharon Byers*—and the date they'd left Nashville: February 7, 1962, three days earlier. If they were indeed in Las Vegas, they probably had registered as Mr. and Mrs.

The first thing we did after collecting the retainer money from Western Union was call McCarran Field and find out what flights into Las Vegas on February 7 had departed from Nashville. Next we called and asked one of our friends at the department, Tim,* to check the passenger lists of those flights to see if our subjects had been aboard—information the airlines would not supply to us, but would to Tim, a police officer.

"Tim," I said. "I need a favor. How busy are you?"

"Busy as hell. Since you motherfuckers decided to make money, I'm swamped."

"That's what this is about. Making money."

"Now that's different. What do you need?"

"We want you to check some airline manifests to see if a passenger from Nashville named Robert Robinson arrived on February 7. Maybe try the car rentals too. We need to find out where he's staying. You know the routine."

"Jesus Christ, Lake, I'm swamped, half-a-dozen reports behind."

"Cut out the overworked and underpaid baloney."

"Okay, okay. Call me about midnight and I'll let you know what I've got."

It was seven hours before midnight and I had nothing to do until then. Zeke went home for dinner. I drove to my ex-wife's place and took the children out for hamburgers, french fries, and malteds. I felt on top of the world, and I think Lake III, Anthony, and Rod did, too. It was almost exhilarating, knowing I'd have more time for my sons and be able to provide support—bicycles, travel, maybe even college educations— they previously would have had to do without. Maybe I ran ahead of myself—after all, T. L. Byers was our *first* client— but I felt confident our venture would work out.

I returned to the office about 9:00 P.M., sure that Tim would come through, we would find the missing couple, and Byers would marvel at our superb detective work. While waiting, I indulged in a mental composition of our report to Byers, which of course I'd write in standard law-enforcement vernacular. The language of police varies from that of the general citizenry; it sets the cop apart and contributes, in my opinion, to an us-versus-them confrontational mindset. For example:

POLICE TALK	TRANSLATION
Land line	Telephone
Vehicle	Car
Exited the vehicle	Got out of the car

Took suspect into custody	Arrested the bastard
Weapon	Gun, knife
En route to	Going to
Under surveillance	Being watched
Used necessary force	Beat the shit out of
Appeared to be	Looked like
Proceeded to	Went to
Applied restraints	Handcuffed the asshole
Arrived at the scene	Got there
Dispatched	Sent
Interrogated	Talked to
Dispersed the bystanders	Teargassed the crowd
Confidential informant	Rat, snitch, fink
Procurer	Pimp
Subject	Person
Received information	Was told
Male caucasian	White man
Male negro	Black man
Routine patrol	Drove around
Late and unusual hours	After dark
Unit	Police car
Usual place of abode	Home

Besides promoting the us-versus-them attitude, the result of what amounts to employing a secret code is that most people unaccustomed to reading police reports, or listening to police officers, come away confused and unenlightened about what actually took place.

Zeke arrived at the office a little after 11:00 P.M. "I hope there's more where this came from," he said. "We make more on this case than we would in two weeks at the sheriff's department."

I called Tim a few minutes before midnight.

"Those people you're interested in," he said, "came in on TWA flight 415 on February 7. They're traveling as Mr. and Mrs. Robert Robinson."

"Where are they staying?"

"How the hell would I know? Can't you guys do anything yourselves?"

"I thought you'd check car rentals."

"Private investigators don't tell the police how to conduct their business," Tim said testily. "But for your information, I did check car rentals. Negative."

Zeke and I had to check the 300-plus hotels and motels in town until we located our quarry. He looked up numbers, which I then dialed to ask if a Robert Robinson was registered. It didn't matter that it was after midnight. Las Vegas, the City Without Clocks, never closes.

I called the major hotels first, starting at the far end of the Strip with the Hacienda and ending at the Sahara. Then I called the ones downtown. No luck.

"Shit," I said. "Nothing's ever easy."

"Quit bitching," Zeke said. "The pay's good."

We were still at it at 4:10 A.M. when a horn honked outside the office. A discreet, personal honk.

"Got to be Tim," I said. "I'll be right back." Zeke and I had agreed to toke him $100 from the $500 we had received.

Tim was double-parked in front. I opened the car door and slid onto the seat next to him. "How do you feel?"

"Lousy," he said.

"Same as always, huh?"

"It's the fucking job."

"Why don't you quit?"

"Is that why you got me over here?"

"No. I wanted to thank you for doing that airlines work." I leaned over and tucked a $100 bill into his shirt pocket.

"Okay. That's the first fucking good thing that's happened tonight. Let me know when you need anything else."

From the yellow pages Zeke alphabetically fed me motel names and numbers; we finally lucked out at 6:45 A.M.

We went to the motel, laid $10 on the desk clerk for a copy of the room-registration card, and began our stakeout. We located a parking place directly across the court from the couple's room, and Zeke set himself up in the backseat so he could take pictures through the rear window. We sat on the room until 9:00 A.M. when they came out, and Zeke's telephoto lens zoomed in for several shots that would have been hard for anyone to misconstrue. The first had them framed in the open motel doorway, and a later one had them kissing near the pool.

"T. L.," I was saying enthusiastically on the phone less than an hour later, "I think we've got what you wanted."

"Not necessarily what *I* wanted," he said. "What my lawyer wanted. And probably what I was afraid you'd find."

"You got it, T. L. Room-registration card. Photographs. We know the airline and the flight they took. Seats were reserved in the names of Mr. and Mrs."

"Well, I guess you should just send it all along to me."

"We'll have the film developed and get everything out there to you. We'll also submit a final bill for time, mileage, and expenses, of course deducting the retainer you wired."

Our total bill was a little more than $700, a big figure, we thought. But just a few days later we acquired an account that convinced us our decision to establish the Las Vegas Detective Agency was akin to genius. Actually, we were just lucky.

Lieutenant Keith Campbell of civil division visited our office on Valentine's Day. Campbell was an old-time Vegan, a friend of Ralph Lamb's, who had the unique distinction of being hired as a *lieutenant* when the sheriff was appointed to office. He was also unique on the sheriff's department, as far as I know, in that he never carried a gun.

Campbell came right to the point. A number of coin-machine companies that owned slots, pinballs, and consoles (a gambler could play blackjack and craps on the console machines) were being cheated to the verge of bankruptcy by crews of hustlers. Devices such as shims (a feeler gauge inserted into the machine to make it pay off), drills (to create the opening for the shim), keys (obtained from dishonest company employees and used to open the machines to loot them), and wires (used in the same manner as shims, but because of manufacturing flaws in the machines occasionally effective even when a hole had not been drilled) were being employed to steal large sums of money. These crews of hustlers frequently contained one or more former legitimate coin-machine mechanics now seeking a more lucrative, albeit illegal, livelihood, cheating the equipment they once had serviced and repaired. These former mechanics were effective cheaters because of their intimate knowledge of the inside workings of the machines.

"I'd like you to meet with the coin-machine operators this afternoon," Campbell said. "They need help."

"What do we know about slot machines?" Zeke asked.

"We can learn. We fit the bill because we've run across a lot of these crossroaders while working narcotics."

"Crossroaders" is a term used to describe people who cheat gambling houses, and dates to Old West days when most inns (where gambling flourished) were located at intersections—crossroads—and hustlers traveled the circuit on horseback from one to another.

We met five coin-machine operators in the offices of United Coin Machine Company on Highland Avenue, one block west of the Strip. The problem was much as Keith Campbell had explained. Our prospective clients were financially well off. They had been on the winning (the house) end of gambling for a long time, but the crossroaders were doing to them what an individual, no matter how high his or her I.Q., or a betting system could never accomplish. They asked if we could reverse the situation back to the unbeatable status quo they formerly had enjoyed.

We were not sure, but since Campbell's visit we had given the matter some hasty thought and were determined to sell ourselves to these people as best we could. Zeke's job was to nod knowingly while I did the talking.

"Obviously," I said, "we can't put a man in each joint to watch your equipment, but what we will do is visit every place. We'll talk to the bartenders and all other employees, educate them on what to watch for, and make sure they know we're on twenty-four-hour call. We'll slap a sticker on each machine warning that it's protected by the Las Vegas Detective Agency and offering a reward for the arrest and conviction of anyone tampering with it."

"That last sounds like a good idea," one of our prospective clients said.

True, although the value was mainly psychological. Many people reading such a sticker don't know what it means and perhaps imagine that tampering with the machine would cause bells to ring, skyrockets to explode, or even a Las Vegas Detective Agency employee to pop out from inside the mechanism and grab them. The idea was to create an aura of security when in fact very little existed.

"Because of our experience working narcotics," I continued, "Zeke and I probably know more about crossroaders than anybody else in the business. We can't protect your equipment mechanically; we're not slot mechanics. And besides, when one hole is plugged these hustlers discover three more. But you know that; you've been trying it for years. If plugging holes worked, you wouldn't have us here now. What we *can* do is put a lot of heat on the people responsible. With the cooperation of the sheriff's office, we can locate them, get them rousted, and make it uncomfortable for them in Las

Vegas. They're not stupid people. Maybe they'll give Reno their action."

"What's this going to cost?" asked Barney Shapiro, who seemed to be the spokesperson for the group. Barney owned United Coin, a large and very successful company.

"A thousand a week," I said. Zeke and I were hoping for $500 a week, which would more than double our combined pay at the sheriff's department.

"Give us a few minutes to confer," Shapiro said. "Take a tour of the building."

Zeke and I left the room and began bickering.

"I was pretty good in there," I said.

"You were fair."

"I convinced them," I said. "They know they need us and that we can help them."

"Need *us?* Do you know how many clients we presently have?"

"Zip."

"Right. So why scare away a good prospect by asking for a thousand a week?"

Before I could answer, we were both proved wrong. Shapiro sent his right-hand man Doyle Davis out to ask us back in.

"Our group," Shapiro said, "is prepared to pay seven hundred and fifty dollars a week to combat this problem. So you don't think we're haggling about price, this figure is based on the amount of equipment each of us has on location. We're paying two dollars a week for each console you protect, and a dollar for each pinball and slot. That comes out to an aggregate seven fifty, each of us paying his fair share."

"We'll try it for seven fifty," I said, much to my partner's relief.

The deal worked better than Zeke or I could ever have imagined. We did what we said we would—visited the joints, talked to employees, laid our stickers on the equipment, arranged for a few rousts—and our clients switched from red ink to black. Our stock rose proportionately. The word spread.

Zeke and I were making more money than we had dreamed possible. But $750 a week? we wondered, envisioning vaster horizons. A dollar to protect a slot machine? There were 10,000 slots in Las Vegas in 1962, and big casinos were as threatened by hustlers as little ones.

An item I invented, but am not proud of, is still being used today in Las Vegas: The Cheaters Book. This was a fat loose-leaf notebook containing some 300 people—and their associates—who had been arrested at one time or another for cheating. Through a colleague in the sheriff's department, we ordered and obtained pictures of all people arrested for cheating, not only in Las Vegas but in Reno as well. Because we included photographs of the associates of the cheaters, this questionable enterprise was probably also libelous.

The Cheaters Book was a best-seller in Nevada. Casino operators ordered them—at $300 a copy—faster than we could have them printed. Our colleague, Zeke, and I split the profits equally.

The Castaways Hotel contracted with Zeke and me to provide security. This entailed hiring *forty* guards, employed by us, to police the hotel and casino. The Mint alone paid us $1,500 a month to provide the services we performed for the coin-machine operators, and the Tropicana retained us at $400 a month just to be on call if they needed us.

The Las Vegas Detective Agency flourished. It owned six cars and had a new Lincoln Continental on lease. We moved to a plush suite of offices at 1111 Las Vegas Boulevard South, the prestigious Heers-Roeder Building.

The job protecting casinos soon involved much more than keeping slot machines from being ripped off. Crews of hustlers—among the most daring and ingenious criminals ever spawned—bedeviled gambling houses the length and breadth of Nevada, but especially in Las Vegas, where the money was (and is), and the gambling game didn't exist that they couldn't cheat. The crews stole tens of millions of dollars each year, at roulette, craps, blackjack—whatever the game, they could rip it off. These people, extremely hard to apprehend, could unquestionably have made their fortunes in the legitimate world. There was about them a certain charm, a Jesse James or John Dillinger appeal as they played David against a mighty Goliath.

The crossroaders employed a deep bag of tricks, and I believe that over time I became more familiar with their methods than anyone else on "our side." At card games they used edgework (marking the sides of cards with a piece of emery board attached to a ring); the punch (a way of marking cards by wearing a ring with a sharp protrusion); sorts (shaving cards so that high cards can be identified); bend (crimping high cards one way, low cards the other); daub (marking cards with a dye, usually hidden in a fake shirt button); and numerous other ways to cheat at poker and blackjack.

Many crossroaders favored the daub. They purchased a dye made from beeswax and secreted it in a shirt button. While practicing (and they spent more time practicing than a pro athletic team), they painted the dye heavily on the cards. As the practice continued, they applied the dye lightly and ever more lightly. The time came when only the crossroaders could spot the dye; it was invisible to everyone else. Red dye was applied to red cards, blue to blue. The beeswax could be purchased in gaming supply stores open to the public; its only purpose, as far as I could tell, was to enable a person to cheat at cards. Craps and roulette were also targeted by the crossroaders.

One of the great cheaters of this period was John Soares, a man who later became a friend of mine. I must say that the dark, handsome Soares possessed balls of iron. He stole millions of dollars in his long career.

Soares developed a move at craps that, literally, could not be detected. When his turn came to throw the dice, he'd rocket them to the other end of the table. The thing was, he only threw *one*. His partner, standing at the other end of the table, would pretend to have been hit by the second die, which Soares in reality still held in his hand. Of course, the porter was unable to find the one that "had fallen to the floor." What Soares did was pass it back to another confederate, who walked it around to the man pretending to be hit.

Now this master cheat was set. Large bets were placed on the "field" (winning numbers included 9 through 12) and again Soares fired the dice—again he threw only one. At the same time, leaning over the end of the table, concealing the action perfectly, his partner was dropping the "lost" die so the 6 showed. Thus, if Soares threw a 3, 4, 5, or 6 (and the odds were two to one in his favor), he had a winner that paid him two to one.

The game didn't exist that the crossroaders didn't cheat. Roulette wheels were tampered with; keno games could be scammed (by putting a few lighter balls in the bowl); even bets on sports events could be sure winners by "past-posting"— making the bet *after* the contest had started, or even after it was over.

I often felt the casinos were shortsighted in their policy toward wages: even today, many people think the job of blackjack dealer is glamorous, but its reality is minimum wage and a constitution able to endure abuse from disgruntled players. The dealers and other casino employees exist in an opulent atmosphere populated by flashy and seemingly rich high rollers, but the employees themselves barely earn a minimum wage. It did not surprise me that many employees agreed to cooperate with crossroaders. A dealer might look the other way while a deck or even a shoe of cards was being substituted, and a floorman had only to take himself to the opposite end of the casino while a slot machine was being opened and rigged.

Crossroaders did indeed feast on every sort of casino action, but slots were their bread and butter. Slots were easy to cheat if the player knew how. Soares and his crew, for example, could open a slot, fix the reels to show a jackpot, and close it back up in less than thirty seconds. Cadillacs were often given away as grand prizes, and unbelievable as it sounds, I estimate Soares and his crew won almost a hundred of these luxury cars. Of course, to avoid detection, the person they had *collect* the jackpot always appeared to be—and was, except in one instance—legitimate. Housewives, businessmen, conventioneers, tourists, all these and more were recruited for the thrill of collecting a one-time jackpot.

Soares never got caught cheating. If he felt too much heat in Nevada, he moved his action to the casinos of London, Turkey, and even Macao. He retired to the good life in California in the early 1970s, and only once, as far as I know, succumbed to the temptation of a comeback. When Atlantic City opened for gambling, he took advantage of inexperienced casino personnel (New Jersey law favored the hiring of local employees to run the games, thus cutting out real pros who might have been more adept at spotting a thief). When the dust settled after Soares's Atlantic City visit, casino managers were shaking their heads wondering what had happened to them.

In any case, the early 1960s were wide-open years in Las Vegas, with the mob running much of the town. Crossroaders obviously had much more to fear from Mafia-connected casino bosses and their tough security guards than from the police or the Las Vegas Detective Agency. Rumors circulated that a few cheats had been beaten severely, then taken up in a helicopter and dropped from 1,000 feet onto a desolate section of desert floor. Crossroaders like Soares may have flourished, but they took terrible risks.

Many of the most successful cheats, I discovered, had learned their skills from casino operators. Soares, for instance, got his start working as a bust-out dealer for the house. Above all else, casino bosses feared a high roller on a hot streak, and when someone began winning serious money, Soares would be called in to deal. He'd second-card the guy a couple of times (deal the second card from the top of the deck) and cool him off.

Most casinos at this time employed bust-out dealers and crap mechanics, and in the small towns throughout Nevada, where travelers might stop for ten minutes or so of gambling, virtually every house employee qualified as a cheat. These out-of-the-way joints were brutal: knowing they had only a few minutes to nick a sucker, they came at him fast and hard. It was unlikely a player would win even a single blackjack hand, much less throw a winning seven at the crap table with the loaded dice the house used.

Out of this tiny desert-town milieu came numerous cheats who graduated to casinos in Reno and Las Vegas and ultimately found it more lucrative to turn their skills against their former employers.

I liked detective work and was obsessed with its possibilities for good—at times the work almost seemed to be in my blood—but partnering a private investigative agency such as we owned soon proved no more satisfying to me than work at the sheriff's department. When I told myself the truth, I had to admit I admired the crossroaders more than some of the people who employed me to catch them. Neither, in a larger sense, were edifying sorts, but there was something about those nonviolent rogues, living by their wits, that placed them a cut above the cold-eyed mobsters with their unbeatable edge—an edge that didn't satisfy their greed, so they employed their own cheats.

Zeke was surprised when I told him I intended to sell my share of our now-thriving business. He was more surprised when I told him what I planned to do: strike out into a totally unrelated field.

"You'll be back in this racket," he said finally, hugging me and wishing me well.

He was right.

4

THE BOUNTY HUNTER

I crossed paths with a semisubstantial sum of money just once in my life and soon we bade each other good-bye. A friend of mine, an "expert" in the lumber business, convinced me we could become timber tycoons harvesting teak trees in Costa Rica and selling the teakwood to U.S. yacht builders. Without adequate thought I invested the proceeds from the sale of my share of the Las Vegas Detective Agency into the venture. We acquired the necessary permits, land leases, and equipment, then headed for Central America.

I loved Costa Rica, even though we quickly went bust. The country is bordered by the Caribbean Sea and Pacific Ocean, and by Nicaragua and Panama. I'm sure bad weather strikes Costa Rica, but it didn't happen while I was there; the norm was sunshine, blue skies, white sand beaches.

Not that we didn't work hard. We did. The problem—fatal, it turned out—was that the equipment we bought wasn't up to the job. It constantly broke down (burned out, blew up); as a result, we spent a lot of time at the beach.

It was during one of my frequent stints at sunbathing that I became friends with a young man who later made a name for himself. A Nicaraguan, he loved his country while hating the government, a dictatorship headed by Anastasio Somoza De-Bayle. My new friend's name was Eden Pastora, and later, as the Sandanista's "Commander Zero," he helped bring down the tyrant. Pastora, an independent type (a dreamer, I think), later joined the Contras, but these "freedom fighters" (Ronald Reagan's words) weren't to his liking either. When he began talking about a "third force" in Nicaragua during the 1980s he nearly got killed—rumors implied involvement by the CIA.

I kept in touch with Pastora for many years. I even talked with him about a writer friend of mine, Bill Hoffman, and me collaborating on a book with him about his adventures. Though his politics were different from Che Guevara's, his activities and idealism, backed by action, had about them a similar aura.

Even in the mid-1960s I had a stubborn streak; I didn't give up easily, which is not always a good quality. I operated the equipment whenever we could make it run, and ended up beating a dead horse, as the saying goes.

Back in Las Vegas in early 1966, I met with a skip-tracer friend of mine, Frank Richards, and told him I needed work. By the way, calling Frank Richards a skip-tracer is like describing Beethoven as someone who composed tunes. Richards ranked as a master at what he did, which was finding people who wanted to stay lost. Of course, he had excellent connections with necessary sources like the police, the telephone company, and the Social Security Administration, but even when all these failed he was still a champion bloodhound and more—he possessed an eerie sixth sense when it came to tracking down criminals.

"I got a friend who can help you out," Richards told me. "I work for him sometimes myself. He can always use reliable help, and I think you'll like him. You guys are two peas in a pod: tough and stand-up."

Two peas in a pod? When I got to know the man he talked

about, I dearly hoped the description was wrong, though "Papa" Ralph Thorson did have some positives—if one looked very hard to find them.

I called Papa Ralph, then flew to L.A. and met him at the North Hollywood house out of which he conducted his business. He was already on his way to becoming a legend, and he made an impression on me right away. Papa Ralph was six feet two inches and 350 pounds, a mean, tough ex–opera singer and heavyweight boxer who called himself "Scorpius" and claimed to capture fugitives through the use of astrological projections.

I winced when he tried that story on me. It impressed some of his wealthy Hollywood clients, a few of whom wouldn't get out of bed in the morning until they learned what the stars foretold for the day. To Thorson's credit he didn't disqualify me as a potential employee because I said he was full of shit. He had enough savvy to know that he needed good investigators; he had more business than he could handle, and none of it could be concluded satisfactorily if he relied on astrology buffs.

Later Thorson became the subject of a book, *The Hunter,* written by Christopher Keane, and a movie based on the book starring Steve McQueen. I thought McQueen, who became Papa Ralph's pal, did a terrific job, though he bore no physical resemblance whatsoever to his subject.

It was 10:00 A.M. when I visited Thorson's home for the job interview, and he had already started on his second fifth of Scotch. I expected him to be loud, filled with braggadocio, but instead he impressed me as rather quiet and thoughtful, hardly the image the press had portrayed—which was why he seldom talked to the media. I guess reporters portrayed the image they wanted to see in the man who was the most famous—and maybe, in the true sense, the last—member of a disappearing profession.

Papa Ralph Thorson was a bounty hunter. He hunted fugitives, usually for bail-bonding companies; when a suspect jumped bail, Thorson went to work, always for a healthy percent of the bond. If, say, the bond were $100,000, Thorson could and did ask for as much as half the money.

The bonding companies were willing to pay. Why not? They never came to Papa Ralph unless they were desperate, in danger of losing everything. In such a circumstance, losing only half was a bargain.

"I need a guy with balls," he said. "The people we chase aren't Sunday-school teachers."

I didn't say a word. What was I supposed to do, tell him I was tough? Besides, I wasn't sure I wanted the job. It seemed too much like being a cop.

"I figure you're okay in the balls department," he continued, pouring himself a glass of Scotch and downing half of it in a gulp. "I hear you worked for Ralph Lamb in Vegas, and he runs a tough crew."

"Yeah." I continued to stare at him, which I knew would impress him more than anything I could say. He wasn't accustomed to anyone looking him in the eye.

"I guess you'll do," he said, making his decision right away. I figured he needed help badly. Also, I never doubted he'd fire me in a New York second if I didn't shape up.

"What do you pay?" I was broke, and child-support payments I'd been making regularly would soon be in arrears. "How about a percentage of the action?"

"Nobody gets a percentage but me. But I'll pay you good."

And he did. It wasn't long before he made me his partner.

Papa, who had a long wild beard, showed me around the office (his house) that first day. The place featured gadgets and lots of guns, books on bridge—he was a tournament-class player—and many pamphlets on food and nutrition. I learned he ate as prodigiously as he drank, and he was constantly popping diet pills, mainly to keep himself awake.

I rented an apartment that evening just off Fountain Avenue and reported for work the next day. It turned out the routine never varied. I'd sip coffee and he'd swig Scotch while leafing through a thick file of fugitives to determine who we'd go after next. He never lacked for work, and I appreciated that we weren't hunting small-timers. The people we tracked had skipped out on *big* bonds, and large bonds meant major crimes. None of the roust or harassment arrests I'd made as a sheriff's detective. The suspects we went after belonged in custody.

I learned a lot about Thorson in a very short time. Physically, he was the strongest man I've ever met. I saw him open heavy, locked doors by swatting them completely off their hinges with an open-handed swipe. He could tear off a car door with his bare hands, and he was unbelievably quick for a man his size. He knocked guys out by *slapping* them.

Papa often accompanied me on hunts with his white shepard dog that he said was half wolf. The dog was trained in both voice and hand commands, the voice commands always issued in German so the animal wouldn't follow anyone else's orders. The dog was huge, vicious, and truly fearsome. I felt sorry for him. I have never felt animals should be used the way Papa used his: to scare and (if necessary) hurt people.

Many of our hunts took us out of California, and we broke some laws bringing fugitives back. Still, I found it remarkable that—legally—we had more authority than regular law-enforcement officers. Superior Court Judge Mark Brandler, a Los Angeles County jurist, pretty much quoted the law in the following opinion: "Out of state bail bondsmen apparently have greater rights with respect to obtaining custody of a fugitive from justice than does a peace officer from another state. Although peace officers must go through the courts by way of extradition proceedings to obtain custody of a suspected law violator, under existing law a bail bondsman can gain custody of a fugitive without the necessity of resorting to state court procedures."

We chased and usually caught—we didn't get paid if we didn't catch them—murderers, armed robbers, child molesters, and kidnappers. A few times we brought them back to Los Angeles in planes, but mostly we drove. Papa often was extremely cruel to these people, and—unintentionally—we became a natural hard cop/soft cop team.

I didn't try to keep up with Thorson in the drinking department, but on long drives we'd imbibe heavily, telling each other it was a way to pass time. Actually, by this time, I'd cut down on my drinking, and soon I stopped altogether. The event that tipped me into becoming a rest-of-my-life teetotaler occurred on a trip with Ralph. A group of people I didn't know beat the shit out of me and threw me into a swimming pool where I almost drowned. I didn't like being so unprepared and gave up alcohol cold turkey.

We were expert at finding people, whether we acted singly or together, but we didn't kid ourselves that we were embodiments of Hercule Poirot or Sherlock Holmes. Papa had innumerable informants and cops eager to help in exchange for his generous tokes.

Papa and I shared many adventures. He related one of them in *The Hunter,* in a chapter titled "The Mission Impossible Snatch." He called me "Ramsey" in the chapter, and he gave Frank Richards (who'd introduced us) the name "Tommy Price." Because it is a good story, and because he took literary license to make it even better, I don't mind telling it again—what *really* happened.

A big-time dope smuggler and wholesaler named Paco Carrera* had been busted in L.A., jumped bail, and fled to his stronghold on the Baja peninsula in Mexico. Carrera's bondsman, standing to lose a fortune, wanted Paco back. It was one thing to snatch a fugitive from Kansas; however, quite another to grab him out of another country. Papa agreed to try for three reasons: (1) he hated drug dealers; (2) he stood to make a lot of money if successful; and (3) he loved adventure, the more danger the better, and this caper promised plenty of danger.

Thorson went all out. He paid for $300 suits for himself and me, rented a limousine, and bought an expensive chauffeur's outfit for Frank Richards. Thorson and I planned to pose as rich Americans wanting to lease land—Carrera had loads of land—and when the opportunity presented itself, we intended to hit Carrera on the head and hustle him back to the States.

I could envision a hundred ways this scheme could go wrong, but Thorson was adamant. Dressed to the nines, we sat in the back of the limo and rode through Tijuana and down the coast to Rosarita Beach, Carrera's headquarters. Richards, a great skip-tracer, didn't have a lot of heart for escapades like this one, and after he complained a few times, Ralph closed the sliding window between front seat and back so he couldn't hear him. Now I had Papa to myself.

"We're likely to get killed on this crazy prank," I pointed out.

"We'll do it just like we did the others."

"The others you talk about didn't employ a gang of killers as protection."

"I told you, we'll wait till we get him alone."

There was no arguing with Papa and, besides, I sort of enjoyed the danger myself. I leaned back, enjoyed the stunning scenery, and listened to Thorson, a very eloquent man, hold forth on the evils of drugs. I knew he meant every word he said, but I didn't think we'd have been making this trip without the lure of collecting a big bounty.

We rented a fabulous suite of rooms with an ocean view just three blocks from Carrera's real-estate office, freshened up, and went calling on the drug dealer. Paco was on his way out the door—for a vacation in Acapulco, it turned out—when our big blue Cadillac limo pulled up in front. Hiding his fear rather well, I thought, Richards hopped out of the driver's seat and held open the car door.

I have to admit, we looked like money. Paco put his Acapulco plans on hold long enough to see what we wanted.

"What do you want?" he asked, shaking our hands warmly.

"Land," Papa said. "We're looking to lease lots of land."

"You are in luck. I have a great deal of land. Wonderful land, your eyes won't believe it."

Carrera led us into his office, and somehow he and Thorson got involved with, of all things, *a discussion of poets.* While they warmed to each other with talk about Keats and Shelley, I kept a discreet eye on Paco's bodyguard Baez,* a short wad of muscle who spoke in grunts.

Eventually Thorson and Carrera got back to the question of land. In his book Thorson quoted Paco, also a rather eloquent rascal (and the quote seemed fairly accurate), as describing his choicest land as resting next to "the unconquered sea. I have two hundred acres of frontier, two hundred acres of the most exquisite terra firma you have ever seen. Cortez stood upon it. Maximilian rode across it. Pancho Villa ravaged it. And the great Zapata made love to beautiful women upon it."

"It sounds wonderful," said Ralph, whose own house and grounds were neighborhood eyesores. "When can we see it?"

"If you like, right away."

Screw the Acapulco vacation. Carrera had two rich Americans ready to be plucked. Paco and Papa walked out of the office, each with an arm around the other's shoulder, while I kept my eye on Baez. No matter what his boss thought, he viewed us with obvious suspicion.

We had to admit the 200 acres were very impressive, and Thorson decided he wanted to buy. He and Carrera dickered over the price, finally arriving at $500,000. Papa said he'd have his lawyers draw up the papers—it would take a week, he said, and meanwhile we'd just take it easy right here in Rosarita Beach.

"A whole week," Ralph later said. "If we're any good at all we ought to be able to snatch him in a week."

Carrera insisted on a cash payment, and Papa acted like that was the most normal thing in the world. As expected, Carrera decided to postpone the Acapulco trip till he closed the deal.

Papa was a strictly need-to-know guy, and I was pleasantly surprised to learn that we weren't ad-libbing everything. When Carrera asked what business we were in, Thorson handed him a business card, and when the drug dealer called the number, Ralph's wife, posing as a secretary, confirmed that we were indeed big-time operators.

Papa and Paco drank like fish; they seemed to revel in each other's company. I began to wonder if Ralph had forgotten why we'd come here, but I needn't have worried. One night, alone in our suite, he said he knew I was keeping my eye on Baez, whom he described as "a stone killer." That's how I'd sized him up, too.

But it wasn't just Baez. Carrera had a dozen or so guys—if he'd been Mafia we'd have called them soldiers—around him at various times. Four days went by and not a single opportunity arose to snatch our prey.

On the fifth day of Papa and Paco partying it was Frank Richards who came up with a plan to speed matters along. He suggested we charter a boat and invite Carrera to go fishing. Only Baez and the charter skipper (no problem with him) would likely come along, and surely the three of us could grab them. Without having to worry about Paco's other goons, we figured it would be easy to sail up the coast and dock in San Diego.

Thorson was usually the most careful of men, but he messed up big-time out on that boat. He got caught up trying to land a sailfish that seemed to be stronger than him, and while he sweated, strained, and cursed he didn't notice Carrera going through his tote bag and finding the big .45 he'd hidden inside. When Papa turned triumphant from having caught the fish, he found Baez pointing a gun at my head, and Paco holding one to his.

Papa did his best. He acted outraged, said he always carried a gun for protection ("Don't you?" he asked Carrera), but Paco didn't buy it.

Here's where Thorson got carried away in his book. He said Frank Richards (Tommy Price in the book) lunged toward Baez, who accidentally killed the skipper before murdering Richards. The force of the bullet, said Papa, hurtled Richards over the railing and out to sea, lost forever.

The truth was more prosaic, and plenty exciting for me: no one got killed; but Richards, Papa, and I were tied securely, taken back to Carrera's office, and thrown into a basement dungeon while he decided what to do with us.

It didn't take a genius to figure it out. With $500,000 cash due to arrive the following day—the seventh day, at 2:00 P.M.—Carrera would keep us alive to sign for it. After that, *adios.* He'd have the money *and* the land.

Of course, there wasn't any money coming. We knew Paco's eventual realization of our bluff would only make him angrier, and that we could count on a slow death instead of a bullet in the brain.

The next day at 1:45 P.M. Baez untied Richards, Papa, and me, keeping us carefully covered with a pistol.

Time had run out. No more second guesses; no more escape

plans. Definitely no more waiting quietly to be killed. Desperate for a makeshift weapon, I spotted a piñata club leaning against the wall. I caught Papa's eyes and guided them toward our possible salvation. He nodded slightly.

I tipped my chair over and crashed with it against the floor to momentarily distract Baez. Papa, lightninglike, went for the club and dealt our captor a hammer blow to the head, a ferocious shot. Buying a couple of seconds paid off; everyone's role reversed.

In our haste to vamoose we made the mistake of not tying up Baez. Instead we grabbed Paco and half-dragged, half-carried him to the Rosarita Beach Hotel parking lot where the limousine waited. This time I drove, fast as I could, Frank Richards in front with me, an enraged Thorson in the backseat with Carrera, administering an awful beating.

Then, as they say, it was like the movies. Baez must have recovered and alerted some associates, because soon I spotted in the rearview mirror an old car barreling up from behind. The guy in the passenger seat was firing a gun in the air; the driver waved frantically for us to pull over.

Sure. I floored the gas pedal and in no time they were miles behind. Unbelievably, Thorson later complained that I should have *slowed down* so he could have fired back.

We drove *around* Tijuana, not through it, figuring Carrera had friends in the border town, and then all that separated us from safety was the international border crossing gate. It's a fact of life that Mexican police are more likely to be corrupt than their U.S. counterparts; with that in mind I didn't want to stop on the Mexican side. In a move Papa *did* approve of, I crashed the limo through a wooden gate and screeched to a halt in the American sector. Soon we were surrounded by border guards from both sides.

Thorson, a silver-tongued devil who never met a cop who didn't know a cop he knew, soon had the U.S. guards on his side. Without seeming to, he name-dropped bigwig customs agents who were his pals, and DEA agents, and he soon had the American guards eating out of his hand. Fact is, they were happy we'd caught Carrera, and without much of a beef from the Mexicans we were waved on through. It was just a short drive from the border to the San Diego Hall of Justice where we dropped off Mr. Paco Carrera and then continued on to L.A.

Not long after this adventure I left Papa Ralph, though we stayed in touch over the years. I had obtained a California p.i. license, and as a sideline to working as a bounty hunter I had conducted a few criminal investigations of my own. I enjoyed the work and felt genuinely needed, something that hadn't been the case as a sheriff's detective, as partner in the Las Vegas Detective Agency, or as a tracker of fugitives with Thorson. Las Vegas survived very nicely without me; casinos prospered even though I wasn't snaring any crossroaders; and I doubted any bail bondsman would go bust because I wasn't out there with Papa.

Defense work was different. Bad things could happen to someone ensnared with the law who didn't have help. Almost as important, I suppose, was the fact that I'd never really done anything all by myself—even with the Costa Rican fiasco I'd had a partner—and I dearly wanted to try. I named my new business Lake Headley, Investigations, and operated out of my apartment off Fountain Avenue.

A final note about Thorson. After his book came out I occasionally called to rib him by saying, "I must be losing my mind."

"Why do you think that, Lake?" he asked, genuinely concerned (but only the first time).

"Geez, Papa, I thought I saw Frank Richards an hour or so ago. I even *thought* I talked to him. But you and I know that can't be. He got killed on that fishing boat in Mexico."

5

MEMORABLE
EARLY CASES

Much of the work I did over the years came from defense attorneys, and I likened my job to that of a hod carrier. I tried to bring lawyers the bricks with which they could construct a solid defense. I did the job of a police detective, although our goals were diametrically opposed. No matter what a cop says—and most, to get a confession, will even profess to be a suspect's friend ("Talk to me; I want to help you")—his or her purpose in life is helping a district attorney convict, and all the odds are stacked in the d.a.'s favor.

I had met several defense attorneys in L.A. while working with Papa Ralph, and after I went on my own I made sure to call on—almost like a door-to-door salesman—many more. I needed to eat, and to help support my children in Las Vegas. Even if I did have a better mousetrap, clients weren't going to beat down a door they didn't know existed.

The following cases from this period of my life have always remained vivid in my mind.

The Honest Cop

Los Angeles Police officer Pete Wilson* ranked as an absolute straight arrow. I knew policemen—I'd spent a lifetime with them (starting with my own father)—and Wilson was what they ought to be and seldom are. Young and good-looking, married, with two kids, he had a spotless ten-year record on the Los Angeles force. "Spotless" records often get achieved by cops who determine very early to rock no boats, grab the pension, and run. Not Wilson. I became close to him and learned that he was a dedicated, Mafia-hating, crime-busting cop who naively believed everyone else shared his ideals.

Wilson's problem—a giant one—stemmed from his use of an informant named Kenny, a Los Angeles burglar and partner of Jack Murphy, Murph the Surf, who stole the famed Star of India. Kenny served as one of Wilson's eyes and ears on the drug activities of the L.A. Mafia. Wilson's mistake, if such it should be called, involved not watching his own snitch closely enough.

The Drug Enforcement Administration (DEA), a government body richly deserving a critical examination, raided Wilson's home on a tip "from a reliable source," the old standby responsible for so many violations of civil liberties. Of course, the warrant-seeking DEA claimed that revealing the "reliable source" would place his life in danger.

When I was using the "reliable source" scam to obtain search warrants in Las Vegas, my source was usually another cop. I'll say this: the cop was *very* reliable. Often he had illegally broken into the house in advance, found (or planted) the incriminating evidence, and now wanted to make the search legal.

The DEA found a kilo of high-grade cocaine hidden in Pete Wilson's refrigerator. Of course they did. As I became absorbed in the case, I became convinced Kenny had planted it there.

I was retained by noted Los Angeles civil-rights and defense attorney Luke McKissack to head the investigation. Meeting McKissack not only marked the start of a long, rewarding relationship, but provided me with a fresh personal and political perspective that changed me from activist for the establishment to defender of unpopular causes. Luke McKissack, in short, put me on the road I traveled the rest of my life.

The Wilson case was difficult to defend. Most people tend to believe their government, and their government, in this instance, said it had found a kilo of coke in the accused's refrigerator. Few citizens were willing to accept that law enforcement, through Kenny, put it there.

I became convinced of it but, sadly, could never prove my premise. I did uncover incontrovertible evidence that the cocaine belonged to Kenny, but the prosecution succeeded in waving this aside and emphasizing *where* the dope had been found.

Knowing I risk sounding loony, I think Kenny served three masters: Pete Wilson; the Mafia; and the DEA. Perhaps the mob learned Kenny was ratting to Wilson, contacted its friends in the government, and set up the honest cop. Thus, the DEA got credit for a bust, and the Mafia ridded itself of a pest.

What Pete Wilson got was a twenty-five-year sentence in Leavenworth.

The verdict made me physically ill. Of course, Wilson was the one who paid the terrible price—my feelings counted zip in comparison. Still, the case came back to haunt me at the most unexpected times. Could I have done more? Why didn't I do this? Or that?

I know two things. Pete Wilson wasn't guilty, and winning beats losing every time.

The United States Versus the Teamsters

This investigation featured murder and busted heads, one of them almost being mine. Teamster officials in Vernon, California, were charged by the federal government under the Hobbs Act with "violence and extortion" and faced *minimum* forty-year sentences for "conspiring to control" the delivery of more than 1,000 truckloads of meat a week. I was hired by the union itself to prepare the defense.

Right away I learned that "conspiring to control" meat deliveries meant primarily that the Teamsters were on strike, a time-honored American method of trying to get more pay from the boss. If the charge was allowed to stick, any union leader who called a strike could be charged with "conspiring to control" whatever industry his workers were picketing.

This strike did indeed feature plenty of violence, about equally distributed on each side. Employers used scabs and free-lance muscle; the union relied on its members. It seemed to me significant that only union people got indicted.

The case drew national attention because of the extreme violence—pitched battles with knives and meat hooks—and ultimately it even was featured on "Sixty Minutes."

I wanted to know what the other side was up to, so I went undercover posing as a sympathizer for the employers. It turned out to be a good move. I was able to tape conversations and meetings where plans were made to disrupt legal union activities.

After I surfaced in my true role as chief defense investigator for the indicted union leaders, I became involved in a potentially deadly game of "bumper car" with a man I'd identified as an FBI informant. He'd been following me for several days and, evidently frustrated, tried to run me off the road. He pulled alongside me on a lonely stretch of road and rammed his car into mine. *Fuck this,* I thought, and slammed my car into his—four times. He careened into a ditch, and I went back to see if he was okay.

He said, unbelievably I thought, "Who's going to pay for the damage to this car?"

"Why not send the bill to the Justice Department?" I suggested.

"I hadn't thought of that," he said.

Another time, leaving my motel, I spotted two large men approaching me with pipes in their hands. I removed the big gun I usually carried (I didn't mind going armed for self-protection, which hadn't usually been the case working for the sheriff's department) and assumed a shooter's stance. The two thugs—dressed in blue suits—smoothly veered in a less threatening direction.

Government prosecutors refused to take our advice (I didn't expect them to) and file charges against management, but they had to back away from the really serious penalties against the union leadership. A chief reason we could claim at least a partial victory was the hundreds of feet of movie film I managed to take of FBI agents illegally interfering with picket lines. That footage, if shown in a courtroom, would have been very injurious to the image of an "impartial" police agency.

The Friars Club Cheating Case

The last thing the venerable Friars Club wanted was a seamy scandal, but that's just what it got in the late 1960s when headlines proclaimed that some of its famous members had been bilked out of large sums of money in rigged gin-rummy games. Founded in 1904 in New York City, this all-male enclave (until 1988, when Liza Minnelli was admitted) provided for major entertainers the kind of ambience that, say, the Harvard Club offers important businessmen. The Friars eventually opened a branch in Los Angeles, where many of its members resided.

The Friars are proud of their history. Irving Berlin wrote "Alexander's Ragtime Band" in 1911 as part of a fund-raiser to build a bigger clubhouse. The clubhouse did indeed get built, and two famous songs were written there: George M. Cohan's "Over There" in 1919, and Bernie Wayne's "There She Is, Miss America."

A list of famous Friars Club members would take several pages to recount. I'll name just a few of them here: Frank Sinatra, George Raft, Milton Berle, Sid Caesar, Red Buttons, Joe E. Lewis, and George Jessel.

My first hint of something amiss came in a phone call from defense attorney Guy Ward, past president of the California Bar Association. "I have a case that's right up your alley," he said.

I resisted asking what my "alley" was—I hoped it was exotic, maybe finding missing heiresses—and instead made an appointment to see Ward later in the day. When I arrived at his rather extravagant office (a relative judgment, I guess, since I still operated out of my apartment) he introduced me to our client. His name was Billy and I'd heard of him. He was a crossroader, a good one, better than good when it came to cards. He had a reputation for being able to do *anything* with a deck of cards.

If I'd needed perking up, the story I heard did the job. Celebrities such as Zeppo Marx, the shoe magnate Harry Karl, Tony Martin, and others had lost hundreds of thousands of dollars in a rigged gin game at the Friars Club in Beverly Hills.

Like most professionals in the crime business, I try not to

ask questions when I don't know the answers, or when I might not like what I hear. I prefer to represent innocent people, and usually I have, but I adhere to the school that says everyone deserves a defense. Regardless, I knew Billy's reputation and had to admit that if I were the cops, I might suspect him, too.

On the other hand, I couldn't work myself into a lather over these rich entertainers being cheated. I'd already met a lot of people with *real* problems.

The thing was, Billy was scared, scared stiff, and this didn't fit the ultracool reputation he'd earned. He dodged questions about what had put God's fear in him. He didn't want to talk, and because I wasn't quick on the pickup I started to get hot.

"They're saying Billy was the mastermind," Guy Ward interjected softly.

That didn't fit.

"Billy is their prime target," Ward added.

Now even slow-as-molasses Headley could figure it out. Billy might have been involved, but he was being set up to take the heaviest rap by some very powerful hitters. He didn't want a long prison stretch, but onerous as that prospect was, defending himself would surely be worse. To defend himself he'd have to name others, and these people killed just for fun.

I've never been accused of diplomacy, but this one time that's what was required. I'm proud to say I believe I passed the test.

Still, I didn't feel on truly safe ground, so I conducted the "fun" part of the investigation first. I gained entrance to the Friars Club, a feat normally beyond my power, because they *had* to let me in. I looked at the peepholes bored into the Friars Club ceiling, peepholes that had been manned by spies who used *bomb sights* to study the players' hands, then transmitted the information to cohorts in the game who were electronically wired to receive it.

Those stars hadn't had a chance.

I even called on some of the stars who had been cheated, not because it was crucial to Billy's case, but because I wanted to be able to say I'd met these celebrities. Interestingly, the chief reaction of one—who lost more than $100,000—was fear that his reputation as a cardsharp would be damaged.

That ended the fun. Right away I'd been able to figure out whom I needed to see, and I didn't relish the idea at all. Indicted as a co-conspirator was Johnny Roselli, one of the top Mafia mobsters in the country, the de facto head of the L.A. mob and a character I knew as Chicago's representative overseeing its interests in Vegas. Roselli was also a powerful figure in the motion-picture industry, of which the mob had a sizable chunk.

Billy D the mastermind? Roselli a co-conspirator? The prosecutors had turned the world upside down. But how to prove it without getting both of us killed?

I knew from innumerable sources in Las Vegas that Roselli was a hands-on killer, though more often he used subordinates. A sophisticated gangster, welcome in genteel circles, he increasingly, and wisely, had others do his hits. Somehow that wasn't any solace.

I figured I had two choices: I could go see Roselli, or quit being a p.i. It always came down to that. Throughout my life, when people said I had courage, it wasn't that at all. What it boiled down to was that if I wanted to be a good investigator—and I needed that more than anything—I could either do the tough things or admit I didn't have what it takes. "This is too risky," I suppose I could have told a defense attorney.

What would he say to that? He *should* say, "Well, pal, I'll see you. I need to find somebody else."

I visited Johnny Roselli in his extravagant Las Vegas hotel suite. A dapper little guy, about five feet seven inches, he wore a powder blue bathrobe over silk pajamas, and when he waved me into an easy chair fronting a big glass coffee table,

I saw through the suite's large picture window that he had a panoramic view of almost the entire Strip. I thought it appropriate. Howard Hughes's "cleanup" (he bought much of Vegas) hadn't yet begun, so who better than a mobster to see what mobsters had wrought?

Roselli had connections with Las Vegas police officials, one of whom had arranged this meeting. I smiled at Roselli. He was a handsome rascal. A little research had told me he was in his late fifties, though he looked much younger. Never adept at dancing around a point, I'd decided to lay my problem right on the line. Well, almost right on the line. I figured the walls had ears.

"That deal in L.A.," I began. "I . . ."

"Right," he interrupted. "I like that guy." Billy. "I appreciate what he wants." Staying out of jail. "A person should get what he wants, long as he doesn't hurt others." Aha! I thought. "You understand?"

"Yes," I said.

"Well, Lake, it's been good meeting you." We both stood up and shook hands, and then Roselli led me to the door. He said to come see him any time I wanted.

"Right," I said, and that's the last time I ever saw John Roselli. A person couldn't help reading about him, though. He later got implicated in a plot with the CIA to assassinate Fidel Castro, and just days before he was scheduled to testify in front of the House Assassinations Committee looking into the murder of JFK, his chopped-up body was found floating in an oil drum in a Florida swamp. Obviously, he'd become a problem to somebody.

For me, he'd been a problem *solver.* What he'd told me was that Billy and I could do whatever we wanted as long as it didn't hurt *him.* That's all we needed. We pointed out to prosecutors, often and vigorously, that they'd look foolish trying to make Billy the mastermind of a plot involving the

notorious John Roselli, whom we called a "Mafia chieftain."
We called him a lot of bad things (never for publication), and
the prosecutors ate it up. We didn't have to persuade them
that Roselli was a bad apple. They didn't ask for proof; they
figured they *knew,* and that was good, because this pal of Sam
Giancana and Meyer Lansky would have taken umbrage if
we'd offered anything solid.

It all worked out for Billy. He never appeared in court. The
prosecutors let him plea-bargain and he received a suspended
sentence. Later he told me I'd saved his life, but it wasn't true.
Johnny Roselli had saved his life.

The Army Versus Billy Dean Smith

If I ever took part in a "Mission Impossible" case, it was this
one. No one gave us a chance. Everyone, and I mean everyone, told Luke McKissack and me that our client was doomed
to life in prison. Our job, friends said, was to make political
points, namely, that the war in Vietnam was unjust. Win the
case? Forget that. It wasn't possible.

Our client was a black man, a twenty-four-year-old U.S.
Army private named Billy Dean Smith. A former bus driver
and mechanic, Billy Dean was accused of having thrown a
hand grenade into quarters occupied by three officers. The
event occurred at 12:50 A.M. on March 15, 1971, at Bienhoa
army base in South Vietnam.

Two of the officers died in the blast: Lieutenant Richard E.
Harlan of Dallas, Texas, and Lieutenant Thomas A. Dellwo
of Mechanicsville, Tennessee. A third officer, Lieutenant Peter
B. Higgins, was wounded. Smith was charged with two counts
of murder, assault (for the wounds inflicted on Higgins), and
two counts of attempted murder. The prosecution claimed his
intention had been to kill two other men: Captain Randall

Rigby, Jr., of Fort Sill, Oklahoma, and First Sergeant Billie E. Willis of Big Stony Gap, Virginia.

Prior to the army's charges against Smith, it had admitted there had been 551 previous "fragging" incidents, in which fragmentation grenades had been thrown, resulting in 86 deaths. A number of these were unsolved. A few of the alleged perpetrators had been court-martialed, but always overseas, and all had been convicted. Billy Dean Smith's court-martial, held at Ford Ord, California, would be the first heard in this country.

The chief prosecutor, Captain Richard Wright, believed he had a pretty straightforward case: Billy Dean Smith had accused Rigby and Willis of being racists, had talked to friends about "getting" them, and had thrown the grenade into quarters he thought the two occupied. Wright had a witness he said would testify that he'd seen Smith running from the murder scene shortly after the explosion. Wright also said he could link a grenade pin found in Smith's pocket to a grenade lever discovered near the murder scene.

Pretty powerful stuff. But that wasn't what worried us most. Research into courts-martial told us that defendants were almost always found guilty. When someone got charged, it meant that higher-ups approved, and court-martial panels (the juries) would be insane to go against the wishes of their superiors. Insane, that is, if they wanted to continue upward climbs in their military careers.

Billy Dean Smith's case was even more daunting to the defense. Top brass badly wanted to make an example of him. The fragging, which approached epidemic proportions, just wasn't acceptable to the military.

The army had one problem. Billy Dean Smith, despite the alleged formidable array of evidence, wasn't guilty. But the defense had an even larger problem. We had to prove he wasn't guilty. McKissack and I didn't kid ourselves about this. High-sounding ideals like the burden of proof resting with the prosecution didn't apply in the real world of court-martial.

Physical evidence is always the most difficult to overcome, so I first investigated whether a grenade pin could really be linked to a grenade lever. I flew to Japan, where the grenades had been manufactured, and learned the claim was nonsense. To be fair, it wasn't that the prosecution was trying to flim-flam us: they mistakenly believed that markings on grenade pins fell into the same category as striations on bullets; i.e., that a certain bullet can be absolutely linked to a certain gun. In fact, any pin would look like any other, and the same held true of grenade levers. McKissack and I decided to let the prosecution present its hand-grenade "evidence," and then destroy it with our three experts.

Japan for me was like a different planet. The pace was faster than I was used to, and even though I'm just average height in my country, I was eyeballed almost like a freak in Tokyo.

I flew from Tokyo to Saigon and interviewed many GIs. Talking to these young men brought back memories of when I'd served in Germany as a member of our army of occupation. I couldn't help but think how much tougher these men had it than I had. My army buddies never doubted that what we did was right, nor did I. *All* the GIs I interviewed in Saigon questioned the justness of the war.

Visiting Saigon was helpful to us, just as traveling to Tokyo had been. Soldier after soldier told me that Billy Dean's alleged threats against officers counted for nothing. *Everybody* bullshitted with buddies about "getting" this officer or that. It was as common as griping about the weather.

"Would you testify at Smith's court-martial," I asked, "if we called you?"

Not a single GI refused. "Everybody," they said, knew about threats against officers.

That left the "eyewitness" who had "seen" Billy Dean running away from the explosion site. Luke McKissack said he thought we'd be all right. He believed that the man had been pressured into the statement by zealous army investigators, and that he could be shaken on the stand. I hoped so. I'd gotten to like Billy Dean, a quiet, committed young man.

Luke McKissack and I usually operated on identical wavelengths, but just before the court-martial began we had a major disagreement. In fact, I almost threatened to quit. I would have if it had been just between him and me, but I wanted to stay at Billy Dean's side. The beef was over the composition of the court-martial panel. We had the right to petition for a panel of Billy Dean's peers, enlisted men, but Luke said we'd go with what was normal: all officers.

I thought he was crazy and told him so. A class system exists in the military—the armed services even admit it by assigning ranks from private to general—and the classes stick together. There are even crimes involving "fraternizing" with officers.

Officers weren't going to sympathize with an underprivileged private from the heart of the Watts ghetto, I shouted to McKissack, especially one who doesn't seem particularly saddened by the deaths of Lieutenants Harlan and Dellwo.

McKissack kept his cool better than I did. "That hand-grenade evidence you found," he said. "I want a panel that can understand it. I want the most intelligent people I can find to judge Billy Dean."

Of course, that set me onto another shouting tirade. I called Luke an "elitist," someone who bought the unofficial military line that GIs were just grunts while officers were "gentlemen."

The decision was his, however; I was no more than hired help. What we got were seven officers. Worse than that, if only five of these officers voted guilty, Billy Dean Smith was gone for life.

The court-martial of Billy Dean Smith attracted worldwide attention. I had never seen anything like it. There were demonstrations at Ford Ord every day, and angry confrontations between political activists and hard-line military personnel. Once, entering the building where the trial was taking place, I saw a lieutenant, without provocation, push one of the protestors. Acting on instinct, I grabbed the lieutenant and told him I was making a citizen's arrest. To my surprise, the assault charge stuck, and arresting government employees soon became a trademark of mine.

I believe the Billy Dean Smith court-martial was Luke McKissack's finest moment—and maybe mine, too. Only Wounded Knee and the Bolles case come close. Everything went as we planned. The prosecution several times had to ask for delays to try to find GIs who would say that barracks threats weren't as common as leeches in Vietnam. They didn't find any.

McKissack used what I'd discovered in Tokyo to destroy the grenade evidence. Three unimpeachable witnesses took the stand to say that grenade pins were to levers as apples to oranges.

How about that grenade pin found in Smith's pocket? We called witnesses—I kid not—who showed that Billy Dean was just being a good soldier. GIs in Vietnam regularly carried spare grenade pins to disarm live grenades from which the pin had been removed but on which the "spoon" had been held depressed so the explosion process hadn't yet started.

Billy Dean Smith had an alibi for the time of the killings and, with the help of military records, I found him. Henry McClay of Chicago testified that he and Smith had been smoking a joint in their bunker at the time of the explosion.

I also located Private Hubert E. Brown of Washington, D.C. Let the *New York Times,* October 20, 1972, take up the story: "Mr. Brown, who was also stationed at the Bienhoa Army base where the attack took place, testified that he saw two men running from the scene just after the explosion and could not tell whether they were white or black.

"He said that he offered the information to investigators at the time, and that instead of accepting his statement, they placed him in a line-up of suspects along with Private Smith."

If the trial had been a boxing match, the referee would have stopped it. The final blow was landed when the prosecution called its eyewitness. Luke was ready to cross-examine fiercely, but he didn't have to. The witness, twenty-year-old Bradley Curtin of Thousand Oaks, California, said he had been in his room at Bienhoa when he'd heard the explosion. "I sat there for a couple of minutes," he said, "then I went outside and I saw a lot of people milling around and a colored man running. The man I saw running was not Billy Dean Smith."

The court-martial panel voted 7–0 to acquit. Billy Dean, cool to the end, stood and gave Luke a hug. Then he hugged me.

That for me was the highlight, but there were others. Representing Billy Dean Smith gave me the opportunity to meet fascinating, committed people who otherwise never would have crossed my path. I was able to have long conversations with Angela Davis; Huey Newton, chairman of the Black Panthers; and numerous other activists I came to admire.

Fatalistically, which is how I tended to view things, I figured life couldn't get better than this. Wrong. Right around the corner was what I consider my most rewarding moment.

6

WOUNDED KNEE

The Western Airlines 707 broke through the cloud cover and began its descent into the bright sunlit sky below. The pilot delivered the customary "fasten seat belts and no smoking" speech, as well as the ground temperature of 83 degrees in Rapid City, South Dakota.

"We're here . . . almost," Luke McKissack said apprehensively as we began the approach to Rapid City.

"What did *Time* magazine have to say about Wounded Knee?" I asked, trying to sidetrack his fear of flying.

I knew full well what *Time* had reported, and *Newsweek, Business Week, U.S. News & World Report,* even the *National Lampoon.* Since Luke had been invited to Wounded Knee, and had extended the invitation to me, I had read everything I could put my hands on about the subject. This included Dee Brown's *Bury My Heart At Wounded Knee,* a good book describing the confrontation between Sioux Indians and remnants of Custer's seventh Cavalry that left hundreds of dead Indian men, women, and children strewn in the winter snow. I knew that American Indian Movement (AIM) leaders had carefully chosen the Wounded Knee site for the just-ended confrontation because of its historical and public-relations value. I knew also that AIM was composed of members from all tribes united into a somewhat militant organization determined to better the deplorable conditions Indians lived under in the United States.

The American Indian Movement was born in the Minnesota State Prison in the 1960s. AIM's reputation for action had been firmly established long before Luke McKissack and I boarded that Western jet from Los Angeles to Rapid City in May, 1973.

AIM members had staged the occupation of Alcatraz Island, the now-deserted California state prison in the bay off San Francisco. AIM put together the Trail of Broken Treaties, and the taking of the Bureau of Indian Affairs building in Washington, D.C. It received the dubious distinction of being placed fifth on a list of one thousand subversive organizations compiled by Nelson Rockefeller's Intelligence Committee. The militancy to which I would soon be exposed made me wonder who the first four were.

The 707 slowed to landing speed, and Luke gripped his knees so hard that his knuckles turned white. Luke on a plane was always a good show. His morbid fascination with air crashes had led to a statistical expertise that would have been frightening had anyone cared to dwell on the topic.

Being one of the nation's leading criminal defense lawyers, who travels to trials all over the world, Luke has to fly often, but I doubt if he will ever learn to enjoy it.

Luke's name was always included in evaluations of great lawyers, those breathing in that rarefied atmosphere of Edward Bennett Williams, William Kunstler, Percy Foreman, Louis Nizer, Lenny Weinglass, and F. Lee Bailey. Thus, when 650 felony cases came down from the seventy-two-day occupation of the Trading Post at Wounded Knee, Luke was among the first invited to participate in the defense. Because he valued the quality of investigative work I produced, he asked if I would go along. It was a wonderful opportunity for a p.i., and when Luke offered to pay expenses, that settled it.

It ranked as quite a distinction for a lawyer to be invited to participate in a case with the magnitude of a Wounded Knee, Attica, Chicago Seven, or any of the political trials so commonplace in the late 1960s and early 1970s. A lawyer had to possess certain qualities and qualifications even to be considered for the defense team. Political position and prominence are major factors because the attorney, in the course of the defense, must necessarily make statements in behalf of, and with the explicit consent of, all the defendants. Frequently these statements will have a greater impact on the outcome of the trial than the evidence put before the court. It was important to keep in mind that these trials resulted from acts committed for political motivation, not personal gain. The defense consequently had to emphasize this motivation, and the guilt or innocence of the defendants must fit within that framework.

A lawyer for the defense team in such a trial must be able to sustain himself financially over a long period of time. Political trials seem to run forever, partly because so much needs to be said that prosecutors attempt to exclude. *Why* an act was committed is something diligent prosecutors will go to byzantine lengths to keep off the record.

Poverty is usually the reason a political action takes place, and also why the accused is generally unable to assist financially in his or her own defense. This boils down to *no pay*. Often certain organizations support political trials with cash donations, but the money is primarily used for the myriad expenses of defense preparation—not normally for a lawyer's fee.

So the lawyer in such a trial must have some money. Luke had little or none. But he was engaged to a terrific lady, Jeanne Phillips, a woman whose mother is known professionally as

"Dear Abby," the most widely read syndicated columnist (more than 1,000 newspapers) in the world. Mrs. Phillips, "Dear Abby," is very wealthy and not politically aligned with Luke at all, but she became a reluctant supporter of his endeavors at the insistence of her daughter, Jeanne.

We touched down and taxied to the terminal.

"Nice landing," I said.

"Any you walk away from are okay," Luke said.

Luke stumbled and cursed the airplane on the aluminum stairs leading to the ground, hardly a grand entrance for a skillful, cunning criminal lawyer, as comfortable in a workers' saloon as in front of the U.S. Supreme Court (where he had appeared more times than any other California lawyer). Although a frequent visitor to these and other hallowed halls of justice, he was not the least impressed by elegant surroundings. His own small cluttered and chaotic office displayed on one wall an autographed photo of Huey Newton.

Charles Luke McKissack was five feet ten inches, 170 pounds, with brown eyes. He possessed a profound personal and professional contempt for most lawyers who, he believed, created more problems than they solved and were next to useless in the rough arenas of courtroom and criminal law. That is why many high-dollar attorneys often turned to him when clients found themselves in real trouble. Conceiving and executing complicated legal documents was one thing; swaying a judge and jury in a difficult murder trial was another. Luke had handled scores of capital cases, some so hopeless other lawyers would not touch them; and, like his personal idol Clarence Darrow, no client of his has ever received the ultimate sentence.

Luke was vain, self-centered, egotistical, a dapper dresser who fancied flashy cars. Numbered among his talents were speed reading, almost total recall, and a nearly eerie ability to win big cases. A small reason for his success, I liked to believe, was my participation as an investigator.

Just inside the airport gate we saw a very pretty young Indian woman holding a clipboard and obviously looking for someone. "Maybe that's her," I said.

Luke, more positive, walked straight up to her and said, "I'm Luke McKissack. This is Lake Headley. Luke and Lake—sounds like a dance team."

"Yes," the young woman said, smiling. "Perry Mason and his Paul Drake. Well, I'm Frances Wise."

"Mason and Drake?" Luke said in horror. "They were creeps."

"I came to get you," Frances said, "so we could talk before we go to the office. How about a drink at the bar?"

We followed in single file like ducks while Frances Wise talked over her shoulder. "We were up all night getting Stan Holder out. He's my brother. We just got the last of his bail posted. And we should get Carter Camp out today. The bail is $125,000 and the Council of Churches has okayed putting up a cash bond. That will be all the leadership out on bail— Russ, Dennis, Vern, Clyde, and now Stan and Carter. We're so happy."

I could see she was. Her eyes gleamed with pride. She really was a beautiful woman, with braided black hair that fell to her waist.

Inside the bar Frances said, "Let's sit over there. Away from the racists."

A blond waitress came to the table. It was revealing to see her face change when she was close enough to see that Frances was an American Indian. It had not been so long ago that Indians had not, by law, been allowed to purchase alcohol in South Dakota.

"I'll have a frozen daiquiri," Frances said politely, looking right into the eyes of the waitress.

"J&B and water," Luke said.

"A club soda with lime," I said.

"What would you like to know first?" Frances asked.

"Give us a history lesson," Luke said. "But stay with what's going on now."

Luke had great powers of concentration; he could lock his mind into a situation and exclude all else. He would have been a great chess player, a Bobby Fischer. He was *intense.*

"Here in South Dakota," Frances said, "we have two major Indian reservations, the Rosebud and the Pine Ridge. The Sioux people live in the most degrading fashion on both these reservations. The 'rez,' as it's called, is nothing more than an economic concentration camp, a prison. The U.S. government, through the Bureau of Indian Affairs, keeps the Indian people confined to the rez through economic pressure."

I could tell that Frances had given this talk before. Equally apparent was her commitment to the AIM cause.

"The government and the BIA do not gas Indians, but they are committed to the genocide of our people. The life expectancy of an American Indian male born on a reservation is forty-five years. Indians hold the world record for preteen suicide and preteen alcoholism. Indian women are constantly being tricked into sterilization. The poverty is appalling: the average annual income for a family on the rez is less than fifteen hundred dollars, and this includes all the white man's doles and benefits."

I was taking notes. Luke McKissack just stared into his drink. He does not know how to boil hot dogs, read the most simple road map, or change a light bulb, but I knew he would not forget a word that was said.

"Living conditions are miserable," Frances continued, the

words now coming in a torrent. "Pitiable. Six to eight people live in a one-room house that has no plumbing. Hook that up with the chairman of the tribal council, Dickie Wilson, who openly and notoriously uses his position to steal money sent to the rez by the government. Dickie lives in a big house and is robbing a very needy people, his own. Wilson is what we mean by an 'apple,' an Indian who's red on the outside but white inside. Like our black brothers and sisters mean when they say someone is an Oreo."

"Question," Luke said. "Why don't the Indian people just vote Wilson out?"

"They've tried, believe me. But Wilson is a tyrant who uses force and fear to rule. He has the Sioux police, the BIA, the FBI, and U.S. marshals to enforce his will. And he's formed young toughs into a goon squad to take on jobs too distasteful for his government allies."

"Such as what?" Luke asked.

"The burning of houses on the rez. Beating and killing activists who oppose him. The goon squad enjoys its work, its power, and its pay. We've tried the police, the FBI, even the Justice Department, but they do nothing, take no action. Wilson's their man and they love what he's doing."

Frances may have spoken this speech a hundred times, but the delivery we listened to might just as well have been the first, so passionate were her emotion and demeanor.

"These are only a few of the conditions that exist today on the reservations. Later you'll be given specific cases and specific charges. We have literally hundreds down at the office, where we'll go as soon as we pick up your luggage."

While we walked, my thoughts swept back to my former career as a police officer in Las Vegas. I was familiar with the beatings and killings Frances had described. I had done them, my fellow officers had done them; we had been encouraged and congratulated. If a "subject" went to the FBI or U.S. Attorney to complain, it was "handled," or covered up, depending on where you stood.

I was glad I had come to South Dakota, glad Luke had brought me here. When Frances pointed out the ancient car that was our transportation, and apologized that she had nothing better, I wanted to laugh. I knew I would cheerfully have walked the ten miles to the office of the Wounded Knee Legal Offense/Defense Committee. This was what I'd been looking for when I quit the Sheriff's Department, sold my share of the Las Vegas Detective Agency, and bade good-bye to Ralph Thorson.

Frances drove. Luke was next to her, and I was beside the window—scribbling notes. Occasionally I stared out into the graying South Dakota twilight.

"Before the occupation of Wounded Knee, or 'the occupation' as we call it, the people on the rez were completely helpless. We had no hope. We took all Wilson and the government dished out, wept, buried our dead, prayed to the spirits for help, and suffered. Now, since AIM, we have hope. We can go to AIM for help. We are organizing our people into the only thing your government understands—a group of warriors dedicated to action, militant if necessary."

"So that's how the occupation came about?" Luke asked.

"A group of our people went to AIM and asked for assistance. My brother Stan Holder, Carter Camp, and many of the Warrior Society came to Rapid from Oklahoma. Carter is the leader of the Warrior Society, an ancient order of fighters, the braves who traditionally have fought the wars. These are the same braves who danced around the burning of the courthouse in Custer, singing 'Today's a great day to die.' These are very dedicated and determined men, perfectly willing to die to improve conditions for their people. And they are dying. You'll hear stories that will be very hard for you to believe."

Frances Wise was hard to believe. She was very attractive, almost stunning, yet without any pretensions whatever. She was articulate, highly motivated, clearly quite organized and professional, and I wondered how far she could have gone in a conventional professional career. A long distance, I imagined.

"Carter Camp and Stan Holder came to Pine Ridge and organized the people and formulated the confrontation. Three carloads of warriors then drove to Wounded Knee and captured the trading post and eight hostages. Carter called Pine Ridge on the trading post telephone, and all the people, more than two hundred, came and joined what was intended to be an overnight sit-down. Well, the marshals and the FBI threw *ten thousand* men and armored vehicles around us and refused to let anyone into or out of the perimeter.

"Stan and Carter organized our defense. We had bunkers manned by warriors, night patrols—everything a righteous war would have. My brother Stan was one of the most decorated marines to serve in Vietnam. He volunteered for three hitches, and he knew about war. He was in charge of our defenses.

"Carter Camp, who had been with Cesar Chavez in California, organized the necessities of day-to-day survival, especially getting people in and out with food and ammunition. We established a community, a group of Indian people who for seventy-two days lived a traditional Indian life free of white intervention for the first time in four hundred years. Even though we were fired on every day—with automatic weapons, even machine guns—we were free and it was wonderful.

"Two babies were born at Wounded Knee. We were so proud. But after the government tricked us into surrendering, everyone was very sad. We had tasted freedom and liked it and wanted more. We were hooked on freedom. And one day we'll regain that freedom, forever. The Great Spirit has assured our medicine men and traditional chiefs that the Red Man is forever. We know and believe the Great Spirit. It's like one of the old chiefs said after Wounded Knee, 'I have lived all my life in total darkness. Now, way in the distance, a light has appeared and my eyes see this light and give my heart hope for my people."

I had never heard anyone talk this way. It was impossible to be unaffected by it, and once again I was happy we had come to South Dakota. I was determined to do my very best. I had no doubts about Luke.

Frances parked the car near a small, two-story building that resembled a ghetto duplex.

"Here it is," she said. "We rent this old house as an office and living quarters for the committee. Sometimes we have forty or more people living here."

"Who's the landlord?" I asked, wondering about a possible security problem.

"A fraternity. They attend a small agricultural college here in Rapid, and are the only ones who would rent to us. You'll find out about the townspeople real fast."

As a matter of fact, there was a security problem. A later visit to the local Radio Shack revealed that the FBI had poured several thousand dollars into Rapid City's economy with their purchase of bugging components.

"This is a rough situation," said Luke, not a man given to exaggeration.

"It was rougher inside Wounded Knee," Frances said.

We walked toward our "office." With the exception of the Black Hills, South Dakota is in general not a scenically beautiful state, and this spot was particularly desolate. (Later we visited a lovely area, Custer State Park, with Carter Camp. When I remarked that it was a beautiful place, he said, "It was all like this when *we* had it.")

"Tonight there's a party," Frances said, "if Carter gets out. You'll meet everybody then. Most of them are away now, gathering information, conducting interviews, that kind of thing. But everyone, even Russell Means, will be here tonight. You'll especially like Carter. He's magnificent."

We entered the office where we would soon spend a hell of a lot of time and were introduced to the three people working telephone duty. It took a moment for it to sink in that this was the control center of an operation that had captured the imagination of much of the world. Messages and queries arrived not only from journalists and organizations all over the United States, but from media representatives, and even governments, as far away as Latin America, Asia, and Africa.

We felt absolutely out of place. Luke suggested we go across the street, rent a room at the motel, and come back. Frances said okay, adding that we should take our time, she had some matters that needed handling.

"What do you think?" I asked as we put our clothes away.

"I don't know," Luke said. "She tells quite a story."

"I mean legally."

"The defense theory has to be that the government had no right to be on the reservation in the first place. The 1868 Treaty gives the Sioux sovereignty, or the right to self-government as an independent nation. I think we'll have to prove that this treaty is the highest law of the land. I believe this theory is right, but it will be very difficult to sell, so we have to prove government impropriety that provoked the Indians beyond human endurance to the point of taking action. We should apply the Nuremberg Theory, where we said the German generals owed a higher allegiance to fundamental rights and God's laws than to a corrupt government."

Luke paused to let me digest what he had said, rolled a blue sock and a gray sock together, and tossed the ball into the wrong drawer. I knew he would expect me to comment pro or con—he had come to rely on me as a sounding board—and additionally it would be crucial that my investigation for the defense home in on what we were trying to prove instead of rushing helter-skelter into interesting, revealing, but ultimately irrelevant directions.

"If we argue effectively from these two positions," Luke continued, "I think we might have a chance."

If and *might?* These were not normally Luke McKissack words. The 650 felony cases arising out of the Wounded Knee occupation were going to be very difficult to win.

Luke went on: "I want to talk it over with Lane and Bradon and Kunstler, if he shows up, but I think I like the idea. You give it some thought, Lake, and tell me how you think we should proceed."

That was some defense Luke was talking about. Treaties. War crimes. Civil rights. Government impropriety. Our opponent was none other than the determined United States government, and I began to feel distinctly overmatched. I had said I knew my business, and I'd damn sure better.

One of our first courses of action was to organize an investigative team under my direction, and to concentrate its energies on the leadership cases: these were the first scheduled to be tried in federal court, and involved Russell Means, Sioux warrior and AIM leader; Carter Camp, Oklahoma Ponca, AIM organizer, and leader of the Warrior Society; and Leonard Crow Dog, Sioux medicine man and the Wounded Knee occupation's spiritual leader.

We needed to visit the scene of the so-called crime, and Carter Camp volunteered to escort anyone from the Legal Offense/Defense Committee who wanted to go. My group, the Investigation Committee, went en masse.

Frances and Carter rode the forty-odd miles from Rapid City to the reservation with Luke and me, and other cars followed behind. Carter began the trip by explaining that AIM only participated in such actions as Wounded Knee if requested.

"We want all the Native American people," he said, "to know we are available if they want to use our capabilities—but only if they call us. When the Sioux, namely Russ, came to us, we made it clear to the traditional chiefs that we would act at their request only. They finally agreed, so I came to South Dakota with a group of Oklahoma Indians. I could trust them completely. They're the fighters—maybe sometimes too much so.

"When I first heard about Dickie Wilson and the goon squads, I said they ought to kill a few of those goons and lift their scalps and leave the bodies on the BIA steps for Wilson to find and get the message. If that didn't straighten him out, lift that fat sellout's crewcut and let him join them. In fact, I'd like to have his back on my lodge pole in Oklahoma.

"But Russ wouldn't have it. I guess he thought it would bring too much heat, and it probably would have, too. We could protect the people by laying it on AIM, but Russ said no. So, no it was. We settled for Wounded Knee, and the only mistake we made was to surrender. We should have made the pigs kill us. We knew that at the time, and still let them bullshit us into surrendering. A bad mistake. And no way to change it either."

Carter Camp was one of the most articulate of the Indian people, a fact he attributed to his training as an organizer in California for Cesar Chavez and the United Farm Workers. Carter had enormous admiration for Chavez's courage, and once offered the services of the Warrior Society to him. Chavez refused, but he was impressed, and he became one of the first national leaders to endorse AIM.

Carter explained the difficulties encountered when an Indian left his homeland, trying to escape the total poverty found on reservations. The traveling Indian, he said, is completely unprepared for urban life—no education or trade, a victim of racism, unable to find work, forced to live off welfare—and actually is a displaced person. He often winds up in a ghetto and inclines toward crime, alcohol addiction, drug addiction, and, ultimately, death. Exposure and starvation exact a dreadful toll on urban Indians.

Carter Camp to me was as fascinating as the story he told. He was six feet five inches, 220 pounds, and the only Indian I ever saw who looked like an Indian: long braids Frances combed for him every morning, Levis and western boots—a tough, mean Oklahoma Native American capable of using force when he felt the situation demanded, yet exceptionally feeling and compassionate where the interests of his people were involved. He was a realist-philosopher, fighter-thinker, warrior-poet. I was honored that he considered me his friend.

Carter Camp told me how he had been in charge of the 1972 takeover of the Bureau of Indian Affairs building in Washington, D.C. John Ehrlichman had negotiated with Carter.

"I understand you're the boss," Ehrlichman said.

"If that's what you understand," Carter answered.

"You people are in tough shape."

"You're going to tell me about my people?"

"Look," said this future Watergate subject, "this is embarrassing. How much money will it take to get your people out of here and back on their reservations?"

"Just a minute and I'll tell you," Carter said. He went into a hurried huddle with the head men, traditional chiefs, and medicine men, and arrived at the figure of $25,000.

"We'll need fifty thousand dollars," he told Ehrlichman.

"I'll have it for you in thirty minutes." The occupation of the BIA building was bad press for a publicity-conscious administration grappling with a citizenry that had turned against the Vietnam War.

"We won't take a check," Carter advised.

"We don't do business in checks," said Ehrlichman.

Thirty minutes later there was Ehrlichman, accompanied by an appropriate entourage, bearing an expensive briefcase that contained five-hundred hundred-dollar bills.

"Why don't you count it?" Ehrlichman asked.

"I trust your government," Carter said.

But the government should not have trusted Carter Camp; although he divided the money, he kept Ehrlichman's briefcase. He displayed it to AIM members as a symbolic trophy, a scalp, something special extracted from the oppressor. Indian people appreciated one of their own tricking a white man, and it gave Carter stature as a leader.

Sooner than I wanted, we arrived at the trading post. We were joined by others, ten or twelve in all, and we walked about the little community: five or six small houses, a church, and the remnants of the trading post, burned down as a symbol of white exploitation during the seventy-two-day occupation. This was the first time the Indians in our delegation had returned since the surrender, and the moment was fraught with emotion.

Two Indians had been shot to death by government forces during the occupation. Carter Camp said the government had fired *ten thousand rounds of ammunition daily,* and after listening to tape recordings of the battles I believed him. It was hardly the government's most splendid moment. South Dakota ranchers were allowed to come to Wounded Knee with their deer rifles and use the Indians for target practice.

Journalists were permitted inside Wounded Knee. "The only reason you're alive," one of them told Carter Camp, "is because we're here. The government doesn't want us reporting a bloodbath. I want you to know I'm on your side, I think you're doing the right thing, and I won't leave until this is all cleared up."

"That's good," said Carter.

A few hours later the government issued an ultimatum: either surrender or the trading post would be stormed. Carter noted that the newsman who thought the Indians were "doing the right thing" was the first person to leave after this report was received.

It was amazing how the Indians had maintained their morale while under siege. A number of them with absolute conviction told me they had seen Crazy Horse riding in the hills. They believed the great Sioux war chief had returned to help his people. It was impossible to doubt that the Indians were willing to die for their cause.

The venerated Leonard Crow Dog was spiritual leader at Wounded Knee. He conducted a Sun Dance Ceremony, part of which consisted of holes being gouged in an individual's chest by an eagle's claw. I could imagine that much of this ceremony was very painful. The holes I saw in Carter Camp's chest looked like bullet wounds.

Leonard Crow Dog was a follower of the old ways. He spoke very little English; his language was Lakota. It was Crow Dog who conducted the ceremony where warriors painted their faces and hung beads, ornaments, and feathers on their bodies.

I was taking a picture of Carter, Frances, Ellen Moves Camp, John Thomas, and others looking at the ruins, remembering the occupation, when a blue sedan roared up and skidded to a stop. Two men in blue coveralls jumped out. Then came another sedan, with men wearing jumpsuits and baseball caps and carrying radios and guns—all the equipment. And then another sedan. And another. Soon there were twenty men in blue, men who identified themselves as U.S. marshals. These were very angry people.

One of them, a "Heat of the Night"-type cop, walked straight up to Luke. "Okay," he said, "just what the fuck are you and this bunch of hippies doing here?"

Luke didn't fluster easily. "We're lawyers and clients," he said calmly in the voice of a teacher talking to a schoolboy, "and we're visiting what's alleged to be the scene of a crime charged in an indictment, a right very basic in trial preparation."

"I don't give a fuck about that," the marshal said. "I want you people out of here and right fucking now!"

As he said "now," his hand slid to the butt of his gun. The meaning was inescapable.

We left, Carter saying there were women and lawyers there and we would not have a chance—these cops wanted to and would, sure as hell, kill us, all of us.

This was the first time I was ever afraid of "my government." I had felt the unadulterated hatred, had even seen it, clearly visible on the faces of the men in the jumpsuits. They had wanted to destroy us. I had been afraid, but even stronger was a sense of revulsion.

Carter Camp later pointed out the sites of all the government bunkers on a map of Wounded Knee, and my crew (a group of dedicated volunteers from all over the country) and I sneaked out one night and dug up those sites, like archeologists searching for tombs. We did not find tombs, but we did uncover evidence that unlawful weapons had been fired by the FBI and marshals—and something else: many, many whiskey bottles.

As a graduate of the Light and Heavy Weapons School at Fort Benning, Georgia, I felt something had been overlooked in my infantry training—no one had told me it was okay to dig in, get drunk, and kill Indians. But someone did allow those U.S. marshals and FBI men to do just that.

We boxed up the evidence and took it to town for safe-keeping.

I went to the reservation on other occasions also, but never without a sawed-off twelve-gauge shotgun. I knew those people in the jumpsuits were extremely dangerous—that working on the investigation was very dangerous.

7

VICTORY AT
WOUNDED KNEE

One day at dusk, just before the mosquitoes got too thirsty, I was sitting on the lawn in front of the office having an enjoyable talk with Mark Lane, a lawyer most famous for his landmark book on the JFK assassination, *Rush to Judgment.* Mark was my height, five feet eleven inches, and had brown hair, a gray beard, and a terrific sense of humor that he would casually verbalize in a succession of very funny one-liners. He was an excellent public speaker, very popular on the college lecture circuit, and the fascinating individuals he knew and had represented made him an endless source of interesting information. Mark was a hard worker, very dedicated.

Jeanne Davis and Fritz Fieton, our volunteers from San Jose State University in California, dropped to the ground beside us. "I think we're staked out," said Jeanne, who had a degree in criminology. "We saw cars on all four corners surrounding this building, each with two or three men in them. I'd guess they're FBI. We got close enough to one to look inside and saw a police radio."

"That's just great," I said angrily.

What were they thinking about? Every day here was a year on a powder keg, with short-fused Indian leaders visiting the legal committee almost hourly. If Banks, Means, or the action-oriented Camp learned about this intrusion on their rights to counsel, there would be trouble.

"It's got to be what they want," Lane said. "They're looking to kill one or more of the leaders. They're angry about that FBI man who was wounded and is paralyzed. They're hotter than hell and out for revenge."

"It could be something else," I said. "We'd better identify them for sure."

"Who else could it be?" Fritz asked.

"A vigilante group. But regardless, if there's trouble, we'd better know who it's with. Let's get license numbers, and I'll run them for name and address through Los Angeles."

"Fritz and I can walk by and get the numbers," Jeanne said. "Maybe they won't suspect a couple."

"Okay," Mark said. "But let it cool out some. They just saw you, too, you can bet on it."

"While we wait," I said, "we can take my car and you can show me where they are."

Jeanne and Fritz got in the front seat. I drove, and Mark stayed at the office in case help was needed from that end.

Just as Jeanne and Fritz had said, there was a car parked on every corner. I also believed they were FBI, but it wouldn't hurt to be certain.

"You know what might be interesting?" I said. "Jeanne, why don't you call the Rapid City police and tell them a carload of men just made indecent proposals to you as you walked past their car? Refuse to give your name; say you don't want to be involved, but you are upset that the streets of Rapid City aren't safe."

I wondered why no one had ever thought of doing this to me when I had been on stakeout in Las Vegas. At the least the lingering doubt would have been introduced that maybe there was basis for the call.

We went to the nearest phone—pay, of course. Jeanne laid the story down, and before we arrived back at the office we heard sirens in the night air.

"They're out there," I told Mark. "At least four cars, maybe more."

Mark is very well known. He was Lee Harvey Oswald's attorney and wrote the screenplay of "Executive Action," a movie starring Burt Lancaster, Robert Ryan, Will Geer, and other big names. Mark would earn the distinction of appearing on Richard Nixon's "enemies list."

Mark looked up from his legal papers. "You'd better tell Luke. I'll stay here and keep trying to raise Banks and Means to wave them off."

I told Jeanne and Fritz to collect those license numbers, and then I headed for the apartment on the outskirts of Rapid City my girlfriend, Elizabeth Schmidt and I were sharing with Luke and his fiancée, Jeanne Phillips. The place had three bedrooms and two baths. One bedroom we used as an office away from *the* office.

I had met Elizabeth Schmidt seven years earlier at the Horseshoe in Las Vegas. She had come from Milwaukee, and I was lucky enough to capture her almost immediately. We took up housekeeping, and when I moved to Los Angeles to open a detective agency, she elected to come along.

Elizabeth, whom we all called Sue, had long brown hair and great green eyes. We called her Sue because she'd had to use a friend's I.D. to work in Vegas. She'd been twenty and the law says twenty-one.

Sue was a big factor in my liberalization. We had a lot in common and a lot not in common. But she was an extremely brilliant woman who listened more than she talked, asked more than she answered, and learned more than she taught. Anyway, she was right by my side through all the rough, serious business from Wounded Knee to the SLA.

I got everyone up and out of the apartment in record time and filled them in on the way to the office.

"What did you tell the two kids?" Luke asked, referring to Jeanne and Fritz.

"I told them to be plenty careful. That we didn't know who was messing with us. I told them to walk around the block once, to go slow, hold hands, and look like lovers."

"What if they're not the FBI?"

"I really don't want to think about that."

I really didn't. A vigilante incident could trigger those hundred or so warriors Carter Camp had in the area into a righteous, old-time raid, but with full automatic weapons and explosives.

By the time we reached the office, Jeanne and Fritz had been arrested and were being held in the Rapid City jail. Bail: $5,500 each. Charge: tampering with a motor vehicle, a state beef, and interfering with a federal officer, a federal felony, punishable by up to five years in prison and a $5,000 fine, or both.

Luke, Jeanne Phillips, Sue, and I left the office and returned home. No way to get Fritz and Jeanne out of jail until tomorrow, the FBI had told Mark when he'd gone to the jail. Tomorrow was Saturday, but the FBI agent Mark spoke with assured him he would do his best to get the U.S. magistrate to arraign Jeanne and Fritz in the morning. Despite Mark's best, most persuasive arguments, nothing could be done to improve that arrangement.

Saturday we went to the jail, where a very stern and sarcastic FBI man told us the U.S. magistrate was "out of town."

The same thing Sunday. But this time we ran a writ forcing the government to charge Jeanne and Fritz, and thus set bail or release them, preferably the latter.

On Monday morning Jeanne and Fritz were arraigned

before the U.S. magistrate in Rapid City, and bail was confirmed at $5,500 each. Also confirmed were the charges: tampering with a motor vehicle, and obstruction of justice. All this for writing down the license numbers of cars probably illegally engaged in violating the civil rights of our clients, namely the right to consult freely with an attorney.

The committee promptly posted bail, and Jeanne and Fritz were released.

We walked back to the office, the subject of the unlawful surveillance we had tried to break up—at great personal expense to Jeanne Davis and Fritz Fieton: three days in one of the nation's worst jails. Not to mention the $11,000 bail the committee had had to cough up, plus much worry by all of us.

"Well," I said, "tell us what happened. The FBI said you were trying to break into that plainclothes car when they grabbed you. What do you have to say in your defense?" I was ribbing these two nice kids, caught up as I was in a cause that a year ago we had not known existed.

"We never touched that car," Jeanne said, "and they know it. We were never closer than three or four feet from the thing."

The reason for the stakeout remained a mystery for several months. We finally learned that it had sprung from intelligence information the FBI had received that a Los Angeles attorney—Luke McKissack—had brought a Los Angeles hit man—me—to Rapid City to assassinate federal officers. The FBI had staked out the office to watch for Luke and me!

As we walked back to the office, we passed a sign blinking "Motor Hotel—Rooms."

We could not help notice a neatly dressed young man carrying what seemed to be a cardboard box of groceries to the open trunk of a car parked at the curb. "That's one of them," Fritz said, "one of the FBI cars we saw the other night. The guy with the box is an FBI agent. He was at the jail."

We watched as he put the box in the trunk of the car, closed the lid, and headed back to the motel. Our paths crossed. "Moving?" I asked.

"Why don't you get a haircut, hippie?" he said. Hippie!

Little did any of us know that I was about to set a world record.

"Let's go in the motel," I said to Mark. "Looks like he's been here for a while, maybe running a wiretap on the office telephone. Bring your camera."

Mark nodded, then asked the others to go to the office and bring help.

Just inside the door, two men—talking to a female desk clerk—were checking out from what obviously had been a long stay. Boxes of cooking utensils were stacked alongside boxes of groceries on the counter and floor.

The two men were upset by Mark's furiously clicking camera. The one I had met outside said, "What the fuck do you want in here, hippie?"

Good. He remembered my name. "To rent a room. Isn't this a motel?" I said and thought, *This is it: what we've been waiting and preparing for.* The FBI man thought he could scare us, but he was wrong. He was dealing with someone who knew him, had not long ago *been* him, and he was about to become part of that world record.

I once had forcibly performed a citizen's arrest on an army first lieutenant, and remembering that incident I'd had one of our research people pull out the South Dakota state statute on citizen's arrest. I'd had copies made, and one of them was in my pocket.

It looked like I was going to need it, if the fire dancing in that agent's brown eyes meant anything.

"Get the fuck out of here, hippie," he snarled. He grabbed my arm and shoved me toward the door.

I spun his hand loose and moved in close to use my height

advantage. I now had hold of *his* arm. "You're under arrest, pal," I said. "Assault and battery. A citizen's arrest for a crime committed in my presence."

I damn near quoted that statute verbatim.

The other agent stepped forward and hit me on the shoulder with an open hand. "You can't arrest him, punk. He's an FBI agent."

"You're under arrest too," I said, and told the desk clerk to call the Rapid City police.

"Leave that phone alone," the FBI agent ordered.

"State law," I said, "requires that these suspects be turned over to the police."

All the time a very cool Mark Lane was clicking, clicking, clicking. Tension was escalating in that office, and our lives were very much in danger.

"Call the police," I told the woman again.

The second FBI agent suddenly vaulted the counter, grabbed the phone, dialed a number, spoke briefly in a low tone, and then hung up. "He'll be right down. We're to wait here. This has gotten out of hand."

"It's not out of hand at all," I said. "You two are busted, and she's going to call the police."

"Fuck off, hippie," the first one said. That name again.

"It's the law," I said. "She has no choice and neither do you. So call them, lady, like you're supposed to do."

She did call. And not two minutes passed before a Rapid City police car roared to the curb and a pair of officers came running toward the motel office. We went out to meet them.

Just then about twenty committee members arrived. "Lake just arrested two FBI agents," Mark told our friends. "The police are here to take custody of them."

I approached the two Rapid City officers with my most professional front. I had to convince them to take custody of my prisoners, or the whole thing would fizzle and die right there. My theory was that the government is very adept at taking the ball and running to the goal—the conviction—but that it is thrown off balance when it encounters opposition. I hoped my citizen's arrests would provide the shoestring tackle that saves ball games, for that is just what this was—a game. If they won, someone went to jail, or worse, for a long, long time. If we won, nothing happens, but there is profound personal satisfaction that comes from defeating an opponent as rich and powerful as the U.S. government. It was that anticipated satisfaction that kept us going despite bad working conditions, poor pay—if any—and the constant knowledge that playing the game could cost our lives.

I chose the dark-skinned officer first up the walk. His hand was on his pistol and there was no telling what the dispatcher had told him.

I was lucky. He turned out to be a full-blooded Sioux, the grandson of one of the traditional chiefs of the Great Sioux Nation.

Stopping well short of him, I presented my private investigator's identification, carefully designed to resemble the I.D. used by federal officers. In fact, we bought our leather cases from the same luggage firm on Seventh Street in Los Angeles where the feds shopped for supplies.

I introduced Mark Lane to the officer, and we recapped the events, meticulously sticking to the truth, knowing that if we got it on with these officers they could check and confirm what we told them.

The officers, of course, knew about Mark, and maybe me also. We were already off to a bad start. But Mark confirmed my story right down the line. I lucked out having an attorney *and* a photographer present at the confrontation, even if they came in one package named Mark Lane.

I showed the police officers a copy of the state statute regarding citizen's arrests, and demanded that they do their duty. They thanked us and went inside to talk to the FBI men.

Mark talked to the committee members. "By now you all know that Lake has just made a citizen's arrest of two FBI agents. He's trying to turn them over to the Rapid police. That's why they're in conference right now, inside. We'll probably have to go to the police station to sign a complaint. Judging from what we heard earlier, there will be a lot more FBI agents here at any moment. This has them crazy. I want one of you to go to the office and get on the WATS line and contact all the media—ABC, NBC, CBS—and make sure they know what's happening. Tell them about Jeanne and Fritz. Let's see what kind of bail they set for those two suspects inside. But most of all, avoid trouble."

The two Rapid City officers came out of the motel and walked up to Mark and me. "Okay," the dark-skinned one said, "I talked to the lieutenant and he said for all of us to come down to the station so we can get statements. I've advised the FBI men they're under arrest and they've given their word they won't hassle it here."

So that was my world record, although I did not realize it until later: most FBI agents arrested by a citizen!

"They'll ride in another car," the cop said, "so if you, Lake, and Mr. Lane will come with us, we'll start seeing if justice can be done." This officer was becoming very similar to a human being.

I thought I understood him. I remembered when I had been a cop how the brass shit whenever the FBI came around. That was not infrequent at all in my case. They were always investigating some civil-rights violation one of my arrested subjects had reported, with good cause, and all of us knew nothing would come of it.

Mark and I got into the uniformed car. The Sioux picked up the microphone and signaled, "Unit twelve, ten-eight, ten-ninety-eight, ten-nineteen, with the victims." Translated into

English that meant car number twelve was in service, finished at the last assignment, and returning to the station with Mark Lane and Lake Headley.

Our driver relaxed on the way to the Rapid City police station. "You know, Lake," he said, "I'm Indian—Sioux. I asked last winter for time off so I could participate in the Sun Dance Ceremony on the reservation this year. The captain okayed my request, no problem. Then the FBI came to Rapid City this summer, and I mean in force. Had six agents in Rapid City before Wounded Knee, and a hundred and sixty after. Plus all the ones who come in from time to time from Minneapolis. There's not a rental car available in this part of the country."

He stopped on an amber light. He was in no hurry at all.

"I had the time off and everything okayed. My family was coming from Pierre to be with me at the Sun Dance. I fasted and did the sweat lodge all year as required by the medicine man. I was ready and my family was ready."

He stopped for a sign. I was on the edge of my seat, and so was Mark.

"Yes, everything was ready, and then the FBI went to the captain and got him to cancel all days off through the Sun Dance. They said they had information that the Indians were bringing a hit man from Los Angeles to kill FBI agents."

This was the first I heard about a hit man. Not until later did I learn that *I* was the hit man.

"The whole thing was pure bullshit. I tried to tell those FBI men that if the Indians wanted them killed, they'd do it themselves. But the captain went for it and canceled all days off, and I missed the Sun Dance. I can't say I have much sympathy for those FBI men back there."

By the time we were inside the police station, we learned that other members of our committee had upped the score to *four* FBI agents arrested. One had grabbed a camera from a committee member, and another had pushed a woman down some stairs.

Actually, I had never seen FBI agents behave as some of these men did. Usually they have a pretty good hold on themselves, unlike local policemen. But these FBI men were wild, guns stuffed haphazardly into hip pockets, cursing, shooting committee members the bird.

Before giving my statement I decided I needed a pack of cigarettes. I walked out the front door of the station and into a wave of applause from committee members sitting and standing on the police department steps. Most of them had cameras and wanted to get shots of the action everyone was sure would soon take place.

I started into the crosswalk and a nice-looking young man with short hair stepped out of a four-door sedan parked at the curb across the street. He met me about halfway into the intersection and stood in such a way as to block my path. I did a left-right, left-right dance, which he matched as if we had rehearsed the routine.

The young man wore a short-sleeve light blue shirt, cuffed chinos, white socks, and wing tips—not at all resembling the South Dakota rancher he was trying to emulate. He was six feet two inches, 220 pounds, with light brown eyes and hair, a thirty-inch waist, and shirt-busting shoulders. I knew for sure that this was the first team.

I was close enough to see scar tissue over both his eyes. This young agent was tough. He probably had boxed or wrestled his way through college and into the FBI. Then I saw his eyes.

Yes, man, I thought, *here it comes. This is really a badass.* You recognize them right away when you've seen as many as I have. The eyes and face are frozen—sometimes stony, or placid, smiling, laughing, or frowning—always punctuating an "it don't bother me, brother" expression, just frozen there. I recognized it, and he knew I did. I've been told that I look the same way on occasions. But why not? Hadn't I been like him not so long ago?

"Headley," he said softly, "where do you think you're going?"

"To get cigarettes," I said, and tried to step around him. No luck.

"Cigarettes are hazardous to your health, Lake," he said, letting me know that he also knew my first name. "Real hazardous. And I wouldn't want anything to happen to you prematurely."

This was the start of the thinly veiled threats that always irritate me. I kept looking steadily into his eyes, and tried to sidestep him. He did a shuffle and stayed in front of me.

"Why don't we go back to the alley and talk about this?" he suggested.

All right, I thought, *here goes.* "Listen, pal, I don't know you, I don't want to know you, because already I don't like you. But if you don't get out of my way, I'm going to rip your fucking ugly head off."

Then he made his first mistake: he got hot. A person loses control when he's angry. His theatrical smile disappeared and his eyes glazed. I had seen such an expression on the face of my pit bull, Ty, just before he was about to attack.

His second mistake was reflex. I don't know what he saw or how he interpreted what he saw, but his hand moved ever so slightly up his side toward a big pistol under the shirt worn outside of his pants. The pistol was hung in a forward-tilt quick-draw holster.

Such a reflex is called a "tell" in high-stakes poker. A "tell," because the movement tells your opponent something about you, something you usually don't want that opponent to know.

What the movement told me was that the FBI agent was

scared, not of me, but of any confrontation that might cause him heat, might land him in trouble with Washington, D.C. I wanted to laugh. This big FBI agent had just lost our little game. Our cliff-hanger was over, but I wanted him to realize that I knew what had gone on.

"Listen, punk," I said, "either pull that piece out, or get out of my way, because I'm not going into any alley with you. I don't hang around in alleys. What I *am* going to do is walk right through you, and then you're going to be an ex–FBI man, because you were stupid enough to get involved. So make up your mind. I've got things to do."

"Don't think this is the last round," he said weakly. "I promise you, I'll see you again. You made a big mistake today."

"The only mistake I made was thinking you were tough."

He stepped back and to my left. I continued across to the drug store and bought six rolls of 35-mm film for Mark Lane and two packs of cigarettes for myself. The FBI agent was nowhere in sight when I headed back to the police station.

Committee members asked about the big man in the street. I said I'd explain later.

"Who was that?" Mark asked when I was inside. He had witnessed our *High Noon* meeting through a window.

"FBI," I said. "He wanted to take me into an alley."

"Can't you stay out of trouble?" Mark laughed.

I wished I could. But I was not the one who'd set up an illegal surveillance that not only interfered with our clients' constitutional rights to counsel, but was practically guaranteed to provoke a violent reaction from the volatile Indians. Nor had I started the strong-arm tactics in that motel office. And certainly I hadn't sought out that muscleman in the intersection. The FBI had initiated each of these confrontations, expecting no resistance, and I felt it was necessary to

show they could not get away with it. As a matter of fact the
FBI did become more cautious, less aggressive, in the days
that followed.

We wrote out our statements in the office of Chief of Detectives Stanley Zakinski, who was surprisingly fresh and open in
his appraisal of the situation.

"We've done our best," Zakinsky said, "to keep the trouble
on the reservation from spilling over into Rapid City, but it's
very difficult. There are three times as many FBI agents here
as we have police officers, and people resent that. We've tried
to cooperate with the FBI, we have to cooperate with them,
but some of the things that have happened make it very difficult."

He wasn't going to say more, but this was quite enough. He
resented the FBI, as that Sioux police officer had, and we were
encouraged that maybe the city attorney would actually prosecute the agents we had arrested.

One of them *was* prosecuted. He was charged with assault
and battery, but never went to trial. On the very day the
arrests were made, all four agents were transferred out of
South Dakota.

But we remained in Rapid City. Luke McKissack and I
stayed for five months. He helped perform the myriad intricate legal tasks necessary to have the leadership cases ready
for trial. We felt if we could win these, which were first on the
docket, the others would be easier.

I led the investigation, conducting interviews, securing
statements, collecting affidavits, and gathering evidence: there
were those shell casings and whiskey bottles surrounding the
trading post, but we also uncovered wiretaps, examples of
unlawful surveillances, and instances of the government in-
timidating witnesses. The investigation committee worked all
day, every day; it was a very dedicated group. At Mark Lane's
request, I conducted classes on investigative techniques for the

twelve or so volunteers on the committee. All of this comprised one of the most rewarding experiences of my life. *This* was what a detective *should* do.

I testified at a pretrial hearing for three hours about wiretap violations we had uncovered, but I was not present for the actual first trials of Leonard Crow Dog, Carter Camp, and Russell Means. When after five months we returned to Los Angeles from Rapid City, it had not yet been determined which lawyers would appear as the trial defense team. If Luke had been one of those attorneys, I would have had to come back to South Dakota with him, but it turned out that counsel consisted of Ken Tilson, Mark Lane, and William Kunstler. I settled for the considerable satisfaction of knowing that the evidence gathered by our investigative committee contributed to the judge's dismissal of the charges against Crow Dog, Camp, and Means because of government impropriety. It was an enormous victory for us, representing clients who were financially quite poor against a wealthy, free-spending prosecutorial entity that at times seemed willing to go to almost any lengths to secure a conviction.

Before Luke and I returned to Los Angeles, some twenty-five Indians—veterans of the Wounded Knee occupation—gave a party for us at our apartment. These warriors were a rough bunch, and the landlady came around to complain when our singing of AIM songs became too loud. Our exuberance evidently had disturbed some of the building's tenants, perhaps the dozen or so FBI agents who rented apartments in the same complex. Regardless, I knew I would miss these Native Americans. I had learned to admire their culture, had even attended a Peyote Ceremony (a traditional Indian religious rite in which part of a cactus is ingested) and a Euweepe (flesh offering) Ceremony. I learned later that my being allowed to attend these sacred rites was an honor rarely accorded to a white man.

Carter Camp was at the apartment party, and four years later he related to me the disheartening fates that had befallen twenty of the twenty-five Indians who had come to see us on our last night in Rapid City: they were either serving long prison sentences or had met violent deaths.

But this was in the future. As we drove back to Los Angeles, I was filled with satisfying memories of our stay in South Dakota. And there was plenty of time on those long, straight Western roads to think back to my earlier life, a life I had not been proud of, and about how different it had become.

8

THE SLA

The weather was cold the night of February 4, 1974, in the university town of Berkeley, the cradle of the modern American protest movement.

Nineteen-year-old Patricia Campbell Hearst and her lover Steven Andrew Weed, twenty-six, felt warm and secure in their handsome $250-a-month apartment. They heard a tapping at the duplex window, and Weed rose in response. The Princeton University graduate peered out through the glass at a shabbily dressed young white woman.

"Hi," the woman said. "Something's wrong with my car. Can I use your phone?"

"Well, I don't know, you see . . ."

Two black men dressed in commando gear materialized out of the darkness, smashed rifle butts through the glass door, drove Weed to the floor. Hearing the noise, a man from next door rushed in: the attackers beat Weed and the neighbor unconscious with a wine bottle.

Weed was knocked out perhaps thirty seconds, then he lurched toward the apartment door while the kidnappers were occupied with their struggling victim, and he ran for help. The commando unit dragged the screaming Ms. Hearst toward a waiting getaway car. The abductors fired bursts of gunfire from their automatic weapons at alarmed neighbors who had crowded to the doors and windows of adjacent apartments. The neighbors took cover, but most of them saw Patty Hearst stuffed into the trunk of the getaway car.

Ten weeks later Patty's voice was heard on a taped communique sent by her abductors, the terrorist Symbionese Liberation Army: "I have chosen to stay and fight with my comrades. My name is now Tania."

Accompanying the terrible taped message was the now famous color photograph of Patty-Tania dressed in guerilla costume and holding a Chinese AK-47 automatic weapon. Behind her hung a banner picturing a seven-headed cobra, the symbol of the SLA. The name "Tania" was associated with the woman who had loved and died with Che Guevera in the jungles of Bolivia.

The kidnapping of Patty Hearst crowded other important stories off the front pages of the nation's newspapers. Who could resist such a story? It was the first political kidnapping ever engineered inside this country.

Sensation built upon sensation. There were fiery pronunciamentos from SLA Field Marshall Cinque (Donald David DeFreeze), and he quickly proved himself more than just a man of words. He forced Patty's father, the fabulously wealthy Randolph A. Hearst, to distribute more than a million dollars in food to needy residents of Oakland. Despite then-governor Reagan's statement—"The people of Oakland are too proud to accept a handout"—tens of thousands showed up to receive free turkeys.

Then Cinque's band pulled a daring armed robbery of the Hibernia branch of the Bank of America. Photographed participating in the robbery was Patty Hearst. She became a hero to many on the left.

I didn't know what to think. Were these revolutionary

Robin Hoods stealing from the rich to feed the poor? Then I got a call from the outstanding activist/author Donald Freed (co-author of *Executive Action,* among many other works), and soon I was up to my ears in a story truly stranger than fiction.

"What do you think of DeFreeze?" Freed asked.

"Cinque? He has a certain panache, I guess."

"He's a police agent," Freed said.

I let that roll around in my head for a while.

"We'd like you to look into this kidnapping," Freed continued.

"Who's 'we'?"

It turned out to be a group called the Citizens Research and Investigation Committee; I was impressed by some of the names Freed mentioned and agreed to meet with these people. One of them, an excop named Danny Stewart, repeated what Freed had said: "This guy Cinque is a police agent. Call him an agent provocateur, if you want. Whatever, he's no revolutionary, like the cops and press want us to believe."

The date was May 2, 1974, and though my pay would be zero, I agreed to head the investigation the Citizens Research Committee had begun. I had lots of energy that had carried over from the bracing experiences at Wounded Knee, and maybe there was something here. After recruiting two veterans of Wounded Knee, Elizabeth Schmidt, and Jeanne Davies, we went right to work.

What we quickly learned—and most of it came from public records—painted an unmistakable picture. In 1964, *ten years* before the Hearst kidnapping, DeFreeze had been a police informant, ratting on friends and associates. This information came from sources I had inside the LAPD, but it wouldn't have taken even the most dense p.i. long to figure it out. We looked at Cinque's arrest record:

3/31/65: West Covina, California
836.3 P.C., 211 P.C., 459 P.C., 12020 P.C.
DeFreeze arrested with bomb, knife, and sawed-off
shotgun.
Probation: 6/7/65

DeFreeze continued as an occasional informant to the LAPD
on the sales of contraband and stolen arms.

6/9/67: Los Angeles, California
211 APC - Robbery, charged 12020 P.C.
Two counts possession of explosives, one count possession of a concealed weapon. Two bombs and a gun.
Probation: to expire on Sept. 14, 1970
#X379-471.

DeFreeze, already on probation, now received three *more*
years probation, despite his violation.

On December 2, 1967, DeFreeze was arrested for the *fifth*
time on an arms charge. He had robbed and beaten a prostitute. He was driven to the 77th Street station by arresting
officers Toles and Farwell, but he escaped while they were en
route. He was recaptured shortly afterward but not charged
with anything.

On December 6, 1967, DeFreeze set up his partner, Ron, by
telephoning and then leading police to Ron's apartment.
There a cache of 200 weapons belonging to Ron and DeFreeze
was found. These weapons had come from a surplus store, one
among several that had been robbed to supply guns to a black
cultural nationalist organization.

DeFreeze, evidently a reincarnation of Houdini, escaped
once again. When he was recaptured he was given *five more
years of probation.* How could this be possible? Ask any police
officer—and I used to be one—and you'll be told Cinque was

somebody's snitch. An out-of-control snitch, no doubt, but a snitch nonetheless. Somebody wanted him out on the street; if allowing a prostitute to be beaten and robbed was the price, someone was willing to pay it. Any of the arrests we uncovered, in normal practice, would have remanded DeFreeze to the penitentiary for parole violation.

I came to believe that during this period—December, 1967—Donald David DeFreeze was a certain Los Angeles police detective's informant on Black Liberation politics. Why did I think this? I called the detective and he implied as much. Unknown to him, I tape-recorded our conversation (May 2, 1974), which featured the following line: "I am reluctant to say anything because the guy is, he is going to be killed."

DeFreeze joined a stable of black agents recruited after the Watts uprising, that worked out of the "black desk" of LAPD Intelligence. DeFreeze's main activity was to report on black militant activity in south-central Los Angeles. This only months after DeFreeze had been discovered to have a supply of 200 guns including automatic weapons. In an event I thought was related, on May 2, 1967, California law enforcement was thrown into an official uproar when a delegation from the Black Panther Party legally demonstrated at the Sacramento State House by carrying *unloaded* guns inside the legislature to protest a piece of pending legislation.

DeFreeze, an ex-con with *200* guns, was given very low bail and, later, probation. In 1968, DeFreeze was arrested, armed, for the *sixth* time:

> 4/10/68: Inglewood, California
>   Burglary: 836.3—459 P.C.
>   Released no charge.

DeFreeze was being run in the ever-mounting campaign against the fast-growing Southern California Chapter of the

Black Panther Party. At the same time DeFreeze was allowed
to ply his arms trade for profit.

DeFreeze was arrested again in August, 1968:

> 8/16/68: Los Angeles
>   487.3 P.C.: Grand Larceny.

Nine days later DeFreeze's wife wrote to the authorities
reminding them of her husband's occasional work for them
and the protection that the couple had been promised by the
police. DeFreeze was released again.

During the early fall of 1968, the LAPD detective and his
agents, including DeFreeze, became part of a new subversive
supersecret unit—the Criminal Conspiracy Section (CCS).
DeFreeze's job involved moving guns and grenades to be used
against the Black Panther Party.

Despite every indication of his instability, DeFreeze, on
December 13, 1968, was given five years probation on the
200-gun charge. The staff opinion from DeFreeze's psychiat-
ric report was that his constant involvement with "fire arms
and explosives" made him "dangerous." Disregarding every
indication of danger, the criminal conspiracy section put De-
Freeze back on the streets into an extremely volatile political
situation developing in Los Angeles. In December, 1968, the
Black Panther Party leaders Jon Huggins and Alprentice
"Bunchy" Carter were gunned down on the campus of UCLA
with guns that I suspected but could not prove had come from
DeFreeze.

> 4/20/69: Los Angeles
>   12031 APC
>   Unlawful possession of a dangerous weapon—"military
>   type semi-automatic M-68 nine MM rifle, which was
>   fully loaded; and attached clip contained 32 bullets. This
>   gun was described as specifically designed for military or
>   police work."

Thus, DeFreeze was arrested for a *seventh* time for an armed offense that carried both state and federal charges. But De-Freeze told the judge that he had "registered" the gun with the police *under his own name,* and that the gun was actually intended for a police-officer friend. DeFreeze was charged with burglary at this same time in April, 1969. Despite consistent and massive violations of his probation, despite demands from New Jersey (where he was also wanted) to hold him, DeFreeze instead was provided medical help by the criminal conspiracy section. During this period, I learned, he threatened CCS with exposure unless they came to his aid. That DeFreeze got released again was unprecedented, according to law-enforcement experts I interviewed.

DeFreeze went to New Jersey:

> 5/9/69: Newark, New Jersey
>> DeFreeze and another man, posing as Black Panthers, were accused of assaulting an employee of a Jewish synagogue with a shotgun, demanding $5,000, and information and aid in a scheme to kidnap a well-known Newark Jewish rights leader. Upon completion of the kidnapping, DeFreeze's plan was to submit a ransom communique purporting to be from the Black Panther Party.

DeFreeze escaped authorities in Newark, crossed state lines in violation, once again, of federal law, and in October, 1969, surfaced in Cleveland, Ohio:

> 10/11/69: Cleveland, Ohio
>> DeFreeze appeared on the roof of the Cleveland Trust Company Branch Bank with a .38 revolver, .25 caliber pistol, an eight-inch dagger, a tool kit, and, in violation of federal law, a hand grenade.

Cleveland police had, in this period, been on extreme alert because of the Ahmed Evans affair (black militants involved

in an ambush and shoot-out with police). Yet DeFreeze was
released on very low bail ($5,000), and charges were *later
dropped.* DeFreeze was wanted, at this time, on a capital
charge in New Jersey as well as for probation violation in
California, but he was *not* held in Cleveland.

DeFreeze fled back to California, and only days later, while
high on pills (his own admission), he robbed a woman at
gunpoint of a $1,000 check and, using false identification,
tried to cash the check at a Bank of America branch.

> 11/25/69: Los Angeles
> A252519: DeFreeze exchanged gunshots with a bank
> guard and was wounded. The gun used in the shoot-
> out was a .32-caliber Beretta automatic pistol. [This
> gun (A63944) was still another gun left over from the
> earlier 1967 200-gun robbery. DeFreeze had obviously
> been allowed to keep a number of guns from this
> cache.]

On December 3, 1969, DeFreeze was ordered imprisoned at
the Vacaville, California, medical facility. Over a period of
eighteen months he wrote long letters to the sentencing judge
in his case detailing his problems and his fanatical Christian
religious convictions.

According to DeFreeze, in 1970, at Vacaville, he was recruited by an alleged CIA operative Colston Westbrook to
lead a behavior-modification experimental unit entitled the
Black Cultural Association. At this time, on orders from
Westbrook, DeFreeze publicly espoused a militant antiwhite
cultural nationalist ideology (his private letters, during the
same period, were saturated with Christian theology).

The Black Cultural Association, DeFreeze said, attracted
outside prison-reform support during this period, and De-
Freeze began operating as a double agent: (1) for Westbrook
and the CIA, and (2) for the California Department of Cor-

rections and the Bureau of Criminal Intelligence and Investigation (CII) responsible to the attorney general of California.

By May 10, 1974, I knew enough about Cinque to be pretty sure of what lay in his immediate future. With our committee's approval, I called a remarkably well attended press conference (the *Los Angeles Times* and *San Francisco Chronicle* were there, among others) and ran down Cinque's past. I ended with a prediction that, "He'll be killed, probably in a shoot-out."

I never doubted that sooner or later, more likely sooner, Cinque would be murdered. He could not be allowed to live, any more than Lee Harvey Oswald could be allowed to survive and start talking.

I take no satisfaction in ultimately being right. On May 17, 1974, Angelinos, including myself, sitting down to enjoy Friday dinner, instead sat transfixed in horror at the "shoot-out" being brought live into our homes via TV.

Six people died in the flaming wreckage of that house at 1466 East 54th Street: Cinque, Angela Atwood, Nancy Ling Perry, Patricia Soltysik, Camilla Hall, and Willie Wolfe.

Elizabeth Schmidt, Jeanne Davies, and I now had to split up the scope of our investigation. Previously we had concentrated on DeFreeze's bizarre history, but the killings on 54th Street meant we'd have to broaden our focus. We agreed that Elizabeth and Jeanne—two attractive white women—would probably be more effective as on-scene investigators, interviewing witnesses and checking out the scene of the slaughter. I'd resume my research on Cinque.

Using contacts in the California radical community, I was able to interview Vacaville prisoners familiar with DeFreeze and the mysterious Colston Westbrook. These inmates told me that DeFreeze had seemingly broken with Westbrook and the Black Cultural Association over matters of policy, and DeFreeze had then gone to department of corrections authorities to complain about the BCA. Other inmates in the Black Cultural Association had charged that DeFreeze was unacceptable to them because of his extremely provocative and ultramilitant positions. Authorities at Vacaville, however, had not found him unacceptable, and had proceeded to set him up with his own outside project. This project, named "Unisight," was supposedly concerned with problems of the families of black prisoners.

In reality Unisight was an organizing magnet for white radicals in the prison movement. Ultimately, Unisight became the Symbionese Liberation Army.

In December, 1972, DeFreeze had been transferred to the maximum-security prison of Soledad in order to inform and entrap black militants incarcerated in that facility. I located a Soledad inmate who gave the following sworn statement:

> While Donald DeFreeze was here, I had a few conversations with him. I have always questioned his departure as being a simple walk-away. I didn't come in contact with him personally until his last couple of weeks here. There weren't many who would associate with him. He tried to give the impression of being super-cool, and he came across as cold. When I met him, he was working in the maintenance shop. I asked him if he was happy on his job, because if not, I might be able to find him something else. He replied that within a few days, he was going to be assigned to work in the boiler room at the South Facility.
>
> I questioned that, because he didn't have enough time here to be given that trust. I know cons that have been turned down for that position. He wouldn't comment; he only gave me a big smile. I should explain that no prisoners were kept at the South Facility at that time, because it had no security. No gun towers were in operation, and there were no guards posted.
>
> A few prisoners with proven records of trust were taken from Central Facility to the South Facility to perform certain duties; then they would be returned to Central after their shift. A few

days later, DeFreeze did get that job: midnight to eight A.M. shift, in the boiler room at South Facility.

On his first night, he was dropped off at midnight, and given a few instructions. His job was automatic; it only required an overseer. Then he was left to himself, and when an officer returned an hour later to check on him, he was gone.

I learned that the South Facility of Soledad, only for trusted inmates, is a holding section for informers.

DeFreeze "escaped" from Soledad on March 5, 1973, and moved underground in white circles in the Bay area.

Then in November, 1973, he was involved in the assassination of Oakland school superintendent Dr. Marcus Foster. This killing came just *after Dr. Foster had acceded to reform demands made by the Oakland black community and the Black Panther Party.* The next time the world heard of DeFreeze, he'd taken the name "Cinque" and kidnapped Patty Hearst. Maybe his adopted name was appropriate, because the actual Cinque, an African Mendi chief in the 1830s, had two faces: the first acquired when he led a rebellion on a slave ship; the second when he himself became a slave trader.

About this time my son, Lake III, age twenty-two, moved from Las Vegas to Los Angeles and joined the investigation. From then on, he was with me for parts or all of every case I handled. Plenty was happening on my end of the SLA probe, digging into DeFreeze's police-agent history; and Elizabeth and Jeanne were unearthing nuggets on their end.

According to the official version of the "shoot-out," six suicidal fanatics of the Symbionese Liberation Army had attacked the Los Angeles Police Department, thus precipitating the bloody confrontation. In reality, the SLA suspects fired fewer than 50 rounds against some 5,000 incoming, and the police fired first. Millions of taxpayer dollars spent, destruction of property, loss of life, a black community under fire: all this resulted from the decision-making chain headed by police chief Edward Davis. Let's look at the facts.

By May 10, many people Jeanne and Elizabeth interviewed in the vicinity of what was to become known as the "death house" said they were aware that "important" visitors would soon be arriving. This completely contradicted the official story that the house was rented at random one day before the police raid.

At no time did the FBI or LAPD honor their oft-made and well-publicized promises to alert the families of SLA members to stand by to attempt to talk suspects out of a bloody confrontation. Three of the suspects' families were less than an hour away at their homes in California. Instead, as the *Los Angeles Times* reported the next day, "He [a police officer] dropped to one knee almost directly in front of the yellow stucco bungalow at 1466 and fired a tear-gas round through the front window. Then he scrambled to his feet and ran for his life. As soon as he was out of the way scores of policemen and F.B.I. agents started pouring bullets into the house."

Police claimed 9,000 rounds of bullets were exchanged, 4,000 fired by the SLA. Jeanne and Elizabeth, after the most careful on-site investigation, believe the official report was correct in one respect: the cops fired 5,000 rounds. The SLA, however, fired perhaps 50. No officer was hit, by the way, a virtually impossible result if 4,000 rounds had been fired.

So much was wrong with the official version. Police said communication was difficult between themselves and the terrorists, yet *our investigation* found that there was a working telephone in the death house. Couldn't the cops, as per normal procedure, have begun negotiations with the trapped fugitives?

I don't believe they wanted to negotiate. Donald DeFreeze talking to the press would have unleashed a scandal even the government couldn't have contained. But let's stick to the facts. The LAPD said it repeatedly asked the fugitives to come out of the house. To surrender. What the police didn't reveal was that the SLA tried to comply. Nancy Ling Perry, Angela Atwood, and Camilla Hall all attempted to come out, and were driven back inside by a hail of bullets.

I personally visited coroner Thomas Noguchi after the so-called shoot-out. The model for the TV series "Quincy" (his role was played by Jack Klugman) and one of the world's most respected pathologists, Dr. Noguchi told me that Nancy Ling Perry had died in the backyard of 1466. She'd been shot in the back as she'd tried to flee from the very people who had urged her to come out. I asked Noguchi if she had been armed. He said no.

How much warning had police given the SLA? "Fifteen minutes," said a LAPD spokesman. But *Newsweek* magazine reported that "moments" after *one* warning was issued, the police fired tear gas.

Puzzled police officials talked a good deal about the "mysterious start" of the fire that raged unchecked at 1466. There should have been no mystery at all. The police had used Flite-rite projectiles, and the manufacturer's own manual, which we obtained, plainly warned of the danger of fire when these weapons are employed.

The police assault began at 5:53 P.M., and Elizabeth and Jeanne estimate that all the SLA members were dead by 6:20. The house had become an inferno, and no one inside was returning fire. Fire-fighting personnel and equipment had arrived on the scene, but the fire fighters were not allowed to approach the blaze for *thirty minutes,* despite a clear danger that it could spread. While there was some evidence of ammunition exploding inside the house, the bullets posed no threat to fire fighters, who had the capability to put out the flames from a distance.

Police continued to pour gunfire into the house throughout

the conflagration. Some of them, we later learned, had been whipped into a fury by a superior telling them that Cinque had murdered, a few days earlier, Officer Michael Lee Edwards, whose body had been found in the vicinity. I later learned that this same inflammatory technique was used in the police raid and killings of Black Panther leaders Fred Hampton and Mark Clark in 1969.

Elizabeth and Jeanne interviewed several fire fighters who said they had wanted to battle the blaze, but had been threatened with arrest when they'd started to try.

Elizabeth and Jeanne talked to virtually every resident in a four-square-block area. The upshot: *every* person with knowledge of the shoot-out said the cops fired first; so much for the idea floated by authorities that "romantic" SLA members had a "death wish" and wanted "to go out in a blaze of glory."

I thought the investigation conducted by Jeanne and Elizabeth would show conclusively to any fair-minded individual that the government didn't want anyone coming out of that house alive. Meanwhile, my own area of specialty, I believed, was producing equally startling conclusions.

In its December/January 1975–76 issue, *Argosy* magazine writer Dick Russell, after studying our investigation, wrote: "The history of the SLA begins with a onetime CIA employee named Colston Westbrook, a burly, fast-talking 36-year-old specialist in Black English now teaching at the University of California at Berkeley.

"Early in 1966, Westbrook was hired as a 'personnel administrator' by a civilian firm—Pacific Architects and Engineers, Incorporated, of Los Angeles—which was operating out of South Vietnam. According to Washington intelligence sources, Pacific Architects was a subsidiary of the Pacific Corporation, a multi-national consortium headquartered in Delaware and wholly owned by the Central Intelligence Agency."

Pacific Architects provided "logistical support for the CIA's Phoenix program," whose goal was assassinating "so-called Viet Cong sympathizers." Colston Westbrook's returned from Vietnam at the same time the CIA launched a new program called CHAOS. The June 1975 *"Report to the President by the Commission on CIA Activities Within the United States"* identified one of the goals of CHAOS: "Acquiring Assets in the Peace and Black Power Movements in the United States," and went on to say, "Individuals without existing dissident affiliation would be recruited and, after recruitment, would acquire the theory and jargon and make acquaintances in the 'New Left' while attending school. . . ."

The purpose was to spy on antiwar groups. Forget that it was illegal. The CIA's charter forbade it from participating in domestic operations.

Colston Westbrook came from Vietnam to work as a tutor to the Black Cultural Association at Vacaville. At the prison he met the police snitch Donald DeFreeze. It was Westbrook who introduced the future Cinque to Willie Wolfe. When DeFreeze left the BCA he formed Unisight—which became the SLA—and a little more than a year later "escaped" from a low-security section of Soledad, where he'd been transferred.

At Soledad, DeFreeze renewed acquaintance with General Khan (they'd known each other in 1968). Khan was DeFreeze's right-hand man at Soledad, and when DeFreeze died in that flaming house, Khan took over as the SLA's new field marshal.

One of our committee's investigators, Rusty Rhodes, located General Khan.

"Don said he wanted to hit Hearst," General Khan told Rhodes, "for the recognition that would be involved. He said he wanted to see her beaten and broken to the lowest thing on earth, lower than even himself. We discussed the complete plan of action early in 1973. It was obvious Don was going to split Soledad, that he had a lot of help. He would set up 'safe houses' in Berkeley, and once that was done I would get word and lead the 'second wave' out. There were eight of us who would escape and make our way to San Francisco, and we'd all meet Don at a flophouse next to the Greyhound bus station. Don and his group would snatch Patty. The second wave, my command, would grab the two younger Hearst girls. Both commands would then set up in the area, but I'd go to Colorado and find a place."

So why didn't it happen that way?

"I caught DeFreeze and [a lieutenant] talking in the custody room," Khan said. "They were discussing the SLA when [the lieutenant] saw me and ordered me into the recreation yard. DeFreeze told [the lieutenant], 'No, let him stay. He knows everything, he's the second man.' So then [the lieutenant] looked at me and told me I was going to escape. I didn't trust [him]. I quietly started warning some of my people that the department of corrections knew our plans."

If I was right, it was more than the department of corrections that knew the plans. I believed the CIA through its CHAOS operation was deeply involved.

Why? The CIA doesn't tell me why it does things, like hire my old pal John Roselli to kill Fidel Castro, but I could guess it had something to do with discrediting the left in the eyes of a middle class becoming increasingly disenchanted with the Vietnam war.

At the least, the CIA had lost control of the monster it had created—illegally.

And, yes, Cinque was a monster. A rapist (he raped Patty Hearst). A murderer (he helped kill Marcus Foster). Snitch, bank robber, gunrunner, dope peddler, mugger—you name it, that was Cinque. In his rantings he even called for the murders of Angela Davis and Huey Newton. He wanted the entire movement to follow him.

The whole scenario Khan had talked about soon resurfaced in our investigation. It came about when the enterprising Rusty Rhodes interviewed inmate Robert Hyde, a jail-house lawyer who actually had practiced law in California courts.

"The California Department of Correction," Hyde told Rhodes, "approached me about a deal to recruit 'snitches' " in 1971. "They wanted me to enlarge my legal assistance efforts to include all races and organizations inside the prison, so I could bring them 'tips.' At first I refused, but their 'goon squad' beat me and threw me into isolation. I stayed there for seven months. I knew I couldn't get out alive unless I made a deal, so I agreed. . . . In late 1971, (I was ordered to begin recruiting inmates for a new organization called the Symbionese Liberation Army. I was very successful. I recruited one hundred or more SLA members. When I became suspicious of all this recruitment, I got word to . . . the FBI in San Francisco. [It] didn't respond, but in early 1972 a Secret Service agent named Miller came in to see me and I gave him all the information I had."

Hyde couldn't explain why the Secret Service had come. No, he wasn't mistaken. Miller said he was Secret Service.

In late 1973, with Cinque now "head" of the SLA, Hyde again contacted the FBI, and two men came to question him. In a letter to his San Jose attorney, Elliott Daum, the convict described what happened: "The day after I talked to [FBI] agents . . . I was taken to segregation (O-wing, the hole) . . . it has been decided I know too much and must be silenced."

Congressman Ron Dellums was notified of Hyde's plight, and his intervention may have helped get Hyde out of segregation.

Perhaps the most fascinating of all the witnesses we found was Wayne Lewis, a former FBI undercover agent. He contacted me through his attorney, and when we met he produced letters from both FBI director Clarence Kelley and assistant director William A. Sullivan confirming that he'd been a bureau employee. I obtained a statement from Wayne Lewis that he was prepared to testify in court to the following:

- He had been in contact with Cinque several times *after* the Patty Hearst kidnapping, in the role of informant operating under orders from the FBI's Los Angeles office.
- He said he was told that DeFreeze was an FBI informant who had gotten out of hand and needed to be "removed."
- He said he was asked to take Cinque's place after he'd been "eliminated."

Early on in our investigation we were retained by Dr. Peter Wolfe, the father of Willie, or "Cujo" as he was known to the media. Dr. Wolfe wanted to know what had happened to his idealistic son. He knew for sure the authorities weren't being straightforward. I felt a good deal of compassion for this decent man, who assured me he only wanted the truth, and I did my best to give it to him.

With Dr. Wolfe's blessing, our committee spent many months trying to bring our findings to the public's attention. We held numerous press conferences, spoke at dozens of universities, held teach-ins and seminars. What we asked for, *pleaded* for, was a genuine official investigation that would root out the truth.

We got an investigation, all right. The government investigated *us*. Elizabeth, Lake III, and I were followed twenty-four hours a day. Our phone was tapped, our mail tampered with. A helicopter hovered over our home.

There were times I felt like stepping outside and shooting it down.

9

RED LODGE

The "heat" finally got to me in Los Angeles, and I began to wonder if our lives might be in danger. Maybe it was paranoia, but I've heard that the Greek definition of the word is "a heightened sense of awareness." Anyway, our residence had become the hub of more police activity than some precincts experienced. Six officers took turns on a round-the-clock stakeout, and there were never fewer than two plain-clothes cars parked outside the house. A helicopter, plus at least one patrol car, followed us each time we took a drive. I grew tired of the constant company, and so did Elizabeth and Lake III.

"I bet the doughnut shop and their greasy-spoon hangout over on LaBrea have been mighty quiet lately," said Lake III, watching the shift change through the living-room window. "Lots of take-out orders."

"Yeah," I chuckled. "Maybe we should petition the city to install a dumpster on the sidewalk and portable toilets for their comfort."

Even though we occasionally joked to break the tension, being under the unsleeping watchful eye of the LAPD got to be a real pain. One afternoon I decided to confront a cop

141

who'd been tailing me. I stopped my car; he stopped right behind me. I got out; he got out. I went to write down his license number, he blocked my way, and we did a little dance in the middle of the street. I hoped he'd push me, or do something else that would allow me to arrest him, but all he did was block my way. *This is ridiculous,* I thought, jumped in my car, swung a U-turn in heavy traffic and lost him. Of course, I wasn't really rid of him. The helicopter still followed overhead.

I definitely needed a break. I'd been running full throttle since May, 1973, with the Wounded Knee case and then the SLA. Both had been extremely stressful and dangerous, and the SLA investigation, especially, had put me much in need of a long rest.

Elizabeth, Lake III, and I decided we could use some country living, an "escape" spot far from big-city pressure and big-city cops. But where?

The question of our destination was answered right away, almost magically, by Don Wogamon, a friend for whom I'd helped out six years earlier. Wogamon, a well-to-do Montana rancher, offered a rent-free piece of property where we could catch our breath.

The next day, January 15, 1976, the three of us, pulling a U-Haul behind my 1971 LTD, drove to Red Lodge, Montana. We arrived two days later to a crisp, cold, smog-free little town I thought might have been transported whole from heaven.

Red Lodge, sixty miles south of Billings in the south-central part of Montana, nestled right on the edge of Yellowstone and the Custer National Forest, was an old mining town of only 2,222 people, the county seat of Carbon County. It featured a ski run and several Old West bars. This was cattle country— quiet, with a crime rate of zero.

We found Don Wogamon at his home, and he took us to

a trailer on a 250-acre spread he owned five miles northwest of Red Lodge.

"It's yours for as long as you want to use it," Wogamon said.

"The trailer?" I asked. "Thank you . . ."

"No. The whole spread. Kick your shoes off, let your hair down, whatever it takes to unwind." Wogamon offered Lake III a job tending one of his properties, and a place to stay in the main ranch house.

It was simply beautiful, idyllic and unspoiled. There were rolling pastures, large clusters of aspen and evergreen trees, and a crystal-clear creek brimming with trout. The trailer perched on high ground overlooking a creek where all manner of wildlife—ducks, beaver, deer, rabbits, fox, elk—came to drink and bathe.

Elizabeth and I had the trailer to ourselves. Her cleaning and getting us settled in turned it into a comfortable mobile-home hideaway. I soon fell into a routine of relaxing, reading, and working on a manuscript about the SLA investigation. Our nearest neighbor lived a mile away. The only traces from our past were the few sticks of furniture we'd brought along, and our three pets: two pit bulls and a kitten called Little Cat. What were the pit bulls like? Once, when a cop broke into our Los Angeles home, they cuddled up to him.

With my problems behind me, I thought we might just stay forever in this wilderness. If I could make a little money writing, and thus pay Wogamon *something,* I reasoned that I wouldn't be tempted to return to major crime areas like L.A. or Vegas. Through spring, summer, and fall we continued to be in love with each other and our peaceful place.

About midnight on December 4, 1976, as I was driving over to Don Wogamon's to pick up my wallet, which I'd accidentally left there, a car packed with cops pulled me over at the entrance to a country cemetery.

"What's up?" I asked a man who identified himself as a DEA agent.

"You're gonna be up," he growled, "or we're gonna drag you out of that fuckin' car."

I got out and he prodded me in the stomach with a shotgun. "Over there," he said, pushing me with the gun barrel until we were *inside* the cemetery.

A dozen thoughts ran through my head, prime among them grabbing this guy's weapon. But there were other cops with rifles and shotguns pointed at me. My best hope, I figured, was offering no resistance, in spite of believing they intended to kill me. I know now it didn't matter, but all the time I kept wondering *why?*

Standing in the darkness among the gravestones, I caught a break. A deputy sheriff, whose name I later learned was Charles Adcock, pushed his way between me and the DEA agent to shield me from the shotgun. Some sort of unspoken communication took place between Adcock and the DEA officer, and then, obviously unhappy about what was going down, the federal narc told me, "You're under arrest for the sale of dangerous drugs."

"Drugs!" I said, flabbergasted. "What the hell are you talking about?"

"Shut up, asshole! Turn around." He recited *Miranda* while cuffing me.

Unknown to me—I guess I'd let my guard down—two Carbon County sheriff's deputies had sneaked onto the property a few weeks after we'd moved in and said they'd found two marijuana plants growing near the creek bed. This startling discovery then led to *180 days* of surveillance by county cops, who hid a mile away and spied on us through a "spotting scope" from dawn till dusk. I don't know if these Montana sleuths were better than their L.A. counterparts, or if I was just lulled to sleep by the tranquil surroundings, but I never knew we were being watched.

In the Carbon County hoosegow, I was gradually able to glean that Montana law equated growing marijuana with selling marijuana, and the penalty for each offense was up to life in prison. A semifriendly guard told me that the state intended to go for *consecutive* life sentences in my case. I also discovered that this incredible law provided a life term for anyone who grew a lone pot plant, or even "offered to give" a single joint to another person.

I took these charges seriously—I'd read about draconian sentences handed out to marijuana smokers—and area newspapers confirmed my fear. The next day a Montana newspaper said I'd been arrested for growing "more than 2,000 marijuana plants" with a "street value of about $450,000." The same article credited local authorities, a DEA agent, and top narcotics officers from other state jurisdictions with wiping out a "pot plantation," and indicated that drug "magnates" would be targeted for prosecution.

Had I stepped into Rod Serling's "Twilight Zone," or what?

At the same time I was being busted in front of the cemetery, six cops and a DEA agent arrested Lake III at Wogamon's home, and another team of cops busted Elizabeth at the trailer. Arrest warrants had been issued but not served on Don Wogamon and his son Timothy, who were out of town at the time. They were charged a few days later upon their return to Red Lodge. All of us potentially faced life terms. The team that entered Wogamon's home to arrest Lake III said their search of the premises had uncovered two joints and a marijuana leaf.

Lake III, Elizabeth, and I endured ten long days behind bars before Wogamon could post our bail—$25,000 each.

I spent my jail time calling lawyers and trying to get bail posted. I itched to get out and do for myself what I'd done for other criminal defendants: a thorough defense investigation. Also, I feared for the lives of Elizabeth and Lake III. I had good cause. The jailers where my son was being held constantly left his cell door open, inviting an escape, which I believed would have led to his being gunned down. When he was too smart to fall for that setup, he got a cellmate who brought in valium, which he offered to share. Though I could never prove it, Lake III and I felt sure this cellmate was a cop.

The first lawyer who came to see Lake III was grabbed by one of the sheriff's men. "You're not talking to anybody," he was told.

"I've got the right . . ." the lawyer began.

"You've got no rights here," the officer said, pushing the lawyer out the door.

When Elizabeth and I were bailed out and returned to the trailer, a lawyer I'd called from jail was waiting for me. "I'm your attorney," he announced, extending his hand.

"Man, I'm glad to see you."

"This your first arrest?" he asked.

"First one."

"We'll make a good team. This is my first case."

Geesus. I didn't want to hurt this nice young man's feelings, but facing two life sentences I figured I could use some experience on my side. I called George Vlassis in Phoenix, noted civil rights lawyer Bill Rittenberg in New Orleans, the Montana ACLU, and *Playboy* magazine. I called *Playboy* because of its campaign against outrageous drug laws, and because from experience I knew it never hurt to have a powerful media ally. *Playboy* listened to my story, checked it out, and soon sent one of its top editors, Bill Helmer, to report on the situation. Helmer, a book author and the country's leading expert on bank robber John Dillinger, became one of my best friends,

In 1961 Lake Headley II (2nd row, standing
1st from left) was employed by the Clark
County Sheriff's Department.

Lake II with activist/author Donald Freed.

Above, L.A. police, guns poised, watched while flames devoured the house at 1466 East 54th Street. The fire took the lives of six SLA members occupying the residence. *Below left*, the seven headed cobra—the symbol of the Symbionese Liberation Army looms behind Patricia (Tania) Hearst in this infamous 1974 Photo. *Below right*, Don Bolles, 47, investigative reporter for The Arizona Republic. *Photos: UPI/Bettmann*

Bolles never arrived at his scheduled appointment concerning a story that he was working on in June of 1976. Detectives study the remains of Bolles's bomb-damaged Datsun. *UPI/Bettmann*

On January 15, 1977 Max Dunlap (left) and James Robison, were falsely accused of the bombing murder of Don Bolles. After being arrested both men were brought from Maricopa County Jail where they were held without bond pending a preliminary hearing on January 24th. *UPI/Bettmann*

Max Dunlap and Lake II conversing freely.

Above, the investigators (from left, back row): Lake Headley, Naomi Devereux and Don Devereux; (in front) Terri Lee Yoder (later Terri Lee Headley) the day that The Arizona Supreme Court overturned the convictions.

Below left, former model Vicki Morgan. *Right*, Alfred Bloomingdale. *Photos: UPI/Bettmann*

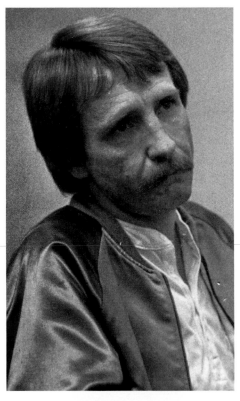

Accused with the killing of Alfred
Bloomingdale's mistress Vicki Morgan,
Marvin Pancoast listens to police testify that
his fingerprints were not found on the bat
used in the brutal murder of Miss Morgan.
UPI/Bettmann

Below left, the Soviet translator Violetta Sanni
was a Foreign Service National employed by
the U.S. Embassy.

Below right, Sergeant Clayton John Lonetree,
USMC. Clayton's affair with Violetta Sanni
was tarnished when the Marine sergeant was
charged with revealing U.S. secrets to his
girlfriend. The case soon developed into a
struggle for Indian rights.

Clayton's grandfather, Samuel Lonetree in
tribal dress and his father Spencer Lonetree
speak with reporters at the Quantico, VA
marine base. *AP/Wide World Photos*

Below, Sergeant Lonetree with the primary
members of his civilian defense team, (from
left) co-counsels William Kunstler and
Michael Stuhff, and Chief investigator Lake
Headley II.

Above left, Donald Frankos wedged between Jimmy Coonan, head of the notorious Westies, and Kevin Hanley. After this 1973 photo Donald "Tony the Greek" Frankos participated in many murders including that of Jimmy Hoffa. *Photo courtesy of Donald Frankos   Right*, Jimmy Hoffa after being convicted and jailed for jury tampering in the 1960's. *AP/Wide World Photos*

Below: (from left) Lake Headley socializing with an old friend George Vlassis, senior editor of *Playboy* Bill Helmer, Hugh Hefner, Christy Hefner, and Russ Million.

William Hoffman and Lake Headley with Frankos's cousin Alice Pohl.

(from left) David Chesnoff, Judge Harry Claiborne, and Lake Headley at Lake's birthday party given to him by his dear friend Nicholas Behnen.

Lake Headley with Victoria Cerinich holding the award given to Lake at the International Society of Private Investigators for "Outstanding Investigator of the Year" (1991).

and later threw a number of *Playboy* investigations in my direction.

What I first wanted to know was *how* all this had come about? Why was I facing two life sentences? I only had one life, and they wanted to take two.

I suspected I'd been targeted because of dossiers maintained on me by a variety of law-enforcement agencies ever since I'd become involved in political cases. At Wounded Knee, I'd discovered I'd been described as a "hit man" in one of these dossiers, and I figured there had been plenty of damaging, equally erroneous updates since then. I pried loose more dossiers, a job harder than pulling teeth, and discovered that, sure enough, I was now described as a "local criminal" (I'd never been charged with a crime) and an "enforcer type" who is "connected to a family in the Organization."

Where did they come up with this stuff?

Anyway, I discovered that these "confidential" dossiers had been liberally distributed to Montana police agencies immediately upon my arrival in the state, which explained why I'd been put under surveillance.

I remembered Deputy Sheriff Charles Adcock, the man who had stood between me and the shotgun-wielding DEA agent, and I went to see him. I knew not all cops were caught up in "following orders," and I believed Adcock might be one of these.

Adcock was reluctant to talk. "Well, pal," I said, "I've got a hunch you saved my life that night."

"I was afraid it might end up in a killing," he admitted.

"My killing?"

"Yeah."

I tried to get him to say more, and finally he did: "That night in the cemetery, I had disobeyed orders and worn my uniform. Also I loaned the DEA agent the shotgun he used like a cattle prod; but first I made sure it was unloaded."

"Thanks again for intervening with that hothead," I said.

"I wasn't staying just between you and him," he confessed. "There was a second officer who had you in his sights, and his gun *was* loaded."

I tried to cultivate Adcock and become a friend of his. The following excerpt from a *Playboy* article on the case describes what happened: "The man who might have been able to answer many questions about the case, Deputy Sheriff Charles Adcock, died of an apparent heart attack at the age of 51 the morning after he began to testify as a defense witness during pretrial hearings. On the stand, he said that he and Red Lodge police chief Tim Ortner had just searched the spot in Wogamon's house where Federal drug agent Don R. Friend found a joint of marijuana lying in plain view on the floor. At the time, Adcock's death seemed highly suspicious. Only hours before, he had confided to a reporter from Billings, 'If I told you everything I knew about this case, I'd be dead tomorrow.' His symptoms seemed inconsistent with a heart attack, and his body was sent for embalming less than 30 minutes after death without notification of his wife, Carol, but extensive medical tests found only natural causes for his death."

If foul play had been involved in Adcock's death, and his demise intended to further a cover-up, the strategy didn't work. Adcock's wife said her husband had often received mysterious calls from federal agents who would tell him to go to another phone and call them back. When Carol Adcock asked her husband why he dealt with the feds, he replied, "So I can stay in contact, so I'll know what they're up to."

The death of Deputy Adcock also shook up Red Lodge police chief Tim Ortner. He agreed to testify for the defense, saying that the drugs the DEA allegedly had found at Wogamon's had not been there moments before, when he had searched the same spot. The indication was clear: the "evidence" had been planted.

Ortner got upbraided by his boss, Sheriff John Moe, for his testimony. Moe contended that Ortner shouldn't have testified that the evidence "wasn't there." He should have said, "I didn't see it."

Ortner was warned not to talk to the press or the defense team, but he ignored the ban and flew to Chicago to tell *Playboy* his story. A pink slip waited for him when he returned. Unfortunately, getting fired ranked as the least of his worries.

"One night shortly after he returned to Red Lodge," Helmer reported in *Playboy,* "Ortner, 36, was also stricken with an apparent heart attack but survived. Friends who took him to the hospital saw a sheriff's-department car parked almost in front of their house with its lights out, but the officer inside offered no assistance and ignored the fact that they nearly rammed his car in their rush to the hospital. Medical tests on Ortner found no cause whatever for the seizure, and no signs that it had been a heart attack."

Playboy called in Russ Million, a first-rate private detective from Austin, Texas, to work with me investigating the case. Astute, sympathetic—a very modern p.i.—Million proved a godsend to the defense. Not only was he convinced that we were victims of a frame-up, he had the courage to plunge ahead in a very dangerous atmosphere. Hatred for us "outsiders," as we were called, was palpable in this little Big Sky community.

None of us knew whether the greatest threat came from the police and federal agents, or from the good citizens of Red Lodge. Many younger citizens sympathized with our plight, but older residents groused behind closed doors—and sometimes openly—about those "damn drug dealers who moved in and started the moral decay of our lovely, law-abiding town."

A vigilante began cruising by our mobile home. Occasionally he'd stop and stare at the door. After I talked to Ortner about this character, he went to the guy and said, "You'd better not fuck with those people. They have guns, legally registered firearms, and they won't hesitate to use them."

The defense team was warned that local "patriots" planned to celebrate the Fourth of July by shooting Don Wogamon and me. We averted this denouement by reporting the threat to law-enforcement agencies *and* the media, and were relieved when the holiday ended without incident. A week later, however, a vacant house owned by the Wogamon family got burned to the ground, apparently by an arsonist.

Clarence Darrow, one of my heroes from books, believed in attacking the opposition whenever justified. He didn't feel a defendant needed to pose as a punching bag, and when the prosecution's hands were dirty—which was often—he put the *state* on trial. Thus, when I discovered that the prosecutor's wife, who worked at the local Western Union office, had divulged to her husband the contents of a telegram sent to the defense team, we fought back by filing a $7.5-million lawsuit against Western Union and the prosecutor. Attitudes among older heads in Red Lodge began to change when at the end of 1976 it was revealed that $60,000 had been expended from the county budget to prosecute us, and that the cost might run much higher. Carbon was not a wealthy county; taxpayers didn't take long figuring out where the money would come from. On top of that, here was a $7.5-million lawsuit that could bankrupt them.

"We're not rich people," a concerned citizen told me one day outside the courtroom. "Why are you doing this?"

Why was *I* doing it? I hadn't asked to be threatened with two life terms on drug charges of which I was completely innocent.

We weren't the only victims of the attempt to "get" us. Tim Ortner, after losing his job, wrote a moving letter to the *Clarks Fork Bonanza:* "All that I have done is tell the truth, and as a result, I have been fired, threatened with arrest, and all but shunned by the people of Red Lodge. . . . I hate to think that I gave up eight years of law enforcement because I told the truth, not to prove some person's guilt or innocence but to try to correct a very bad situation—planted evidence. Why can't people understand that this could happen to them or their children?"

Early on I decided to represent myself against the charges. Defense lawyers I'd worked for had often joked that they felt they worked for me (I guess I did often become bossy and insistent, but I reasoned it was in the client's interest), so why not see how *I* could do in court? Actually, I reasoned that if I was going to jail for two life terms, I wanted to be the "lawyer" who lost the case. Too often I'd listened to inmates complain about the quality of their legal representation, and I didn't want to be one of those.

But before the issue of representing myself could be argued, there was the question of which judge would preside at the trial. We got the first judge assigned to the case disqualified after we discovered that he had recently sentenced a defendant to twenty-five years in prison for possession of one joint.

We had a second judge disqualified after *his daughter* came to us and said her father had called marijuana a "devil drug."

Talk about a generation gap.

"Would you really call a member of my own family to testify?" this judge asked.

"Yes," I said.

The third judge seemed about as fair-minded as we could expect. He began by allowing me to represent myself, while suggesting strongly that I take advantage of the expertise of the several high-powered attorneys who stood by to assist. I appreciated his concern, but I wasn't a fool. Of course I'd take advantage of the skills of these lawyers.

It didn't take long for this judge to dismiss the case on the grounds that we'd been victims of illegal surveillance, and that the search of Wogamon's home had been unlawful. That should have been that.

But the prosecutor wouldn't give up, and I can only attempt to guess his motives. Did he fear the wrath of citizens outraged by the big bucks this case had cost? Was he urged on by higher authorities? Or did he really feel he'd stumbled upon a gang of drug kingpins? I suspect it was reasons one and two.

Anyway, this prosecutor appealed the decision to dismiss to the Montana Supreme Court. In the appeal the date of the alleged crime was changed to conform to a police surveillance report stating that plants believed to be marijuana were seen growing near the creek. We countered with a lawsuit accusing the prosecutor of "malfeasance and misfeasance in office, of ordering the sheriff to perform illegal acts, of encouraging false testimony, preparing false affidavits to obtain arrest and search warrants and of attempting to conceal a variety of illegal acts by himself and others."

Even the most prejudiced Montanan—and the case was hot news in this huge state—had begun to question the wisdom of the drug charges against us, but still the prosecution plunged ahead. We countered with *another* civil-rights suit (we were stacking lawsuits up like planes circling LaGuardia), pointing out that we had been placed under surveillance even before we were allegedly suspected of growing marijuana. None of the defense lawyers thought the government would be eager to reveal why they had decided to watch us.

I've always considered the Red Lodge case a typical example of how, unfortunately, the criminal justice system often functions: the side with the most manpower and money usually wins. What made the Red Lodge case different was that the defense outgunned the government; most of the time it works the other way; the state has the advantage. It has tax-payer-funded police to conduct thorough investigations, taxpayer-funded lawyers to prosecute. The normal citizen can't afford investigators or high-powered attorneys. It's always been fascinating for me to observe the trials of rich people. Their "win" ratio is much higher than the average citizen's, and when they are convicted, the sentence is much less.

The rich have the money and the clout, and that's what we had at Red Lodge. I might have wound up spending my life in some Montana prison if I hadn't known to call for help, and if that help, in the form of dedicated civil libertarians, hadn't responded to my cry.

Before the matter got settled, I turned up the heat one last time on the prosecution. Employing the old citizen's-arrest standby, I busted FBI agent Merrill Reese during the noon recess of a pretrial hearing. Wogamon's wife Margie suffered a cut nose when she tried to take a picture of Reese and he pushed the camera away. I grabbed the G-man, pinned his arms, and charged him with assault. As at Wounded Knee, the agent was transferred out of the area and never brought back—though charges pended—to stand trial.

The defense had become a formidable team: the Playboy Foundation; NORML; the ACLU; and several independent civil-rights lawyers.

The government wanted out. Maybe it figured we'd own a good portion of the state if they kept persecuting us. Whatever, the prosecution offered to drop all charges if we'd scuttle our phalanx of lawsuits.

"It's up to you," other defendants told me, and that of course was what the lawyers said.

I thought long and hard about what to do, and ultimately three factors persuaded me to accept the deal: (1) I wasn't in this business to get rich, and I knew a big monetary award would furnish ammunition to government detractors; (2) a monetary award wouldn't cost the prosecutors a dime—it would come out of the pockets of already strapped Montanans; and (3) I'd received a phone call from my childhood friend, attorney George Vlassis, who told me I was needed to look into the murder of a newspaper reporter named Don Bolles.

The fight against state and federal law-enforcement agencies had set my juices flowing again, and I was ready for a new challenge. The victory in Red Lodge, and that's what it was, made me feel good. The only thing I regretted about the case was that it ended my relationship with Elizabeth Schmidt. At least for a while, she'd decided she'd had enough of my kind of life, and decided not to accompany me to Arizona.

10

THE MURDER
OF DON BOLLES

"Telephone my wife. They finally got me. The Mafia. Emprise. Find John Adamson."

These were the last words of ace Phoenix, Arizona, newspaper reporter Don Bolles, uttered to attorney Max Klass and others who on June 2, 1976, rushed to Bolles's side after they heard a bomb go off. Klass had run by a "ball of flesh," part of the reporter, and found him lying facedown in the Clarendon Hotel parking lot in downtown Phoenix, the remains of his burned, mangled body half inside, half outside his demolished Datsun.

The tremendous explosion had shaken the ground with earthquake force, smashing windows hundreds of feet away, sending parts of the Datsun and pieces of Bolles atop a four-story building across six lanes of Central Avenue.

The assassins, who had planted the explosive device underneath the car, directly below the driver's seat, must have calculated that six sticks of dynamite would blast a human body apart. They couldn't have dreamed that Bolles would live, much less, like the good reporter he was, be able to gasp his final story: *Mafia. Emprise. Adamson.*

Emprise, by the way, was a large sports concessionaire rumored to have mob connections.

Bolles survived eleven days, but never spoke again. Doctors amputated his leg, an arm, the other leg, but the reporter clung to breath as tenaciously as he had pursued his investigative stories. When he finally died on June 13, his personal physician, Dr. William Dozer, said, "He put up the most courageous fight for life I have ever seen."

The murder of Don Bolles, who earlier had been nominated for a Pulitzer Prize, journalism's highest award, remains the most famous killing in Arizona history. It garnered national and international headlines. President Gerald Ford expressed outrage and sent a long telegram of condolence to the widow of the slain reporter.

Still, despite national and international attention and the most massive police investigation in state annals, the murder remains *officially* unsolved. In February, 1993, more than *sixteen years* after the bombing, two men, Max Dunlap and James Robison, are scheduled for trial on the homicide charges. Many, perhaps a majority, of Arizona residents believe these two are innocent, that the real killers remain at large. How such a tangle came about, and why public opinion is still so sharply divided a decade and a half after the murder, comprises a story that promises to take its place among all-time crime legends.

At first, when the search for the murderers began, it seemed that the case would soon be solved. Just two and a half hours after Bolles died, the police picked up local hoodlum John Harvey Adamson and charged him with murder. Adamson had been mentioned in the reporter's dying words, and the prosecution quickly built an airtight case against him, including proof that he had lured Bolles to the Clarendon with the promise of an important story and had personally planted the bomb under the reporter's car.

But who had hired Adamson?

In what turned out to be a critically important decision, a Phoenix police detective granted partial immunity to a prominent attorney, Neal Roberts, a close associate of Adamson's, in exchange for the lawyer's *theory* of who had masterminded the bombing.

Neal Roberts suggested it might be Phoenix building contractor Max Dunlap and one of Arizona's richest men, rancher Kemper Marley. The *Arizona Republic,* Bolles's own paper, featured the theory in a major story.

Adamson waited seven months, then, in a plea bargain, named Max Dunlap and Kemper Marley as his accomplices, plus a local plumber, James Robison, who Adamson said had detonated the bomb.

Based virtually entirely on the testimony of confessed murderer John Adamson, Robison and Dunlap were indicted and, on November 6, 1977, convicted of first-degree murder. Both were sentenced to die in the Arizona gas chamber. The wealthy, powerful Marley wasn't indicted—"not enough evidence," said the prosecution.

It appeared Arizona justice had done its job.

After the convictions, a group of citizens calling themselves the Dunlap Defense Committee contacted George Vlassis, and he called me in Red Lodge. The committee waited till afterward, they said, because they didn't believe Dunlap could possibly be found guilty.

"Max is a dear friend," David Frazer of the defense committee told me. "He's the most decent man I've ever met, and simply incapable of killing anyone."

The Dunlap Committee was comprised of solid, hard-working, middle-class citizens, mostly from the Class of 1948 at Phoenix North High School. Max Dunlap had been class president, a football star, a "straight, honest guy" who'd formed his own successful contracting business. His friends remained that 1948 crowd from Phoenix North—doctors, lawyers, store owners, housewives, accountants. For thirty years Max had extended friendship and a helping hand to them; now they had come together to support him.

As my meeting with the Dunlap Committee neared a close, emotions became heated. These law-abiding, solid citizens typical of modern suburbia, many of whom probably had never been committed to a cause before, had become zealots, crusaders with a mission.

"Let me tell you about Max Dunlap," said Dr. Ken Olsen, a psychologist. "Outwardly he was a rugged kid, captain of the football team; but on the inside he was a sensitive, caring person. In the summertime when swarms of pesky June bugs bothered us, Max was the only guy who refused to kill them. He'd carefully brush them off, so we nicknamed him Juney. Why, Max wouldn't even swat a fly. That's the kind of gentle man the police say blew up Don Bolles."

Everybody had a story. Businessman Harold Bone: "I've known Max most of my life. He's been a good friend to me, but more, to everyone in the community. I can't remember his ever refusing to lend a helping hand, and often unsolicited. When you meet him you'll see: he's incapable of commiting this crime."

Tire-store owner John Sullivan: "I remember one year at the state fair. A little girl had won the blue ribbon for her prize steer, but she was crying. Max asked her why. 'He's been bought,' she said. 'The new owners will slaughter him.' 'It doesn't have to be that way,' Max told her. He topped the bid for the steer and gave it back to her."

Clearly the committee members wanted Max Dunlap home with his wife and family. I didn't have the heart to tell them that statistically they faced horrendous odds. From my memory of cases this famous, I couldn't recall a single instance of conviction reversal.

We discussed money. The committee agreed to pay me $2,500 a month, no expenses. I figured I might lose money, but this case was one of those a detective should be willing to work for nothing. The murder victim had been a particularly admirable individual, and if innocent people had indeed been convicted, then a terrible wrong needed to be righted. Also, my good friend George Vlassis had performed numerous favors for me, and I knew he wanted me to take on the investigation. The committee itself, at considerable expense (one woman had mortgaged her home for her friend Max), had already made major outlays, largely for ads in area newspapers to proclaim Dunlap's innocence.

There was one final point to be worked out. I said that in order to work for Dunlap, I'd also have to work for Robison. The state hadn't been able to split them, and I didn't think I should try. I couldn't imagine any conflict of interest, and I understood Dunlap and Robison had become fast friends since the indictment and conviction. Learning the state had charged them as co-conspirators, even though they had never met until their joint indictment, had nearly knocked my socks off.

This settled, I first visited the lawyers for the two condemned men. They weren't happy to see me, but couldn't very well turn down help offered by Max Dunlap's influential friends. One of the attorneys said, "There's nothing you can do. We've done everything. But go ahead if you want."

Soon joined by my new girlfriend, a pretty twenty-three-year-old named Terri Lee Yoder, I holed up in Room 217 of the Westward Ho Hotel (Calvin Coolidge spent part of his retirement there) with a four-foot-high stack of the discovery papers (material given the defense by the prosecution) and began to read.

John Harvey Adamson, of course, was prominently mentioned. Indeed, Bolles had named Adamson in his dying words. Known as Cocaine John, he was a drug pusher, gambler, local thug, arsonist, enforcer, con man, fixer; he also bragged of being a hit man. I described him as a walking-around definition of the word "sleaze."

But Adamson couldn't have acted alone. He had been hired, and with much of the nation outraged by the savage murder of a fighting reporter, the police and prosecution were under heavy pressure to bring all the principals to justice. To accomplish that, they offered Adamson a lenient sentence, a new identity, and $100,000 (money put up by the *Arizona Republic,* which had employed Bolles) to name who'd helped him and who'd hired him. Ironically, the man who had planted the bomb under the reporter's car stood to receive the reward for information leading to the crime's solution.

Attorney General Bruce Babbitt, later governor of Arizona, a 1988 presidential candidate, and a member of President Clinton's cabinet, suggested a slightly different deal: Adamson would receive a 54-year sentence (with parole guaranteed after 20 years) to be served outside Arizona, with immunity from thirty-three confessed felonies, (punishment for which totaled $80,000 in fines and 325 years in prison, two separate life sentences, and death in the gas chamber). Babbitt's offer did not include the $100,000 reward.

In accepting the new deal, Adamson agreed to plead guilty to the Bolles murder and name his accomplices. He also agreed to testify "truthfully and completely at all times whether under oath or not." If he didn't speak "truthfully and fully," the plea bargain read, the entire plea agreement would become "null and void and the original charges automatically reinstated."

On December 28, 1976, more than six months after his arrest, Adamson finally told the prosecution this story: James Robison, an acquaintance of his, a plumber with electrical experience, built the bomb Adamson planted, and Robison triggered the blast; contractor Max Dunlap had hired Robison and Adamson, Dunlap acting as a go-between for multimillionaire rancher Kemper Marley, a crusty, colorful character Adamson said had been enraged by articles Bolles wrote several years earlier implicating Marley in fraudulent activities.

The motive for the crime didn't ring true to me. Why would Kemper Marley, with an estimated worth of $100 million, order a killing because of all-but-forgotten articles now gathering dust in the newspaper morgue? It seemed to me more likely that someone would kill a reporter for a story he *planned* to write.

Like almost every state in America, Arizona law required corroboration of accusations made by a felon against a defendant. However, the Arizona legislature speedily passed what became known as the Adamson Act, a law that eliminated the need for corroboration and enabled prosecutors to obtain death sentences for Dunlap and Robison based solely on the testimony of Adamson, an admitted killer.

What was going on here? I asked myself in the Westward Ho that first night. I had never encountered a law as dangerous as the Adamson Act. Any slimeball with a beef could accuse a citizen of heinous crimes, and according to Arizona the slimeball's word *alone* was enough to convict. The legislation had been enacted specifically to enable prosecution of Dunlap and Robison, and I wondered *why* the state wanted those two so badly, and *who* had the clout to pass such a harmful law.

My first full day on the case involved meeting Max Dunlap in a visitor's room slightly larger than a phone booth at the Arizona State Prison near Florence. I had hardly expected to find a model of the modern maximum-security penitentiary jutting out of the sand, but nothing in my experience had prepared me for the abysmal hellhole I found.

Convict labor built the Florence "correctional facility" from remnants of the Old West's notorious Yuma Territorial Prison, moved some 200 miles—literally stone by stone—across the desert.

Inmates sweltered in sizzling slow summers and shivered when winter winds chased in all manner of wilderness vermin through gaping cracks and crevices. Its only appearances of "modernization": razor wire and closely spaced guard towers topping the institution's ugly stone walls.

Death row, where Robison and Dunlap existed in six-by-ten-foot cells, came equipped with aggressive desert rats and a menagerie of small, shyer creatures skittering across the floor, over grungy walls, and along a crumbling ceiling that leaked copiously whenever the rains came. Except for a few minutes of fresh air and outdoor exercise in a hurricane-fence enclosure called the "dog run," inmates stayed locked down twenty-four hours a day.

I had called ahead, and after a wearisome row with Carolyn Robinson, a warden's assistant, had obtained an okay to visit Max and Jim. I suspected the battle hadn't ended, however, and sure enough, as soon as I'd entered the administration building, a surly captain told me, "You can't be here."

"I'm already here," I pointed out, and attempted to reason with the man. He griped that what I wanted was "something out of the ordinary." Logic seemed beside the point as I tried to convince him that he had no say in the matter—one of his superiors had already granted permission—until at last he called Carolyn Robinson. (I grew to know her well in the next year and a half and almost became fond of hearing, "You back again?") Although she remained riled that I'd gained entrance into their domain—she must have checked around and learned that (1) I couldn't legally be stopped and (2) my reputation suggested I would sue if they tried—she told the captain to send me through.

Max Dunlap was six feet tall and husky, with hair turned completely gray from the ordeal. He was an extremely likable individual who was very, very scared: for himself, naturally, but more for his family—his wife, Barbara, and his seven children. Listening to Dunlap express his love for his family (later I heard it reciprocated many times), I thought that if this all-American guy, with his all-American family, could be framed, then it could happen to anybody.

Dunlap, speaking softly but urgently, began by telling me what I already knew, that he had never met Jim Robison until the two had been indicted for the Bolles murder. Dunlap said that eight days after the bombing, the attorney with the theory, Neal Roberts—also a graduate of that class of '48—had asked him if he would perform a favor. Of course Max would. He enjoyed helping people. Roberts, claiming to be very busy, asked Dunlap to deliver $5,800 to John Harvey Adamson's lawyer. When Dunlap arrived with the money, the attorney was in court. Dunlap told the receptionist the purpose of the visit, and she said John Harvey Adamson was waiting in another room. Dunlap gave the money to Adamson, a man he had never met before. The transaction took five seconds and resulted in a murder conviction: Adamson said the $5,800 was a payoff from the rich rancher, Kemper Marley.

I watched in the close quarters we occupied as Max struggled to find the right words to explain. "Lake," he said finally, "would you do a favor like that for George Vlassis, if he asked?"

"In a hot second," I said, "without looking back."

"Lake," Dunlap said at this first meeting (I visited death row seventy-four times during the course of the investigation), "I've never committed a crime, never been charged with one, and I certainly had nothing to do with killing that reporter. I'm fifty feet from the green door and begging you to do all you can."

"Are there any areas I should avoid?" I asked routinely. The question was one way to determine if he had anything to hide.

"Do anything you want. Go anyplace. Talk to anybody. Even if you think it's leading to me, keep heading forward, because it can't lead to me. I'm innocent."

I next interviewed Jim Robison. He stood five foot seven, weighed 220 pounds, and had big bulging shoulders and forearms and gnarled hands, which had wrestled for years with rusty pipes and clogged drains. A long scar zigzagged through a deep dent on his forehead, as if someone had struck him with a sledgehammer and *then* whacked him with an ax. Robison looked like a rough character.

It was soon apparent that whereas Dunlap was blessed with hundreds of friends and a loving, supportive family, Jim Robison had nobody. Unlike Max, who wore "easy mark" stamped all over his face, nobody would mistake the rugged, powerful Robison for a pushover.

Robison opened the conversation by interviewing me. What had I done? Where had I been? Who did I know? Finally, "Why do you think you can do something for Max and me when nobody else has?"

In day-to-day life I had more friends who resembled Robison than Dunlap. Robison, wise in the ways of the alley, would think twice and three times before agreeing to help a Neal Roberts. Yet I was to discover that Jim wasn't a selfish or venal man. Once you got past the forbidding exterior, you discovered an exceptionally well-read man. He didn't fit the mold of any murderer I'd ever met. There was one thing he shared with Max Dunlap: until his arrest for the Bolles killing, he had *never* been arrested, not even for jaywalking.

Robison told me he had known Adamson for years, chiefly in the role of confidant. Adamson couldn't commit a crime without bragging about it to someone, and that someone was often Robison, who listened, pondered human nature, and kept his mouth shut. On death row he'd become friends with the man he'd never met before, and his concern for Max Dunlap equaled what he felt for himself.

"Tell me about Adamson's testimony," I said.

"He said I detonated the bomb he put under the car with a device like kids use to fly model airplanes. But the bombing occurred during the day, eleven-thirty-four, when I was working, and a hardware-store clerk, Chris Stamps, testified I was buying a brass pipe coupling from him at eleven-fifteen in the morning. No way could I have driven all the way across town in nineteen minutes to detonate that bomb. Regardless, Adamson testified that I was with him at the Clarendon parking lot at eleven-ten."

"How did the prosecution beat the alibi?"

"They said to the hardware clerk, 'How do you know your watch wasn't five minutes fast?' Well, he couldn't know. Then the prosecution had a cop drive the distance, racing across town, flying through school zones, running red lights, a regular bat out of hell. He made it to the Clarendon Hotel with thirty seconds to spare. Phenomenal. Even with all that, though, I couldn't have been there at eleven-ten, like Adamson swore."

Robison shook his head, and I saw his fists and jaws clench. "So I guess I screeched to a stop at the Clarendon, probably sweaty and shaky, and in all of thirty seconds concealed myself in a spot that provided an unobstructed view—the device had to be pointed directly at the vehicle to explode the dynamite—and blew him up."

"Jim," I said, "I'd like to know, did you have anything at all to do with killing Don Bolles?"

"No. Absolutely no."

A guard knocked at the door. We had five minutes left.

"I hope you do some good," Robison said, "but I'm afraid

you're Don Quixote off on a tilt with windmills."

"Maybe not," I said.

"Anyway, I look forward to your coming back, and I certainly enjoyed this conversation. I know I'll be more helpful to you than poor Max—he's just in a state of total confusion."

A major factor impeding a clear-eyed investigation of the Bolles murder was the insistence of the *Arizona Republic,* Bolles's own paper, that the reporter had done no investigative work for seven months prior to his death; thus, no one existed who might want to *prevent* a story. But I did some digging and learned this wasn't true. I found out that Bolles moonlighted as the Phoenix stringer for *Newsweek* magazine and as an investigative reporter for a New Mexico daily, the *Gallup Independent.*

Was it possible that Bolles had kept his information from his bosses at the *Republic?* I called John Zollinger, publisher of the *Gallup Independent,* and he told me that he'd told Bolles's editor at the *Republic* about the arrangement.

Why, then, did the *Arizona Republic* peddle the myth that Bolles was doing no investigative work? In fact, I learned from several of Bolles's associates that he was working on "something big" at the time of his death.

The Arizona establishment wanted to put the Bolles murder behind it, so my investigation began rocking some important boats. Police cars started following me. Anonymous callers warned me to get out of Phoenix . . . or else. The two Phoenix dailies were extremely hostile: editors told me the case had been solved and no good could come from ripping the scab off a painful wound.

I plunged ahead, making as much noise as possible, hoping someone with information was out there and would come forward and help me. Soon I was tipped onto Joe Patrick, one of Barry Goldwater's closest friends, the senator's "wing man" for more than three decades in the Arizona National

Guard. "Isn't it unusual," Patrick said, "that the attorney who got immunity had three cars stolen the day they blew up Bolles?"

"What?"

"Yeah. Three. Neal Roberts reported three cars were stolen from behind his house on the very day."

I went to police headquarters and asked for records of crimes reported on June 2, 1976. The police refused to give me anything. I contacted a detective friend in Los Angeles, and he ran Roberts's name through the National Crime Information Center (NCIC) computer and learned that he had indeed reported three vehicles stolen on the day of the bombing.

Why had this information been withheld from the defense? I began looking into the background of Mr. Neal Roberts and learned that he had powerful friends—one of whom was Barry Goldwater.

"What do you think the odds are," I later asked a reporter, "against two cars and a pickup truck being stolen from one guy in one day? In a classy neighborhood? On the day he's a hot suspect in a major murder? I don't think something like this has happened in the history of the world. Three vehicles. On . . ."

". . . the day Bolles was hit," the reporter completed.

"Let's start with the Cadillac," I said. "Adamson told Robison—remember, Adamson called him a few days after the bombing—he took that car and headed for Havasu, where Neal Roberts had made reservations for him at the Rodeway Inn. The trip was rushed, because one big thing went wrong: Bolles didn't die right away. He lived, and he was talking, and surely he named Adamson. So Adamson made a quick getaway, but the Cadillac overheated. He caught a ride back to Phoenix. That accounts for the first vehicle. Of course, Robison's story is corroborated by where the Cadillac was found: I-10 in the direction of Havasu."

"What about the pickup?"

"Vehicle number two. The cops recovered it at Sky Harbor Airport. Check the color of that pickup: green and white. Witnesses at the bombing scene recall seeing a green-and-white pickup, never located by the police. Obviously, whoever took that pickup caught a plane and got out of town."

"And the Chrysler?"

"Vehicle number three. Never found. Maybe it ended up in San Diego. Or was abandoned in the desert. I can't put a fix on that car, but I can on the pickup and the Cadillac. They were getaway vehicles. Probably not in the original plan, but Bolles's living changed the entire scenario, to the point Roberts got left with his absurd multiple robbery story."

What I needed more than anything was a conduit for the mass of new evidence I was acquiring. What good was this information if the public couldn't be informed? With the *Arizona Republic* unreceptive, I went to the *Scottsdale Daily Progress,* a large paper in the area, and spoke to owner/publisher Jonathan Marshall, a rich transplanted New Yorker who believed the convicted men were guilty. But in exchange for an interview with Jim Robison, which I said I'd try to arrange, Marshall assigned his star reporter, Don Devereux, to review my findings.

"Don, just take a look at what I've uncovered so far," I said to Devereux. "If you really think there's nothing here, I'll quit the case."

Devereux looked, studied, and became a convert. So, too, did Jonathan Marshall. Devereux and his wife, Naomi, soon joined me and Terri Yoder in an intense, nonstop investigation aimed at solving the Bolles case. A delighted Jonathan Marshall consistently scooped his competition with shocker after shocker.

Menacing voices had warned me to drop the case and get out of town. It was worse, at least at the start, for Devereux.

A speeding truck tried to run him down and narrowly missed.

I urged Devereux not to go anywhere alone. "Remember you're an investigative journalist," I said. "That what Don Bolles *was.*"

11

TWO MEN SAVED FROM DEATH ROW

At the beginning I merely felt I *needed* Devereux—what good was my information if it didn't reach the public?—but soon the reporter and I became the closest of friends, bound together by a remarkable, perilous investigation. For reasons that will become obvious, I didn't want to share my information with the police, the prosecution was uninterested, and in the early months it couldn't help the defense lawyers. They had already filed an appeal, about which no one was optimistic, but until the appeals process ran its course, new evidence could not be introduced. The best way to find support was through a big newspaper, and soon the *Scottsdale Daily Progress,* namely Devereux and Jonathan Marshall, no longer doubted the innocence of the two men waiting to die on death row.

From my investigation, the name Hank Landry began to stand out. I located a Phoenix police report, penned by homicide detective Jon Sellers, which forever changed the course of the investigation. His report read: "On 4/11/78 at approximately 3:00 P.M., Hank Landry was contacted by telephone. The purpose for the contact was to determine what knowledge Mr. Landry possessed of the Bolles incident. At this time Mr.

Landry related to investigator that he was present at a Memorial Day weekend picnic of 1976 at Neal Roberts's house at 90 W. Virginia. He further stated that during this picnic there was a conversation between Neal Roberts and John Adamson concerning the [Anarchist] cookbook, as well as explosives. He said that during the conversation, Don Bolles's name was mentioned, and that he interceded in the conversation asking, 'Why not just use a gun and get it over with?' He said that as a result of the statement, Neal Roberts replied he wanted it to be loud and clear."

I read this report four times before being convinced that my eyes weren't deceiving me. The *weekend before* Don Bolles's car had exploded, Adamson and Roberts had talked about blowing him up—using dynamite for a "loud and clear" warning.

Hank Landry passed a police-administered polygraph, but even so, no charges were forthcoming against Roberts.

Often detective work involves the tedious, boring, and mundane, such as reading police reports. In the pile of discovery I found a police report written by Phoenix police detective G. Marcus Aurelius that somehow the defense had overlooked. The report revealed that Bolles had been digging into a potential scandal at Arizona dog tracks. One of the dog-track officials was Bradley Funk, an old drinking buddy of the "loud and clear" Neal Roberts. Bolles had written many stories about Bradley Funk and the dog tracks, which reportedly had mob connections; but at the time the reporter had died, he'd been contemplating writing a real shocker. I discovered a pending $1.5 million lawsuit—prepared shortly before the Bolles murder—filed by Betty Richardson, accusing her ex-husband Bradley Funk of invasion of privacy and harassment, including charges of sexual impropriety toward his own child.

For *fifteen years,* I learned, Betty Richardson had confided in Don Bolles. He helped her through a difficult divorce from Bradley Funk. Bolles was an avid listener and Betty told all about Bradley's sexual aberrations and cruelty.

Betty Richardson quoted Brad Funk as saying, "We're going to have to get him [Bolles] off our back." According to the police report, "Mrs. Richardson said she believes Bradley Funk had become so insanely jealous and vindictive due to the indifference toward him of his daughters that it is quite possible for him to have privately engaged the services of a subject to harm Bolles. She described Bolles as being the only person, other than the lawyers, knowing of the pending lawsuit."

The allegations in Betty Richardson's lawsuit would have destroyed Bradley Funk, and Bolles intended to print them the minute the papers were filed and made public record. Here, I thought, was a *real* motive for murder.

I learned that during the six months given Adamson to concoct his story implicating Dunlap and Robison, Adamson had made a single friend in the jail: James McKay, a trusty, the only person Adamson allowed to serve him his meals. I traced McKay to a prison where I interviewed the man. "I gotta put this story together," McKay quoted Adamson as saying. "I'm not gonna die."

"Why not just tell the truth?" the trusty had suggested to Adamson. "You've already been offered immunity."

"The state gives immunity," Adamson had replied. "My people *don't.*"

I thought I had a pretty good idea what kind of people didn't give immunity, but then, with the help of reporter Don Devereux, I located an individual I thought was the most important witness of all. This was Michael JoDon, who had quite a story to tell.

JoDon had moved to New Orleans because he'd felt his life was in danger. I flew to the Crescent City and waited for the meet outside Pat O'Brien's on Easter Sunday. A suspicious

JoDon came five minutes late. Behind him two burly young men stopped several yards down the sidewalk. After introducing ourselves, I said, "I'll need to talk with you alone. I want to tape-record."

"I'm alone," the slender, handsome man in his early twenties replied.

"No, you're not," I said, nodding toward his tag-team shadows. "Tell your muscle to go munch on some beignets or take in a strip show. You won't need them for a while."

JoDon sized me up and made a decision. "Okay, Where to?"

"I have a room at the Monteleon. Let's walk."

Against the unique backdrop of the delectable sounds and smells of French Quarter streets, JoDon began to relax and chat about his lifelong dream of being a policeman in Arizona, and how he'd come no closer to a career in law enforcement than working as an informant. Earlier research into his background had already told me that JoDon had proved himself an extremely accurate and valuable informant with the Scottsdale police department in 1972, and that his undercover work for the Phoenix police, state police, DEA, ATF, and FBI had led to several major convictions.

With the tape recorder on a table between us in my hotel room, JoDon told me about being present in the home of his girlfriend and inadvertantly overhearing the discussion of a plan to kill Don Bolles in late May, 1976, *three weeks* before Bolles died. JoDon said that *three times* before the murder he told the Scottsdale Police Department about the plot, and afterward he'd given his information to the Arizona attorney general's office, but neither agency had seemed interested.

JoDon passed a lie-detector test, and I had him questioned under hypnosis by a leading clinical psychologist who said that in his expert opinion JoDon told the truth.

My revelations were printed regularly in the *Scottsdale*

Progress, a paper subscribed to by members of the Arizona Supreme Court, who were considering the appeals of Robison and Dunlap. I continued digging, and lips began to loosen as Phoenix realized I had no intention of going away.

A local bar owner called and told me to come to his establishment at 7:00 P.M. and sit alone. I complied, and found myself talking with a Phoenix police detective who said his conscience had never given him a respite since he—on orders from superior officers—had removed evidence implicating Bradley Funk from the Bolles murder file. This officer said he and another detective had done as they were told. I checked with the other cop, also conscience stricken, and he confirmed the story.

The *Scottsdale Progress* printed the story, and the Phoenix Police Department had to admit the purging of the file. In short, they had destroyed evidence.

What brought me to Downey, California, on November 17, 1979, was a critical August 17, 1976, police report which, incredibly, *had not found its way to the defense until recently, more than three years after Bolles died:*

> On 8/17/76, investigator flew to Downey, CA after receiving a telephone call from Det. Gary Morrow of the Downey Police Department. Det. Morrow related to investigator that he was in touch with a Bill Wright who allegedly was in an alcoholic hospital with Bradley Funk shortly after the Bolles incident. He related to investigator that Mr. Wright was giving him information concerning statements that Bradley Funk allegedly made to him during their stay at the hospital. . . .
>
> A tape recording of the conversation held with Mr. Wright was made and the tape was retained for future reference. For a complete verbatim account of what was said, please refer to the tape. The following are the highlights of the conversation held with Mr. Wright.

He said that on June 7, 1976, he was admitted to the Beverly Manor Hospital located at 401 South Tustin in the city of Orange. He said that the hospital is a private hospital for alcohol and drug-related problems. He said that on June 7, 1976, he was in the detox center and was present when Bradley Funk came into the hospital on June 8, 1976. . . . He said that at the time he did not know this was Bradley Funk but that he and this person were ultimately assigned the same room, Room #211, and spent approx. 25 days together in this room. . . . He said that Funk became very nervous following Bolles's death and bought the paper every day and received numerous clippings from Arizona concerning the Bolles investigation. He related that Funk told him that he felt his family was going to be blamed for the bombing. He said that Funk stated that in his opinion, some dog owners were the ones that killed Bolles. He also stated that there were going to be some big people hurt as a result of this and named Steiger and Goldwater. Wright said that Funk mentioned some land deals and that he at some time during the conversation believes he mentioned Max Dunlap's name. Wright was unable to be specific as to the conversation or how it took place. He did maintain, however, that at no time did Funk implicate himself or his family in the bombing of Bolles and simply stated that they were going to get the blame for it.

Wright stated that he remembers Funk telling him that he believed Bolles was blown up by a controlled device and remembers him telling him that the explosives or something were purchased in San Diego. He further stated that one time during their stay together, when they were on pass, Funk took him to a hobby shop when he was buying some material for a model boat that he was putting together and at this time Funk pointed out to him a remote-control device, stating that it was something like the one that was used to blow Bolles up. He said that Funk only pointed to the device through the case and did not handle or examine the device. Wright described the device as being brown but later changed the color to black and was shown a photograph of the remote-control device which investigators suspect is similar to the

type that was used. At this time, Wright said that the device that
Funk showed him was similar to the one that investigator had a
photograph of.

The Phoenix detective had concluded that a follow-up interview with William Wright wasn't necessary.

I concluded differently.

Through a contact I had at the California Department of
Motor Vehicles, I attempted to run Wright down using his
date of birth and former address, obtained from the report.
But the DMV had no information on his current where-
abouts.

Knowing he was a retired trucker, I contacted Teamsters
Local 896 in Los Angeles and talked to Frank Martinez, a
union steward. Years earlier Martinez had helped me with an
investigation I'd conducted for the Teamsters. The Justice
Department had charged them with shaking down packing
houses by refusing to move meat unless paid a bribe. I was
able to show that the Justice Department informants had lied
to obtain lenient sentences for themselves, and charges had
been dropped.

Through Martinez I obtained Wright's current address. I
didn't want to just show up on his doorstep, unannounced,
but I couldn't call and make an appointment because he had
an unlisted phone. So I went to a contact at the telephone
company—who charged a hundred dollars per number—and
got Wright's listing.

I don't like this procedure, but the police use it, and they
don't have to pay.

I set up a meeting with Wright at the Downey police station.
There he introduced me to Detective Gary Morrow, who
seemed protective of the truck driver. Morrow expressed dis-
enchantment with the Phoenix police's handling of this witness and remarked that Wright's anxiety stemmed from the

mob connotations in the Bolles bombing.

"Mr. Wright," I said, "I read Jon Sellers's report of his interview with you."

"I'm glad someone's interested. I don't think Sellers liked what he heard from me. He never came back."

"Well, we're shooting for a new trial, and *I* want to talk to you. I can't answer for Sellers."

"It surprised me," said Detective Morrow, "that we didn't hear back from Phoenix. I thought they would check out what Bill told them."

"You were never subpoenaed to the trial?" I asked Wright.

"All I had was that one talk with Sellers."

"When did you meet Bradley Funk?"

"On June 8, 1976, the day after I checked into the hospital."

"What kind of shape was he in?"

"He seemed okay to me. Frankly, I wondered why he was even there."

That Funk had checked into a detox center before Bolles died, thus removing himself from the scene of the investigation, struck me as a coincidence not dissimilar to Neal Roberts having had three cars stolen on the day of the bombing.

"Did Funk mention John Adamson to you?"

"Yes. He said Adamson was just a 'stooge' in the murder conspiracy."

Some of what Wright told me had been contained in the Sellers police report, but not the truck driver's opinion that Funk didn't need alcohol rehabilitation, nor that Funk had called Adamson a "stooge."

On what did Funk base this judgment? He claimed he'd met Adamson only once, at the Stockyards Restaurant, describing the killer as "a slimy-looking guy with mirrored glasses." Adamson, for his part, claimed he had *never* met Funk.

"Did Funk tell you he knew Adamson?"

"He said he saw him numerous times at the dog tracks."

"Did Funk ever mention Don Bolles?"

"That's mostly all he talked about."

"What did he say?"

"Not much until Bolles died. Then he told me he knew his family would be blamed, but he said he believed some dog owners were responsible."

"Dog owners?"

"That's what he said."

"Did he name any of these dog owners?"

"Like I told Sellers, the only names I remember were Steiger and Goldwater. Brad said some big people were going to be hurt."

Adamson owned dogs. But most dog owners revered Bolles, saw him as a champion in their fight for better purses from the Funk-Emprise racing monopoly. Dog owners wouldn't want Bolles dead.

"Did Funk say anything about how Bolles was killed?"

"Yes. He told me he was blown up by a bomb triggered by a remote-control device."

All our work paid off in February, 1980, when the Arizona Supreme Court reversed the Dunlap and Robison murder convictions and ordered new trials. The two men were released from death row after spending nearly two and a half years there, and the prosecution's case was in tatters. "Are we ever ready!" exclaimed defense attorney Murray Miller to reporters when asked what the chances were of acquittal in a retrial.

The prosecution suffered another defeat. John Adamson, who admitted planting the bomb, refused to testify again unless he received an even sweeter deal than he'd gotten before: Adamson demanded immediate release from prison; a new identity, a new wardrobe, money, and a college education for his son.

I wondered what Adamson was up to. Surely he didn't want to reenter the courtroom arena as a lamb against lions. Perhaps, I thought, he'd put an impossible price tag on his testimony to keep himself from being ripped apart on the stand and forced to name his true co-conspirators—the ones who "don't give immunity."

The prosecution threatened Adamson with the revocation of the sweet plea bargain deal he'd received. Adamson countered with an intriguing argument: that he was being subjected to double jeopardy. He had already gone to court and been sentenced for murder. He claimed he couldn't be retried for the same crime.

At a preliminary bail hearing for Dunlap, Adamson took the Fifth Amendment 136 times.

While all this was going on, the California Department of Justice released a document concerning a certain Nicolo Angelo DiVincenzo, described as a "hit man for organized crime" who "allegedly advised that he had been hired to murder John Adamson, arrested for the bombing murder of Bolles in June of 1976. DiVincenzo reportedly stated that he had received the contract to hit Adamson prior to Adamson's arrest because Adamson was a direct link to Funk (believed to be one of the Funks of Funks Greyhound Racing Circuit, Inc.)."

Neal Roberts, who'd said he wanted the Bolles murder to be "loud and clear," was also called to the preliminary bail hearing. He pleaded the Fifth Amendment to the "loud and clear" remark, to "setting up" the "easy patsy" Dunlap by having him deliver that money to Adamson's lawyer, and to questions about the three vehicles "stolen" on the day of the bombing.

On June 21, 1980, while my investigation still steamed full speed ahead in anticipation of a possible retrial, my apartment was set afire and Terri Lee Yoder and I nearly died. Our hearts actually stopped beating before paramedics arrived and rushed us to the hospital in critical condition. We survived, but it was touch-and-go, especially for Terri.

The alarm clock that June 21 never went off—no, the alarm must have gone off, because we figured that's what woke Terri up. I didn't hear it.

Terri Lee doesn't remember any of this, nor do I. But we pieced it together from what neighbors and people at the hospital told us, and the fire department report.

She woke up to an apartment in flames. The blaze had started in the kitchen and roared down a hallway toward the bedroom where we slept. She tried to wake me up, but couldn't.

The place was filled with choking smoke.

Our apartment had two doors to the outside: one exiting from the kitchen, the other opening into a little foyer, which led to the living room.

Terri opened the living-room door, then fled through the one in the kitchen. She ran to a neighbor, having an early-morning cup of coffee on his patio, and shouted at him, "Call the fire department! My apartment is on fire!"

She then raced back to the kitchen door, a life to save, but the intense heat drove her away. She ran around to the front.

A man stood there, mesmerized by the flames. When Terri started through the front door, he grabbed and held her. "You can't go in there! That place is going to burn to the ground!"

"I got to!" she screamed over the roar of the fire. "My old man's in there!"

Terri jerked away from him and plunged inside. She fought her way through smoke and terrific heat to reach me, attempted to shake me awake, and that's where the fire fighters found her, collapsed at the foot of the bed. She was still on fire, a human torch. Overcome by smoke, she had fallen on her left side, and her nightgown was in flames.

They found me still lying on the bed.

Terri and I were each lifted onto a gurney and carried from the apartment. Outside, the man who had tried to stop Terri Lee asked a fireman, "They're going to be all right, aren't they?"

"I don't think so," the fireman said. "Both their hearts have stopped."

It really hit the guy hard. He blamed himself. In fact, paramedics had to give him first aid. He threw up, cried, sat down, and just fell apart. He moaned, "I should have stopped her. I shouldn't have let her go in there. I knew something like this would happen."

After literally jump-starting our hearts to get them beating, they took Terri Lee and me to the nearest hospital, Phoenix Baptist. From there a Medivac helicopter flew her to Maricopa County General Hospital and its highly rated burn unit.

That afternoon a doctor at Phoenix Baptist phoned George Vlassis and asked for the name of my next of kin. He told them Lake III, and said they might reach him through my friend Nick Behnen in Las Vegas.

"He's right here," said Behnen to the caller from Phoenix Baptist, and handed the phone to my son.

"Your father has been in a fire," the doctor told Lake. "Can you come to Phoenix?"

"Sure, I'll be there tomorrow."

"You better come today, if you want to be sure of seeing your dad alive. We can't be certain how long he's going to live."

Behnen drove Lake to the airport and paid for his ticket on the next flight to Phoenix. Vlassis met the plane and brought him to the hospital.

A doctor asked Lake, "Who was this woman at the apartment? What's her relationship to your father?"

"She's his girlfriend, Terri Yoder. What do you mean, what's the relationship?"

"Well, how does he feel about her?"

"He cares a lot for her. Why?"

"Because the girl can't live. She's going to die any minute now. We don't expect her to survive the rest of the day. Your father has a fifty-fifty chance of pulling through, so we want to know, if this girl dies, or *when* she dies, how your father will react. If he regains consciousness, we don't know whether to tell him about her condition, because we don't know how the news will affect his recovery."

"I can't tell you how to handle that. I know Dad thought a lot of Terri; otherwise, he wouldn't have been living with her."

When Lake III first saw Terri, he said she looked "weird." They had her lying facedown in a hammocklike sling up over the bed. She had been burned on the whole left side of her back, from the bottom of her buttocks to the top of her shoulder, and down her left arm.

He asked the nurse, "How is she?"

"Not good. Any minute now. She's a goner."

The nurse pointed to a heart monitor and said, "See the line going across the screen, and that little blip on the line. That's all the heartbeat she has left. When that line flattens out, she's dead."

Lake III told me Terri Lee looked horrible. After they began letting her have visitors, her ex-husband heard the news (reports of the fire appeared in all the papers) and came to the hospital. When he walked into the room, he took one look at Terri's charred body and fainted. He fell against a table and gashed his head, which required stitches. This isn't to say he lacked heart. Terri really did look awful.

I began to recover, but Terri remained critical. I had plenty of visitors: Max and Barbara Dunlap, Vlassis, Mike Stuhff, Devereaux, Dunlap Committee members.

Max told me, "This is because of the Bolles case. I'm sorry. I can't tell you how sorry I am."

Barbara cried. She told me how badly their kids felt for us. The Dunlap children liked Terri; several were her age.

Jim Robison phoned me from prison, where he was being held on a phony assault charge.

My friend Molly Ivins called, as did Bill Helmer of *Playboy*.

I had access to a phone and dialed all over the country talking to people. Trouble was, I didn't make sense. I called friends, talked to them, then couldn't remember what I had said.

My incoherence was caused by smoke inhalation. As it was explained to me, breathing in toxic fumes—mainly carbon monoxide and cyanide, released from burning carpet, wallpaper, and other synthetic materials—had caused my brain to swell. The pressure of the brain pushing against the skull made me goofy at times. The doctors prescribed medication to reduce the swelling and minimize the pain, but the slow recovery process required time and a lot of rest.

I had already used up a lot of time. After hospitalization for ten days, seven in critical condition, I was up moving around and anxious to leave. I desperately wanted to be with Terri, and for some reason thought I could talk the doctor into releasing me because Bill Helmer was coming to town.

So I made my pitch, promising no driving a car for thirty days, no working for six months, and no smoking, ever. I also agreed to take it easy and see him as an outpatient every day for the next month. I said, "Yeah, yeah, yeah," to anything he wanted, just to bullshit my way out.

"I probably shouldn't release you. But since your girlfriend needs you, and your friend is coming to Phoenix, I will. You have to keep the promises you've made."

Lake III, who had faithfully pushed visiting hours to the limit for me and Terri, stayed in Phoenix for two weeks after I got out of the hospital.

He never hesitated to chauffeur me places or run errands—requests I didn't always make at the most appropriate times. And my son kept his broad shoulders available for me to lean on, which I did often.

Finally—it took many months—we nursed Terri back to health. She remembered very little about her stay in the hospital, but other things became less fuzzy for her. I proudly watched her work her way up from waitress to bartender to manager of a bar. I encouraged her—you're doing great, stick with it, keep working—more for the therapy than for the money she earned. I think she knew, after what had happened—she'd saved my life—that if she told me, "I need your left arm," she'd get it.

On the day of my release from Phoenix Baptist, Bill Helmer and I had gone to the burned-out apartment to take a look. The place had been totally destroyed by the blaze. If I hadn't known otherwise, I would have thought a bomb had exploded inside.

In the living room we saw the sky through a hole ten feet in diameter in the ceiling. The TV set had folded in on itself, and the telephone resembled something out of a cartoon: a black blob of plastic that melted and ran down onto the table.

The strangest thing happened as we surveyed the destruction: the telephone rang.

"You going to answer it?" Helmer asked.

"No. You go ahead." I put my hands in front of my face, and took a step backward, feigning fear. He let it ring.

The apartment looked like a war zone. In the kitchen everything had been destroyed, even pots and pans. A total loss.

The dining area also had been wasted. Charred cookbooks, dishes, and boards littered the floor. Terri's beloved plants had been obliterated.

In the hallway, starting about three feet above the floor, the walls had been scorched to black as the fire had headed toward our bedroom. Terri, to reach me, had run through a boiling, churning hell of heat and fire.

Sheets were still on our bed, and burned onto them was an outline of me, a ghostly white impression against a dark gray background, like the chalk figure of a body the homicide detective draws at a murder scene.

"I don't know why you're still here," Helmer said, eyeing the bed and sniffing the stale, water-soaked odor of dead smoke permeating the ruined clothes in our closet.

Smoke had discolored papers on a table where Terri and I had been working. The top sheets were singed black, and any exposed edges of those underneath had curled into distinctive patterns.

Still, the living room ranked worst of all. Its ceiling featured that fire-made skylight, blackened beams, and boards scorched nearly to soot. Sheetrock had been burned off the walls, and exposed studs had metamorphosed to charcoal, which had crumbled onto the floor.

Helmer kept shaking his head. I suggested we get away from the place and asked where he intended to spend the night.

"Are you kidding? I'm getting out of Phoenix, and if you've got a lick of sense you'll be on the plane with me. I mean, what has to happen for you to get the message? Can't you see they don't like you in this town? Get the fuck out while you still can."

In the official fire-department report, a fire fighter named Rodman stated that after Terri and I had been carried from the rubble, he'd witnessed Phoenix police detectives removing files from our apartment. I discovered, when I checked for myself, that documents I had been keeping there relating to the Bolles investigation were missing. They also had grabbed my pistol and a jar into which Terri and I tossed loose change.

George Vlassis accompanied me to the police station, where with a minimum of hassle they returned the gun and the money jar. But no files. They denied files had been taken, though I knew better.

Fire fighter Rodman "modified" his report. Originally he'd written that he had *seen* police removing files and putting them into a squad car; later he changed this to hearing them *discuss* taking the documents.

No matter. They *were* missing and I knew the police had burgled them.

Fortunately, it was no big matter. I always retain several copies of important reports and never keep all of them in the same spot.

What concerned me most, of course, was the possibility that someone had tried to kill Terri and me. Nine months earlier our apartment had been burglarized; valuables were completely overlooked, but several Bolles case interview tapes had been taken.

About two months after the fire we moved to Flagstaff, and after just a few weeks, a *third* burglary occurred: someone broke into a storage locker I maintained in Phoenix and stole an entire box of Bolles investigative material. The owner of the storage facility said a master key, lock pick, or bolt cutter had been employed in the break-in. The lock itself was never found.

After the fire in our apartment, I didn't think myself paranoid to suspect arson. The first fire fighter on the scene had found two hot-water faucets running. Neither Terri Lee nor I had turned them on, and they would prove significant to an explanation for the fire.

Devereux, concerned about the possibility of a murder attempt, himself the intended victim of a hit-and-run in that alley, sought an opinion on the fire from Anthony Joseph Pellicano, a Chicago private investigator ranked by author and former CIA agent George O'Toole as one of the nation's four best (O'Toole listed me in this same elite company). O'Toole, using uncharacteristic praise, described Pellicano as having "the perceptiveness of Sherlock Holmes" and "the tenacity of the Royal Canadian Mounted Police."

More important to Devereux, however, was Pellicano's acknowledged expertise on arson and bombings.

Pellicano studied the fire at our apartment and said it showed many characteristics of a classic method of arson. The arsonist, he pointed out, opens a container of ether near a hot-water heater, closes the door to concentrate the evaporating fumes, and turns on one or more hot-water faucets. When the draw on the hot-water tank becomes sufficient, the gas flame comes on, igniting the ether fumes and triggering the fire.

Interestingly, the fire department determined that the blaze had begun in a pantry right next to the compartment housing the hot-water heater.

I saw this as the bottom line: *no* explanation other than Pellicano's accounted for those hot-water taps having been turned on.

I studied the fire from every angle I could, concluding that the arsonist probably didn't try to kill us, though he wouldn't have been unhappy with the result. I believed, and Devereux agreed, that someone thought there were incriminating documents in the apartment that needed to be destroyed.

Terri, right up to the present, doesn't remember anything that happened during the three days prior to the fire.

Before leaving Phoenix I wrote a long letter of appreciation to the fire fighters and paramedics, making it clear my quarrel was with the police department, not them. I thanked them for saving my life and Terri Lee's, and requested the fire chief to place a copy of the letter in each of the fire fighter's files.

The prosecution finally "temporarily dismissed" murder charges against Robison and Dunlap. Without Adamson, there seemed to be no case at all, and the confessed murderer refused to go back on the stand.

"I owe Lake Headley my life," said Max Dunlap, back with his family after three years spent fifty feet from the "green door." James Robison expressed similar gratitude, revealing at the same time that prosecutors had offered to spare his life if he would confess and name Kemper Marley as the money man behind the murder. "But Marley had no more to do with this than Max or me," Robison said. "I couldn't lie about him, the way Adamson did about me, just to save my own skin."

Years disappeared, but the Bolles murder would not. It just wasn't acceptable to the public that the state's most famous murder remain unsolved. Not only had Bolles been an especially admirable citizen, but the killing at high noon in the heart of downtown Phoenix had deeply scarred the image of an entire state.

In 1989 the case boiled over again. The Arizona attorney general, facing a stiff reelection campaign filled with charges that the Bolles murder had never been solved, convened a grand jury to look once again into the facts of the murder. For a time Dunlap Defense Committee members hoped that at last the official investigation would take a look at the prominent Arizonans they believed had been behind the crime, but soon it became obvious that the state wanted Robison and Dunlap back in the dock again.

The state first went after Robison, the weaker of the two. The prosecution probably felt it wasn't quite ready to tangle again with Dunlap's army of friends.

Then–Arizona attorney general Bob Corbin went to the grand jury but it *wouldn't* reindict. Anyone familiar with America's grand-jury system knows that these blue-ribbon panels generally do whatever the prosecution wants.

I testified in front of the grand jury Corbin hoped would reindict. I know I'm not a spellbinding orator, but the grand jury seemed fascinated by the story I told. I saw several members gasp almost in horror when I told about Neal "Loud and Clear" Roberts and wondered aloud why they weren't hearing evidence against him.

When the grand jury wouldn't reindict, the prosecutor filed a "complaint," which he contended was all that he needed. Since the charges against Robison (and Dunlap, for that matter) had never been dropped—a Sword of Damocles hanging over their heads—the attorney general said they could be reinstated whenever he chose. They were, and soon thereafter Dunlap was reindicted as well.

Attorney General Corbin chose a time propitious for himself. He faced a stiff reelection challenge from *two* candidates, and they let it be known that his total lack of progress in the most important case he'd ever handled—the Bolles murder—would be a major campaign issue. Thus, when Corbin recharged Robison and Dunlap, observers felt it represented a desperate gamble to establish that he genuinely sought justice for Don Bolles and merited reelection.

I found it damnable that these innocent people, old men now, had to go through the ordeal again. I wasn't so young myself any more, but like an old fire horse I answered the bell one more time, and learned of a potentially damaging development: Bradley Funk had died of a heart attack on December 30, 1989.

A living Bradley Funk would have posed a big obstacle to the conviction Corbin hoped to obtain against Robison and Dunlap. The attorney general may even have breathed a sigh of relief, given another problem he had: a $55,000 campaign contribution he'd accepted from Charles Keating—head of Lincoln Savings and Loan, which became the largest S&L bankruptcy in history—for a campaign in which Corbin ran *unopposed.* Corbin, incidentally, never went after Keating's banking empire, though it was his job to keep tabs on it. When asked if he intended to return the $55,000, Corbin said, "I never promised him anything and have never done anything for him. And I'm just hardheaded enough to think that if you give something back to the man, then it looks like you did something wrong."

God, I hate what Arizona authorities have done to Max and Jim. As I think about the case, in May, 1992 (the state's been in no hurry to proceed to trial), I tell myself these men *can't* be convicted again. But then I remember that the state did it before, and I wonder if the delays don't have something to do with the state of Neal Roberts's health. Roberts is not well and may not live to face withering cross-examination.

Whatever, I would dearly love to live long enough to see my friends Jim and Max acquitted.

Here's what I believe is the bottom line: the state wove a tangled web. Once the decision was made to protect the powerful, all that remained was a sordid vendetta against the innocent.

12

THE BLOOMINGDALE/MORGAN AFFAIR

In mid-July, 1983, I received a call at my Las Vegas home from the noted author, playwright, and investigative journalist Donald Freed. He wanted me to join him as part of a three-man team, funded by a wealthy magazine magnate, to take an independent look into the recent (July 7) murder, in Los Angeles, of Vicki Morgan, brutally bludgeoned in her own bed with a baseball bat.

Donald Freed was someone I had admired for a long time. A fighter for justice. A professor of continuing education at UCLA, he possessed a vast array of writing skills (plays, screenplays, novels) he employed for social good. He was author of the prize-winning Broadway play *Inquest,* and coauthor (with Mark Lane) of *Executive Action.* He also wrote *The Killing of RFK,* and such diverse works as *Freud and Stanislavsky: New Directions in the Performing Arts* and *The Existentialism of Alberto Moravia* (with Joan Ross). Freed and I had each looked into the SLA and the murder of Robert Kennedy, and we wondered how Sirhan Sirhan could be so widely accepted as a "lone assassin" when the fatal bullets seemed to have been fired from a position other than his. In any case, I again couldn't resist the opportunity to work on a case with Donald Freed.

The victim, Vicki Morgan, had been considered one of the most beautiful women in the world, but her fame came not from her stunning good looks but from the people she knew: Ronald Reagan, Nancy Reagan, Gerald Ford, and multimillionaire department-store magnate Alfred Bloomingdale.

In Los Angeles I met former FBI agent Bill Turner, the third member of our team, at Donald Freed's home. Each of us had doubts about the official versions of other "celebrity" homicides—particularly Marilyn Monroe's death—and with the trail still warm in the Vicki Morgan murder we expected to uncover details the authorities would prefer remain hidden, but nothing excessively shocking.

We were wrong. Not only had major violations of national security taken place and top government officials been implicated in a seamy sex scandal, but we became convinced that the police had overlooked the real killers.

Bill Turner and I both checked into the Hyatt Regency on Sunset Boulevard, where I spent the next day going through newspaper accounts of the murder. Mindful that deadline-beating coverage *usually* contains errors, I nonetheless had long ago adopted scanning news clips as the quickest way to familiarize myself with the bare bones of a case.

Murder charges had been filed against a gay man named Marvin Pancoast, who had lived with Vicki in a sharing-expenses arrangement, on the basis of his confession. Pancoast, who quickly retracted his confession, pleaded insanity. He gave the following motives: "The way she talked to her mother when she was over to help us move . . . Her mother came over and packed all her things, and she just sat there like the Queen of Sheba. . . . She needled me and she wouldn't quit."

These reasons seemed flimsy to me, but people had been

killed for less. I did know that confessions, even retracted
ones, were very difficult to overcome in court.

My second day on the case was spent in a musty cubicle at
the Los Angeles County Courthouse in downtown L.A.,
perusing a deposition Vicki Morgan had given in a lawsuit
filed against the now-deceased Alfred Bloomingdale.

Important finds in a complex murder case usually come
after long, tedious digging, but right away I happened upon a
treasure trove: an account, in Vicki's own words, that told me
several other people had much stronger motives than Marvin
Pancoast for wanting her dead.

Vicki had been suing Bloomingdale for palimony (oddly, it
seems, with his blessing), based on the twelve years she had
spent as his mistress, and on oral and written promises he'd
made to take care of her for life. These were guarantees he'd
probably intended to keep, but at the time of the deposition
he lay dying—he had one week to live—and his wife Betsy,
Nancy Reagan's best friend, had cut off the money he'd ear-
marked for Vicki.

The deposition read like a good Hollywood novel, except
this was the real thing, and I sat entranced, caught up in a
story of sex, money, and power that proved truth really is
stranger than fiction.

Seventeen-year-old Vicki Morgan, who hoped to be a top
model and film star, first met Alfred Bloomingdale, age fifty-
three, at the Old World Restaurant on the Sunset Strip in
1970. On an impulse, it seemed, he followed her into the
restaurant and introduced himself, asking for her phone number. She had no idea who he was, nor that he had enormous
wealth and power and was frequently mentioned in society
columns with his friends Ronald and Nancy Reagan.

Vicki stated that at first she'd shunned Bloomingdale, but
after two months of his insistent phone calls—never fewer
than five a day, often as many as twenty—she'd given in and

agreed to meet the much-older man. Their first real rendez-
vous was at Schwab's Drugstore in Hollywood, where a talent
scout had purportedly discovered Lana Turner.

Thus began what would be a twelve-year sexual relationship. But more than that, the Alfred Bloomingdale/Vicki
Morgan love affair took fantastic twists and turns, many of
them, I came to believe, relevant to her murder. At the moment, though, deep in the bowels of the county courthouse, I
had to force myself not to turn the pages too quickly.

Outside of Schwab's, Vicki stated, Bloomingdale had in-
structed her to let a second young woman into her car, and
they'd proceeded to a mansion in Beverly Hills. "Alfred has a
real interest in you," the young woman told Vicki as they
rode, "and I'm here to tell you that he's going to beat you
when he sees you up at that house." But, the woman added,
Bloomingdale also wanted Vicki to know she was "special to
him and that he will make special—what's the word?—allowances."

I'll bet, I thought cynically. I figured I knew the ending to
this tale of Dirty Old Man Meets Tender Damsel, but I
couldn't have been more wrong.

At the mansion, according to Vicki, Alfred came right to
the point. He said he intended to take her as his mistress. "By
the time Alfred and I walked up there," Vicki said in the
deposition, "these two women were nude and I was told to
take my clothes off, and Alfred was already taking his off, and
he asked one of the girls to get the equipment, which is Alfred
Bloomingdale's belt, his ties, and, excuse me gentlemen, but a
dildo."

The women faced a wall, trembling a little, with their arms
raised and their wrists tied, and Alfred beat them furiously
with his belt. "He had a look in his eyes," Vicki said, "and
believe me when I say this, a look in his eyes and his face that
scared me to death."

I knew Bloomingdale had been a top advisor in the Reagan administration, a very close friend to Reagan himself, a president who professed "strong family values." I was keenly aware that this kind of story had the potential to cause enormous damage to powerful people. I thought again of Marilyn Monroe, and what she might have said about the Kennedys, had she lived.

After the S & M session, Vicki testified in the deposition, Alfred dismissed the other women and concentrated his attentions on her. He spanked her and they had sex together.

Vicki was frightened by Alfred, but also felt "irresistibly drawn to him." She believed him "the most fascinating man I have ever met in my entire life. There's no one like him in the world. He's fun, he's childlike. He's a little arrogant but not rudely arrogant. He always needed help doing this or that because he was tripping over his own feet, and he was so worldly. He knew everything."

In addition, he had important friends, and I read about Vicki meeting many of them: director Mervyn LeRoy; Justin Dart, a Reagan "kitchen cabinet" member chain-drugstore magnate; future attorney general Edwin Meese; and numerous other luminaries. For a teenager, for *anyone,* it was heady stuff. Bloomingdale took her to Europe, to Florida, and to the Bahamas. When he was in Los Angeles they only met during the day because his wife, Betsy, insisted he be home at night.

Bloomingdale introduced Vicki Morgan as his daughter, but soon he was promising to divorce his wife and marry Vicki. "He proudly told several of his friends that I was having his child," said the young mistress.

But Alfred had a change of heart and ordered her to have an abortion.

It was inevitable that Betsy learned of her husband's affair. Apparently Nancy Reagan, Vicki testified, realized what was going on in the first year but did not tell Betsy. "Nancy

Reagan," said Vicki, "had seen us together along with quite
a few other people . . . but he would say to his friends that I
was his daughter. I'd say, 'Alfred, I don't look like your
daughter.' "

Vicki broke the relationship off several times, usually because she couldn't accustom herself to his sadistic sexual
demands. Vicki married a young actor named John David
Carson, but this just made Alfred want her more. He got her
unlisted phone number from the telephone company.

Actually, I later discovered, Bloomingdale would have been
a hard individual for almost anyone to lose. He had been a
founder of the Diner's Club, the first major credit-card service
in the world, and very early learned how credit-card receipts
could be used to tell a great deal about a bearer's habits.
Bloomingdale himself seldom ever used plastic.

Vicki told about how her marriage collapsed under the
pressure applied by Bloomingdale, and of moving into the
Beverly Hills mansion of Bernie Cornfeld, a wheeler-dealer
whose financially crumbling Investors Overseas Service (IOS)
had been taken over by swindler Robert Vesco, now one of the
world's most famous fugitives.

She also ended up in the bedroom of the ruler of Morocco,
King Hassan.

Vicki, a high-school dropout, was playing with some very
heavy hitters. At the L.A. County Courthouse I wondered,
ominously, if people like King Hassan, Cornfeld, and Bloomingdale tended toward pillow talk. If so, Vicki could have
heard stories she'd have been much better off not knowing.

Vicki testified that she returned to Alfred in 1976. He paid
her $10,000 a month and promised her, "I'll divorce my wife.
We'll tell her and we'll be married." But, as Vicki lamented,
"he told me that hundreds of times."

The truth was, Alfred had fallen in love with Vicki Morgan.
He could talk to her as he was never able to with his socialite

wife, and Vicki always listened attentively when he had something to get off his mind. What Alfred couldn't do was purge sadistic sex—what scared Vicki—from his life.

In 1978 Vicki fled from Bloomingdale again, this time by marrying real-estate developer Robert Schulman, but, as before, Alfred wouldn't let go. "They grabbed shirts, they were going to fight," Vicki said in her sworn testimony. Soon Vicki was back in the tycoon's clutches.

"I feel like I'm going to end up like Marilyn Monroe," Vicki said prophetically, and certainly with good reason. "Alfred continuously confided in me," she went on, "by telling me his private opinions about influential and important people with whom he was intimately involved, such as Ronald and Nancy Reagan, and he would relate specific instances involving them, and he told me about his involvement in secret and delicate matters such as campaign contributions for Mr. Reagan."

I had started reading in the early afternoon and twilight was coming on. I was almost near the end. In the summer of 1981, Vicki related, Bloomingdale entered UCLA Medical Center suffering from throat cancer. Vicki was barred from visiting after Betsy found out the mistress was often at his side. Vicki beat the ban by wearing a nurse's uniform. Alfred executed a contract leaving Vicki one-half of his equity in the Showbiz Pizza chain, plus a two-year monthly allowance of $10,000 (together, a total of more than $1 million).

Alfred came home briefly, and Vicki related how she managed even to see him there, but soon he was confined in St. John's Hospital in Santa Monica, where Vicki visited in the disguise of a nun.

Alfred died at St. John's and was given a quiet funeral, possibly in revenge for a lifetime of philandering.

It seemed to me, talking to Freed and Turner late that night at the hotel, that we needed to learn a good deal more about

Alfred Bloomingdale. Vicki's remarkable deposition had provided motives for murder stronger than Pancoast being upset
about the way Vicki "talked about her mother."

Turner related the circumstances of Pancoast's confession.
On July 7 at 3:20 A.M., Pancoast had walked into the North
Hollywood police station and announced, "I just killed someone. She's at 4171 Colfax, apartment D in the rear. I killed her
with a baseball bat."

Homicide detective William Welch had found Vicki lying
on her bed. She had been killed by repeated blows to the head,
and her hands and some fingers were broken, the latter consistent with a victim trying to ward off blows. Yet Pancoast
told the police that Vicki offered no resistance because she was
either drunk (her blood alcohol level was .05 percent, far
below the legal intoxication level) or asleep. If asleep, how
come the defensive injuries to the hands and fingers?

What Pancoast confessed to bore little resemblance to what
Detective Welch witnessed at the scene. The baseball bat
wasn't where Pancoast said he'd left it, and there were no
fingerprints on the weapon. Pancoast said he drove his blue
Oldsmobile to the North Hollywood police station, but Welch
located it in the condo's parking garage, several miles away.
How, then, had Pancoast gotten to the station? Most curious,
not a trace of blood was found on the confessed murderer or
his clothes. All the police had was the recanted confession.

The three of us had known (it was in all the newspapers)
that three days after the murder a well-dressed woman had
walked into the law offices of Steinberg and Bugliosi (the
latter the famed author of *Helter Skelter* and the prosecutor
of Charles Manson) and left three videotapes for Robert
Steinberg.

Steinberg viewed the videos—soon known worldwide as the
"sex tapes"—and called a press conference where he announced that they depicted sex acts being performed between

Vicki Morgan, Alfred Bloomingdale, a former U.S. congressman, and two very high ranking officials in the Reagan administration.

Steinberg announced at his press conference that the contents of the "sex tapes" could "bring down the Reagan government." He offered to turn them over to Ronald Reagan himself, but before that could occur, Steinberg reported that his office had been broken into and the tapes stolen.

I felt we needed to know more about Alfred, Vicki, and those videotapes, so I resorted to a method that had served me well in the past: I went on several radio talk shows, including PBS, and made it known that an independent investigation was underway. I said I could be reached at the Hyatt and urged anyone with relevant information on Vicki's murder to contact me. Often witnesses hesitate to talk to the police, fearing exposure, but are willing to confide in a p.i. guaranteeing confidentiality.

One caller insisted on a face-to-face meeting, and reluctantly agreed to come to the Hyatt. She turned out to be a middle-aged employee of the powerful William Morris talent agency, and very, very frightened. She told me she could lose her job, insisted on anonymity, and then said, "I'm talking to you because it's the right thing to do."

The woman, who was indeed a respected employee of William Morris, related a remarkable story. She told me that Vicki Morgan had gone to the Morris agency and suggested the writing of a book to be titled *Alfred's Mistress,* and Morris had begun negotiations to represent her. Then, the woman related, a senior Morris agent received a phone call from former President Gerald Ford.

I learned that Vicki had gone to numerous agents with her obviously commercial property, but after initial enthusiasm, the agents all had backed away. Were they warned off, I wondered, just as the Morris agency had been?

But Vicki remained determined to tell her story, and I wondered if, in the end, that hadn't cost her her life. She reached an agreement with free-lance writer Gordon Basichis and began to record her adventures on tape. She was murdered before the book could be finished. (Titled *Beautiful Bad Girl*, it was published in 1985.)

Another caller, who insisted on being known as "Charley," told me she had seen the videotapes and that prominently featured in the sex romps was U.S. attorney general Edwin Meese. This was before Marvin Pancoast, Vicki's roommate, told his attorney, Arthur Barens, the same thing. On May 21, 1984, *Time* magazine wrote, "Barens told reporters his client maintains that Presidential Counsellor Edwin Meese was among Morgan's filmed partners. Claims Barens: 'We have evidence that the videotapes exist and that the Government has them.' " Ed Meese has denied ever meeting Vicki Morgan.

The motive. I always came back to the motive. It made no sense to me. And the more I learned about Vicki Morgan and the powerful men she had known, the more obvious it became that others *had* possessed strong reasons for wanting her out of the way. Her book, if it had seen the light of day, could have been a wrecker of careers.

Everything Vicki became traced to Alfred Bloomingdale, and I looked deep into his background. He had been a member of Ronald Reagan's so-called kitchen cabinet, an influential group of wealthy men credited with masterminding his amazing rise to political stardom. Following Reagan's landslide election victory in 1980, Bloomingdale had been appointed to the powerful and ultrasecret Foreign Intelligence Advisory Board. Actually, as Donald Freed discovered, Bloomingdale had done undercover work for Reagan as early as 1966, the former president's first year as governor.

California was one thing, I thought, but a top security job in the federal government? Couldn't Alfred's scandalous sex life, his propensity for sadism, be used as blackmail against him? And how much had he told Vicki?

I shook my head whenever I thought of Bloomingdale in a sensitive national security post, and not just because of his tawdry personal life. While working for then-governor Ronald Reagan in California, he was part of a campaign against the United Farm Workers of America, the union headed by Cesar Chavez. Reagan despised this union—he called one of UFWA's strikes an "uprising"—and seemed to look the other way when wealthy growers, who were supporters of his, organized beatings, break-ins, and burglaries. The *union* also uncovered three assassination plots against Chavez—in 1969, 1970, and 1971—but the Sacramento government showed little interest, UFWA officials felt, because the state was working hand-in-hand with the growers.

I also learned as much as I could about Marvin Pancoast. The *L.A. Weekly* reported that he "is known to have been involved in the masochistic side of several S & M relationships," an indication of his passivity. The paper also quoted a friend of the accused murderer: "I couldn't imagine Pancoast doing anything to hurt anyone but himself. He was harmless."

What was Pancoast's role in Vicki Morgan's murder, if any? Intelligent speculation is the best I can do.

Pancoast, in his confession, told police he "went to the store" around midnight the morning of the murder, returned to the condo, "couldn't sleep," and killed Vicki at 2 A.M. One informant, who claimed to be close to Vicki but refused to give an identity ("I'm deathly afraid"), said Pancoast had indeed left the condo at midnight, but had returned shortly accompanied by five other men. The group arrived in two cars and went inside.

Who knows? The police never uncovered any of this, but they weren't looking very hard. While our team had the advantage of reluctant informants willing to confide in us, we were at a disadvantage in *compelling* testimony, even if we knew the individual's identity, which in this case we did not.

But the story made a certain amount of sense. Vicki had a Doberman, given her by Alfred for protection and reputedly very good at its job, that no one heard barking during the fatal assault. Could Pancoast, perhaps the only person besides Vicki who could control the animal, have taken the dog outside while the murder happened?

Turner, Freed, and I spent two months on the Vicki Morgan case, and did everything we could, given our unofficial status. None of us believed Marvin Pancoast had wielded that baseball bat, and oddly enough we also came to the same conclusions about the origins of the "sex tapes."

Figuratively, we suspected, they came from Alfred Bloomingdale, reaching out from the grave. Bloomingdale had genuinely loved Vicki, had tried to provide for her with the bequeathal of his Showbiz Pizza stock. But Bloomingdale, the old spy master, had to know his mistress's life was in danger. He had told her too much. Probably, he figured, she would keep quiet if her material needs were provided, but that possibility ended when the court ruled for Betsy Bloomingdale, not Vicki, in the palimony suit Vicki pursued after Alfred's death. The tapes, we believed, were insurance, protection; they carried the threat that they would be released if harm came to Vicki.

I didn't attend Marvin Pancoast's trial, held one year after the murder. I figured Pancoast had a good shot. *Time* magazine had written: "Beyond his now repudiated confession, there is no hard evidence. A strong motive has not been established, and the investigation of the case was strikingly inept. The police neglected to seal off the scene of the crime and did not recover any fingerprints from the bloodied baseball bat. . . . Deputy District Attorney Stanley Weisberg lamely explains, 'We had other cases more important than this one.' "

I suspected, rather, that the police and prosecution had feared what they *would have* discovered had they conducted an A-1 investigation.

The prosecution won. Like I said, a confession is a hard thing to beat. Marvin Pancoast was found guilty of first-degree murder and sentenced to twenty-six years to life.

I recently contacted Freed and Turner, and the years haven't changed their opinions: Marvin Pancoast did not bash in Vicki Morgan's skull. How could he have smashed Vicki's head to a pulp and not gotten a single drop of blood on his body or clothes? *Cui bono,* the lawyers always say; who bene-fited? I can think of plenty of people, but one of them isn't passive, pathetic Marvin Pancoast.

13

THE IMPEACHMENT
OF HARRY CLAIBORNE

Las Vegas is a hedonist's heaven. Hotels here—and nine of the ten largest in the world are clustered in this gambling oasis—take a loss on relatively inexpensive deluxe accommodations, delicious food, and spectacular shows featuring top-name entertainers, and *still* make out like bandits, posting huge profits from their casino operations. Droves of tourists clamor day and night, frantically emptying wallets in a non-stop quest for cash, a grab at the brass ring, one more pull for the jackpot of jackpots.

Being home based in Vegas sparks instant conversation from strangers everywhere I go. They delight in telling about rollicking vacations, meager wins, and what star they saw perform; or, more often, they whine about a losing hand, coming "this close" to being set for life, or a convention hangover they'd like to forget. In general, people think of Las Vegas as a fun place to visit, not as a place to live. Few stop to consider that the dealer winning most of the blackjack hands (for the house) or the voluptuous chorus girl dancing her way to premature varicose veins also has a family, makes mortgage payments on a three-bedroom, two-bath rancher, has two kids and a dog named Rover, and attends PTA meetings once a month. Behind the glitzy scene in joints downtown and on the Strip, 258,295 residents form a community with ordinary homes, schools, churches, businesses. Just like any other city, blue-collar workers and professionals grind it out in a routine, work-a-day world.

Which brings me to an interesting case I didn't have to leave town to investigate. Until now, its thought-blocking head-lines—such as "Judge Convicted of Tax Evasion"—served to keep most observers confused, with only the foggiest notion of what actually happened. But I was Judge Harry Claiborne's defense investigator, and I think it important to go beyond the headlines and reveal the true untold story.

What happened weaves a tale so bizarre, so Byzantine, that an understanding of it is absolutely vital to obtaining a criminal-justice system of which we can be proud.

My friend Harry Claiborne is an Arkansas country boy who moved to Las Vegas in the 1940s and soon became known as "Nevada's Clarence Darrow," often representing underdogs and compiling a breathtaking (perhaps the best in the country) win/loss record of 494–68. I did work for Clai-borne during my brief costewardship of the Las Vegas De-tective Agency. Investigating his cases was inevitably more morally rewarding than protecting casinos from crossroaders.

Anyway, I know for sure that Judge Claiborne wasn't tar-geted for impeachment because he was corrupt. It usually doesn't work that way. If legislators hate corruption, why not clean up their own act first? The government went after him because he wouldn't go along with its sleazy schemes.

The war between Harry Claiborne and the U.S. Depart-ment of Justice (which lasted almost a decade) began with his firing the first salvo in 1980: "I'm not going to hear any more strike force cases in my court. They're a bunch of liars and crooks."

Judge Claiborne referred to "criminal misconduct" by

members of the Justice Department Organized Crime Strike Force headquartered in Las Vegas. He charged that the strike force used unconstitutional investigatory means, including entrapment, in the cases brought before his court.

Claiborne also protested loudly about the *nature* of these cases. He contended that the strike force wasted the court's time with hundreds of food-stamp violations while "ignoring the big fish preying on the citizens of Nevada." The government team actually brought into Claiborne's court—*United States District Court*—welfare mothers and handicapped persons accused of using their food stamps to purchase nonapproved items such as beer and cigarettes.

One of the worst abuses I uncovered when I began working as defense investigator for Judge Claiborne involved an FBI agent and a gas-station attendant. The agent posed as a welfare recipient receiving food stamps, and asked the attendant to sell him *one dollar of gasoline* for a one-dollar food stamp. When the attendant refused, stating that such a transaction was illegal, the agent pleaded: he said he was late for a job interview downtown and would lose his chance for employment if he missed the appointment. The attendant had mercy on the "unfortunate" (who wouldn't have?), but when he sold him the gas for the food stamp, he found himself arrested. It was this sort of abuse that Claiborne so strenuously opposed.

Eighteen strike forces operated in the United States at the time (1980). The idea of these super-high-powered investigatory teams originated with then–U.S. attorney general Robert Kennedy (one of the first targets he went after was Jimmy Hoffa); their purpose historically has been to investigate top-level political corruption in areas where local authorities could not be relied on to do the job, *not* to "jam up" courts, as Claiborne charged, with minor food-stamp violations. Anyone familiar with Nevada politics knows that in this wide-open state there are indeed plenty of "bigger fish" to fry. The investigators were *supposed* to find these people.

"I'm not going to hear any more strike force cases."

This laying down of the gauntlet brought FBI SAIC (Special Agent in Charge) Joe Yablonsky, known as the King of Sting, into the picture, and the events leading to front-page impeachment headlines accelerated to a breakneck speed. The flamboyant, gold-chain-adorned, cigar-chomping Yablonsky, who kept pictures displayed on the wall behind his desk of various "names" he'd helped convict, boasted openly that he had "a space reserved for the Arkansas hillbilly."

According to Cliff Isbell, a police informant, Yablonsky wasted no time in calling a high-level intelligence-community meeting at a suite in the Showboat Hotel. Federal, state, and local intelligence officers attended this secret get-together. Las Vegas metropolitan police department commander Kent Clifford sent Sergeant Dennis Caputo and two of his best informants, Isbell and James Johnson, to the meeting. Yablonsky announced at this critical conference that the U.S. government would finance sting operations in Nevada targeting Senator Paul Laxalt, Judge Harry Claiborne, former Nevada governor Michael O'Callaghan, and a number of other, lesser Nevada politicians. As the audience listened raptly to the man who had managed ABSCAM (the most famous of the FBI stings), none in the crowd knew that Yablonsky and I shared Cliff Isbell as a source of information. It was through Isbell that I learned much of what the justice department was doing.

Cliff Isbell had served time in the state penitentiary with Nevada's most notorious dealer in prostitution, Joe Conforte, aka The Pimp, The Whoremaster. Isbell confided to Yablonsky that if the Sting King wanted to know about crooked Nevada politicians, he "should talk to Conforte."

Conforte was more than willing. He'd become disenamored with his address at the time, Rio de Janeiro, where he'd moved to avoid a five-year sentence for income tax evasion, and he welcomed the two FBI strike force agents Yablonsky sent to Brazil to talk with him. A deal was struck.

And what a deal it was. I learned after entering the case in Claiborne's behalf (in 1986) that it was one of the most incredible, lopsided trade-offs in the history of plea bargaining. In exchange for Conforte agreeing to testify that he'd paid Harry Claiborne $80,000 in bribes, the FBI promised the following:

- Conforte's bail-jumping case would not be prosecuted;
- he would not be charged with murder in the killing of heavyweight boxing contender Oscar Bonavena;
- he would not have to serve a day of his five-year tax-evasion sentence;
- the government agreed to lower his $21 million tax liability to $3 million, payable at $50,000 a month.

In other words, this eighteen million dollar witness could put the money he'd saved into a simple savings account and *earn* more than a half-million dollars a year.

What did the government get for its $18 million? Not much.

Or, looked at another way, a great deal.

A grand jury returned an indictment against Judge Claiborne on December 8, 1983, for bribery *and* income tax evasion. The income-tax-evasion charge (the basis of the impeachment proceeding), almost every lawyer and judge in the country would agree, should have been a simple civil matter had it been forced to stand of its own weight.

The first trial of Harry Claiborne ended with a hung jury in April, 1984. There would never be a second trial, at least on the bribery charges. It appeared that Conforte's testimony was perjurious, shot full of lies. There were at least a dozen critical events Conforte testified to under oath that simply

couldn't have occurred. The day Conforte said he had personally handed the bribe to Claiborne, for instance, the two men
were thousands of miles apart.

The prosecution's use of Conforte to get Claiborne borders
on the incredible. On the cutting edge of the prostitution
business in Nevada for more than thirty years, Conforte and
his 106-bed Mustang Ranch had roles in the movie *The Godfather:* foretelling the future, Conforte played a brothel owner
who set up a prominent government official. After agreeing to
lie about Harry Claiborne, Conforte sold his Mustang Ranch
for a cool $25 million. Remarkably, he'd earlier been forced
to put the house of ill repute into bankruptcy (the deal with
Yablonsky rescued him), and the U.S. government had run
the operation (Uncle Sam an actual pimp) for some three
years.

Before Yablonsky could make his deal with Conforte, he
needed IRS approval, which proved a major snag. IRS district
director Gerald Swanson objected vigorously; he was de-
moted for his efforts and transferred to Dallas, Texas, where
he supervised 12 persons compared to the 325 who worked
under him in Nevada. Jeffrey M. German wrote in the *Las
Vegas Sun:*

> The Yablonsky-Conforte agreement is similar to others nego-
> tiated almost daily in America's criminal justice system. A suspect
> talks about the alleged crimes of others and gains immunity for
> his own transgressions.
>
> There are differences in this pact, however. One is the extraordi-
> nary witness fee Conforte demands—up to $18 million by IRS
> accounting—for testifying against Claiborne.
>
> Another is the impact that the pursuit of Claiborne has had on
> the lives of others. The road to Conforte's homecoming is strewn
> with the shattered careers and ruined reputations of men who
> stood in his way, men who up until then had enjoyed the honors
> that go with success.

Over the past several days, the *Sun* has chronicled the stories of two such men—former IRS District Director Gerald Swanson and retired military hero Alex Lemberes.

Swanson's "crime" was his apparent reluctance to approve Conforte's demand for a huge cut in his tax bill at a time when thousands of Nevada taxpayers were facing back bills themselves.

The *second* trial of Harry Claiborne involved charges of tax evasion, specifically $106,000 of income not declared on returns for 1979 and 1980. This money came from payment for legal fees Claiborne earned in private practice before being appointed to the federal bench by Jimmy Carter. Like many Americans, Claiborne did not make out his own tax returns; instead he relied on an accountant—in this instance, Jerry D. Watson. Watson swore under oath that the failure to declare the $106,000 was *his* clerk and bookkeeper's fault. It happens hundreds of times every day in America.

Regardless, the total amount owed was $10,126.04 (keep in mind the $18 *million* Conforte avoided paying), which Claiborne sent to the IRS immediately upon notification. Also bear in mind that this $10,126.04 was the *sole basis* for the nationwide headlines and the upcoming impeachment proceedings.

But everything about the Claiborne case was handled in an unusual manner. The IRS's *own guidelines* call for the following steps to be taken in a tax investigation:

(1) Audit
(2) Intelligence Division investigation
(3) Conference for the taxpayer with the supervisor of the Intelligence Division, if the taxpayer requests such a conference
(4) Forwarding the case to the IRS Regional Counsel, who will notify the taxpayer of the investigation and ask if he wants a conference
(5) If the taxpayer does request a conference, the conference will not be denied

(6) After the case goes from IRS Regional Counsel to the office of the United States Attorney, the IRS notifies the taxpayer of this transfer

(7) A pre-indictment conference is held with the taxpayer present

In Claiborne's case, only step seven was taken: a preindictment conference, which shortly preceded the indictment. The government obtained an indictment under the "false statement" statute, which has a markedly lower burden of proof for the prosecution than the tax-fraud statute. The statute under which Claiborne was tried has, according to the book *Tax Fraud and Evasion,* a history of use when "it is difficult for the Government to establish that a tax was in fact due at all or it is anticipated that the taxpayer may have good jury appeal on the deficiency tax issue."

Incredibly, Judge Claiborne had a mistake on an earlier tax return: he had overpaid $23,000.

Harry Claiborne was convicted on two counts of tax evasion in August, 1984, and sentenced to two years in prison. While he appealed this miscarriage of justice, the U.S. Senate brought impeachment proceedings against him. I was honored when he asked me to head the investigation, which uncovered much of the information in this chapter. I think his background is very important.

Harry Claiborne, born in McRae, Arkansas, in 1917, to a farmer father and schoolteacher mother, was guided very early in life toward the law by a legendary local attorney named Flywheel Pierce, a populist, hillbilly sage.

Upon graduation from law school, young Claiborne served five years in the air force during World War II, then moved to Las Vegas where he worked as a police officer for a year before being admitted to the Nevada bar.

In 1946 Claiborne became chief deputy district attorney for Clark County. He was known as an early crusader against drunken driving long before the cause became popular. Later, as a defense lawyer, often representing the rankest underdogs, he posted a win/loss record still reverently discussed in Nevada legal circles. On September 1, 1978, he was sworn in as U.S. district judge for Nevada. As in the appointment of all federal judges, his life history had been closely scrutinized by the FBI and passed muster.

Claiborne's personal life was colorful, as can be imagined for someone who would call strike force members "liars and crooks." He had served as one of Howard Hughes's most trusted attorneys. Like many defense lawyers who do *pro bono* work, Claiborne was able to handle no-pay cases for indigent defendants by falling back on money he'd earned representing people like Hughes. The prestigious *Almanac of the Federal Judiciary,* for summer, 1985, rated Claiborne as follows:

> Courteous to lawyers and litigants. Not influenced by the identities of the parties or the lawyers. Tends to have a current docket; accommodates emergency requests. Has knowledge of current legal developments and a good understanding of the issues in both complex and ordinary cases. Generally rules on motions promptly and knowledgeably. Does not tend to push too hard for settlement. Imposes average to heavy sentences.

During Judge Claiborne's ongoing difficulties, the man who had targeted him, Joe Yablonsky, began having his own problems. Yablonsky, violating several federal laws, tried to influence the result of an election by using his official position to dig up dirt on one candidate for the benefit of the other, earning himself a public reprimand from FBI director William Webster.

Nevadans were quickly getting a bellyful of Joseph Yablonsky. In March, 1983, several top attorneys and law-enforcement agents—United States Attorney Lamond Mills, Attorney General Brian McKay, Clark County District At-

torney Robert Miller, The District Attorney's Chief Investigator Beecher Avants, Sheriff John Moran, and Metro Intelligence Commander Preston Hubbs—publicly rebuked the FBI
agent, criticized him for illegally meddling in a political campaign, and urged his removal from Las Vegas.

Yablonsky's waning credibility bottomed out when it was
revealed he had kept $40,000 that a local bank had mistakenly
credited to his account.

Hank Greenspun, undeniably the most influential and respected newsman in Nevada, copublisher and editor of the
Las Vegas Sun, considered Yablonsky's abusive, high-
handed, dishonest tactics despicable. Greenspun wrote an absolutely remarkable editorial on the Harry Claiborne case:

> The *Sun* is a newspaper in search of a lawsuit.
>
> Newspapers don't ordinarily go out of their way asking to be
> sued for libel, but sometimes it becomes necessary in the interests
> of justice.
>
> This is especially so in the case of federal officials who have
> outrageously abused their powers and whose corrupt superiors
> cover up the wrongdoing.
>
> Often, faced with federal stonewalling at every level, the only
> way to bring out the truth is to invite the wrongdoers to sue you.
> In a courtroom, a jury of our peers can determine just who should
> be prosecuted for criminal activities—the hunters or the hunted.
>
> The *Sun* has published scores of stories about the abuses perpe-
> trated by the FBI and the Justice Department against Nevada
> citizens. We've been threatened with lawsuits by various federal
> officials seeking to silence us and hide the truth. . . .
>
> Well, we're tired of the threats. The Justice Department's whis-
> per-mongers, who deal not in fact but on rumors, defend them-
> selves to their friends by a campaign of threats designed to make
> us cower at the thought of being sued.
>
> I've got news for these scoundrels. This paper has been sued by
> other demagogues and power-mad public officials and has yet to

lose because the truth has always been our defense.

The *Sun* is not a helpless citizen without resources to fight a lengthy battle. We can afford to hold out a little longer than a private citizen with limited finances. Our nerves will not shatter nor our knees buckle under the weight of threats by small people acting in the name of the United States government.

In short, we're inviting Justice Department attorney Steven Shaw to sue us because we accuse him of criminal misconduct.

We're inviting Nevada FBI chief Joe Yablonsky to sue us because we charge him with an arrogant abuse of power and criminal misconduct.

And we're inviting Attorney General William French Smith and his henchmen to sue us because we accuse him of covering up the criminal misconduct of his subordinates.

Shaw, who is an attorney for the Justice Department Public Integrity Section, committed perjury in a federal courtroom in Reno. He also suborned perjury before at least one federal grand jury and has abused his position by threatening to use confidential government information in a private capacity. . . .

FBI chief Yablonsky not only directed the government persecution of various Nevada citizens who rightfully declined to participate in his personal vendetta against a federal judge, but also lied under oath in a federal courtroom in Reno. That has been documented. . . .

At stake is not just the future of a federal judge in Nevada. Far more important is the nature and extent of federal government activities directed against Nevada citizens at the whim of federal agents without regard for fairness and justice. . . .

And why has it happened? It has happened because a federal judge, Harry Claiborne, dared to stand up to abusive tactics of the Strike Force and call that misconduct to the attention of the public.

In September, 1984, the month after Judge Claiborne's conviction, I was working full bore on his appeal when a Las Vegas Metro Police Department (LVMPD) officer contacted me and said an informant named Cliff Isbell wanted a meeting. I hadn't seen Isbell since 1969 (when he'd been an informant for me) so I phoned him right away.

We met at 11:30 A.M. on September 29, 1984, in the Commercial Deli on East Sahara. Isbell said that a friend of his had sent him to ask me if I would keep his name out of the newspapers regarding a federal civil rights suit I'd filed against my former police commander, Robert R. Griffin.

I said I'd think it over, and then Isbell and I talked about "old times." (My talks with Isbell later formed the bulk of an affadivit I filed with the special Senate panel taking evidence for Claiborne's trial.) He said he had been "set up" by Nevada Gaming Control investigators in a slot-cheating scam at the Frontier Hotel and the Las Vegas Club, along with his partner, James D. Johnson.

An ex-felon, Isbell didn't relish returning to prison, so he'd gone to the LVMPD and offered to become an informant in exchange for dismissal of the slot-cheating charges. Isbell said Commander Kent Clifford had readily agreed to use him and Johnson as snitches, and that subsequently the cheating charges had been dropped.

I talked to Isbell for four and a half hours this first day, listening to him recount his adventures as a rat. When we parted I knew one thing for sure: I wanted to talk with Isbell some more.

We began meeting on the average of twice a week. Isbell told me he had been treated as "another officer" by both Sergeant Caputo and Commander Clifford, and had been allowed access to all secret files maintained in Clifford's private office as well as Caputo's political squad files. To prove he told the truth, Isbell supplied me with a transcript of a surreptitiously recorded meeting between Caputo, Clifford, and flamboyant Bob Stupak, the owner/operator of Vegas World.

Isbell's activities fascinated me. He said he'd made cocaine buys that were secretly filmed; one of them resulted in the arrest of a Golden Nugget employee.

I met with Isbell many times and, sure enough, my patience paid off. Gradually I coaxed from him details of a burglary at Judge Claiborne's home in the Spanish Oaks section of Las Vegas. Isbell told me that he, an FBI agent, Sergeant Caputo, and James Johnson had driven to Claiborne's home in a blue metro van, and Johnson and the FBI man had approached the residence. Isbell and Caputo had been lookouts. Johnson had been point man: he'd stood outside the home, ready to rush inside and alert the FBI agent if someone approached the home. The FBI agent had done the burgling.

Although Isbell professed an inability to recall the FBI agent's name, I learned it from an independent source and then confronted the LVMPD snitch.

"That FBI agent who robbed Claiborne's home. Was he Steve Rybar?"

"That name rings a bell."

"Was it Steve Rybar?"

"Yeah. It's come back to me. Rybar. Steve Rybar. That's the name."

He'd known it all along, I would have bet, but there was no sense getting hot with him. Instead I plied him for everything he knew, and dug up another gem: he claimed federal attorney Steve Shaw was aware the burglary had taken place, and illegally obtained photographs of Judge Claiborne's financial documents had been used to prepare the case against him.

I asked Isbell if he would testify to what he'd told me in court and he said yes. Previously, when questioned by the district attorney's office and the *Las Vegas Sun,* Isbell had claimed no knowledge of the break-in. Also, Yablonsky, Rybar, and Caputo all signed sworn statements denying any involvement. But I believed Isbell's story. The evidence used to convict Judge Claiborne had been obtained through an illegal break-in. That should have been it. Case dismissed.

Like I say, that *should* have been it. But I wanted more evidence, just in case, and I went to see James Johnson, who, unfortunately, had failed a polygraph test, despite having been granted immunity for his cooperation in the investigation. The following sworn, signed, and notarized affidavit became an important part of Claiborne's appeal and is reprinted in its entirety:

The undersigned, JAMES DANIEL JOHNSON, being first duly sworn, deposes and states that:

1. I am currently serving a four year sentence at the Southern Nevada Correctional Institute as a result of plea agreement to charges in Douglas County and Elko County, Nevada.

2. I was formerly a friend and close associate of Clifford Isbell. I was a resident of Clark County, Nevada, for approximately twelve years.

3. During the period of time that I was associated with Clifford Isbell he and I agreed to cooperate with and provide information to the Las Vegas Metropolitan Police Department and with the Federal Bureau of Investigation.

4. Clifford Isbell and I met with former Metro Intelligence Commander Kent Clifford in regard to setting up a "sting operation" by purchasing the Rose Bowl Race and Sports Book and wiring it with surveillance equipment.

5. Since the Metropolitan Police Department did not have adequate funding to support a sting operation on such large scale, Commander Clifford brought then Special Agent in Charge Joseph Yablonsky of the FBI into the proposed sting.

6. I met with Cliff Isbell and with Special Agent in Charge Yablonsky and with Commander Clifford in regard to setting up the proposed "sting" operation.

7. Special Agent in Charge Yablonsky agreed to obtain or provide federal funding for the proposed sting. In return for federal participation, he wanted to have credit for the operation.

He also wanted to have certain individuals targeted.

8. The Metropolitan Police Department had targeted several prominent Clark County political figures and business persons, including County Commissioners Manny Cortez and Thalia Dondero, John Moran, Justice of the Peace Bonaventure, as well as the Binions and Steve Wynn.

9. Yablonsky had a much shorter list of people he wanted to get. The most important to him was Judge Harry Claiborne. He also expressed his contempt for and desire to "get" Senator Paul Laxalt although it was not contemplated that Laxalt would be gotten at the Rose Bowl Sports Book. Yablonsky also wanted to get Sig Rogich and another individual whose name I cannot recall at this time.

10. Special Agent in Charge Yablonsky, while discussing his desire to get Federal Judge Claiborne at a meeting with myself and Cliff Isbell at the Jo-Jo's Restaurant on Las Vegas Boulevard near Bob Stupak's Vegas World, asked me if I knew a good "second story man," that is a burglar.

11. I recommended Ray Perrara as a burglar known to me.

12. Cliff Isbell disagreed with my suggestion of Ray Perrara, and Special Agent in Charge Yablonsky stated he would get his own man.

13. Later, I participated with Metro Intelligence Sgt. Dennis Caputo, Clifford Isbell, and another person introduced to me as a federal agent in "casing" the Claiborne residence in Spanish Oaks. The federal agent was introduced to me as Steven with the last name of Riley or similar last name. I have since seen photographs and identified that federal agent as Steve Rybar.

14. After we "cased" the Claiborne residence, Cliff Isbell, Caputo, Rybar, and I returned for the actual entry into Judge Claiborne's home.

15. Cliff Isbell and Sgt. Caputo remained in the van during the illegal entry into Claiborne's home. Rybar and I went through the gate into Judge Claiborne's courtyard.

16. Rybar went up onto a kind of step or platform in the courtyard and went through the door quickly.

17. I remained outside while Rybar was inside the Claiborne residence.

18. While Rybar was inside the Claiborne residence, I observed a vehicle with a decal on the side which I believed may have been a security service vehicle drive slowly past the Claiborne residence.

19. At the time I observed the vehicle, I briefly went into the Claiborne residence to warn Rybar that there might be "heat."

20. I went a short distance down the front hallway, then turned back and went down a side hallway to the left where I heard drawers being opened.

21. I followed that side hallway to a den where Rybar was going through drawers. I told him that there might be heat. He said he wasn't done yet. I left the residence and went outside again.

22. Shortly afterward Rybar exited the Claiborne residence with a small, black camera which he used to take photographs of Judge Claiborne's financial records.

23. While I was imprisoned at the Southern Desert Correctional Institute at Indian Springs, in February of 1986, I was transported by federal agents to Washington, D.C., so that I could be sentenced for a federal misdemeanor charge.

24. I was transported to Terminal Island, California, El Reno, Oklahoma, and other federal facilities at federal expense for the purpose of such misdemeanor sentencing.

25. One of the facilities to which I was transported was Lewisberg, Pennsylvania. While in the infirmary at Lewisberg, Pennsylvania, I was visited by a person who refused to identify himself.

26. He told me where my mother resided, worked and went to church. He told me where my wife resided, worked and where my sons went to school. He told me that I should do a lot of forgetting before I got back to Nevada. He said that the agents who got the federal judge were just doing their job in the line of duty and he asked what I thought they would do to me for what I was doing.

27. Nevertheless, I will testify truthfully in any legal proceeding regarding my prior association and activities with former Special

Agent in Charge Yablonsky, with the agent identified as Steve Rybar, with former Commander Kent Clifford, former Intelligence Sgt. Dennis Caputo, and Clifford Isbell.

Further, affiant sayeth not.

But neither Cliff Isbell nor James Johnson were ever allowed to testify in court, and they were not heard when the U.S. Senate tried Claiborne for "high crimes and misdemeanors." On October 9, 1986, after a short "trial," Claiborne became only the fifth federal official—all judges—removed from office through impeachment, and the first in fifty years.

I sat at the defense table throughout the Senate trial, and I was shocked by the lack of deliberation evinced by this "greatest of deliberative bodies." Actually, adjournment was at hand, and most of the senators seemed more eager to get to various vacation spots than to consider whether they might for all time be besmirching a good man's reputation.

The Senate judged Claiborne guilty of two charges involving underpaying his taxes by $10,126.04 in 1979 and 1980 (forget that it was an accountant's error, that the taxes were immediately paid, and that Claiborne had overpaid taxes in a previous year); a third charge was laughable—that his oversight on the taxes had "betrayed the judiciary and the nation."

Good heavens. In a time when $10,126.04 would probably have been insufficient to bribe any of these outraged politicians, at least they hadn't found this "offense" damnable.

The U.S. Senate, in judging Claiborne guilty, refused to hear any of the circumstances that brought him into the dock in the first place. All of this was ruled irrelevant. Most senators (a handful voted "not guilty") said he'd been convicted of tax evasion and that was proof enough. They refused to hear testimony about *how* the guilty verdicts were obtained (with evidence obtained from an illegal break-in), nor why: because he'd been targeted by an FBI strike force after he'd refused to condone their illegal tactics.

Judge Claiborne served almost two years in an Alabama prison. When he was finally released he returned to Las Vegas, started a private law practice, and began doing what I always felt he did best: defending underdogs.

14

THE LONETREE AFFAIR

The Lonetree case started for the defense with a phone call from Sally Tsosie to my old friend, Las Vegas attorney Michael Stuhff.

It figured that Sally would reach out to Mike. A Catholic seminary student and 1973 University of Utah graduate, Mike had decided upon finishing school to devote a year to helping Sally's long-oppressed people on the expansive Navajo reservation in Arizona. But instead of one year, the idealistic Mike stayed thirteen, earning little money but lots of friends in places like Fort Defiance and Window Rock.

The January 20, 1987, message to call Sally marked the first time Stuhff had heard from her since 1985, when he'd moved from the reservation to private practice in Las Vegas. He had represented Sally, her mother, and Sally's sister, Louise Benally, in the long and heated Navajo-Hopi land dispute initiated by a hastily drafted executive order in 1882 and perpetuated for a century by governmental wrangling and chicanery.

Stuhff had no idea why Sally had phoned, but he looked forward to talking to her. They had ridden out some rough times and celebrated a few victories together. She had been with Mike on one of the land-dispute cases while picketers brandished protest signs *inside* the courtroom. Other times he had to raise his voice over beating drums outside the courtroom.

"Hello, Sally," Mike said when he got her on the line. "I haven't heard from you in a long time."

"Mr. Stuhff, you've got to help me."

"What's the problem?"

"Remember my son Clayton? He went into the Marine Security Guard program."

"Of course I remember."

"He's in trouble." Her voice trembled.

"What kind of trouble?"

"He's being court-martialed."

"Why?"

"He guarded the embassies in Moscow and Vienna. He's charged with espionage."

Stuhff wasn't an expert on military law, but he knew espionage carried a maximum sentence of death. He couldn't believe that Clayton would be involved in such a major crime, an illusion Sally quickly shattered.

"They're talking death penalty." Sally's voice finally cracked.

"Where's Clayton being held?"

"At the brig in Quantico, Virginia. At the marine base. He's in solitary confinement. No one will tell me anything."

Mike had learned that Navajos do not cry. But Sally Tsosie sounded very close.

"How did this happen?"

"No one will answer my questions. I'm his mother and they won't talk to me. They only say he was involved with a woman."

"Who's *they?*"

"The marines."

"Sally, this is very serious. Clayton needs a lawyer who's not part of the military."

"I know. That's why I called you."

Mike said he would contact attorney Michael Kennedy in New York, an expert on courts-martial, first thing the next day.

The next morning, I walked into Mike's office in the Valley Bank Building on Fourth Street and said, "Let's go to the Horseshoe for ham and eggs." I normally didn't eat red meat—I'd long ago switched to a fish-and-chicken regimen— but I knew Stuhff considered the Horseshoe's two-dollar breakfast, with a ham slice bigger than the plate holding it, the best bargain in Las Vegas.

"I'll join you in a minute. First I've got to call Michael Kennedy. Do you want to say hi to him?"

"I'd like that." Kennedy and I were old friends. "Why are you calling him?"

"I'm referring a case."

"Oh?" A private investigator needs to be curious.

"You remember Sally Tsosie. Her son is in the marines. He was guarding the U.S. embassies in Moscow and Vienna."

"Right."

"Clayton's facing a general court-martial for espionage. They say he got mixed up with a woman in Moscow. Now he's accused of giving secrets to the Soviets."

"*Giving* secrets? Or *selling* them?" I didn't believe Sally Tsosie's son would do either.

"Marine authorities are calling it 'sex for secrets,' or some such thing. I guess they're saying he was trying to impress a woman."

Mike wasn't far off. The headlines—and the case soon was garnering headlines worldwide—screamed SEX FOR SE-CRETS.

"Why do you want to pass the case to Kennedy?" I had my own long history of working with Indians, and every time after doing it I had felt better. Actually, my history with Navajos stretched back farther than Mike's. It seemed to me that he and I should be on this case.

"Kennedy just did an espionage. Defending Clayton could cost a hunk, in time and money. I don't know anything about military law. I . . ."

"You guys went to the same schools, didn't you? Took the same courses, right? What does Kennedy know that you don't?"

"A lot. He's got experience."

"Hell, Mike, you're a good lawyer. Catching up on military law isn't that tough. Besides,"—I smiled—"you've got a leading expert right here, in the flesh."

He laughed. "That's right. You worked that fragging case [the Billy Dean Smith case]."

"Mike," I said, "courts-martial aren't much different from regular criminal trials."

"It's financial."

"I think we can raise money. You've got a member of an oppressed minority here. Just like Big Mountain. Or Wounded Knee."

My optimism didn't impress Stuhff. He hadn't gotten rich on Big Mountain, and he knew I'd dipped into my own pocket to help pay expenses at Wounded Knee. For Mike, "raise some money" translated into not having to hock furniture to finish a case. Throughout his career he had handled cases *pro bono,* increasingly wondering if his efforts made a difference, if they really helped. I harbored no doubts that they did, but my view might be a matter of perspective: my three sons were grown and on their own. He had four kids at home.

But Mike and I had gone off on crusades before, and I felt that an important case involving a Navajo rightly belonged to us. Realizing that my attempt to make the financially strapped Stuhff feel like a money-grubbing mercenary wasn't working, I tried a different tack.

"Think about the publicity. Everybody will be watching this one."

Stuhff considered this an even weaker argument. True, the Lonetree case could attract additional business, but it would most likely be the nonpaying kind. Victories won for Native Americans and other oppressed groups usually did not impress better-off clients, i.e., those able to pay.

"I don't know, Lake. I just don't feel up to this one."

"Damnit, Mike, let's take a shot. Sally needs help. She's a friend and deserves the kind of personal attention we'll give her."

I knew Stuhff would do it. And sure enough, instead of phoning Mike Kennedy, he shortly called Sally Tsosie in Tuba City, Arizona, and told her he would represent her son. In turn, she told him she'd just learned that Clayton's father, Spencer Lonetree, had contacted William Kunstler. So that's how it ultimately worked out. Stuhff (Kunstler graciously made him "lead" lawyer), Kunstler, and I would be the defense team, assisted by a marine attorney, Major David Henderson.

On January 31, 1987, Mike and I arrived at National Airport in Washington, D.C., rented a car, and drove forty miles south to check into the Quality Inn directly across the street from the entrance to Quantico Marine Base.

Within the hour we met Marine Capt. Andy Strotman, a military lawyer who had promised to show us unclassified Naval Investigative Service (NIS) files (at this point we couldn't review classified material). The four-inch-thick file Strotman passed on to us at Quantico kept us awake most of the night. Reading NIS's account of Clayton's background and activities in Moscow and Vienna, we immediately realized the defense's major problem: Sergeant Clayton Lonetree had confessed. Summaries of his detailed statements to NIS agents, all tape-recorded, filled more than 250 almost marginless and closely spaced pages.

We received small comfort from our knowledge that confessions obtained during lengthy, isolated interrogations are often unreliable, exaggerated, and falsely incriminating. Confessions are extremely hard to beat.

During our first visit to Quantico, the confessions themselves were classified as secret, and thus not for our eyes. When we finally were able to review the actual confessions, we found evidence of wholesale manipulation, abuse, and "shaping" of Lonetree's statements by the agents who had interrogated him. These agents had extracted "admissions" that Clayton had stolen and delivered top-secret documents *that their own subsequent investigation determined did not even exist.*

Henderson, Stuhff, and I visited Clayton in the marine brig on February 1, Stuhff and I for the first time, in a depressing institutional green room. Lonetree, wearing camouflage fatigues and a yellow plastic badge bearing his name and photograph, hardly resembled the stereotypical rough-and-ready marine. He stood five feet seven inches, looked very slight at 135 pounds, and had straight black hair cut "high and tight," prominent cheekbones, and dark, sensitive eyes. I knew right away this wasn't a hard-boiled spy.

I was struck immediately by Clayton's frailness, particularly his delicate hands, which appeared more suited to playing a piano than manning an M-16. He appeared unfrightened and exhibited extreme politeness—"Sir," "Mr. Headley," "Mr. Stuhff," "Major Henderson." A likable kid. Very shy, almost stoic, eager to please. And not entirely resigned to a bad fate, I was to learn. He said he was still clinging to the hope that the CIA would accept his double-agent offer.

"Double agent?" I said, somewhat amazed.

"Yes, sir," he said.

I questioned Clayton for a long time this first day. His story, it seemed to me, would have softened the hardest heart.

The son of a Navajo mother and a Winnebago father, the product of a broken home, Clayton was primarily raised by his father, Spencer Lonetree, a hard-drinking taskmaster who mercilessly drove Clayton and his younger brother Craig (also a marine) to succeed. Grueling 5:00 A.M. training sessions and relentless pressure to excel in school molded a tough, thoughtful, sensitive, serious boy who "wanted to be all he could be." And more.

Certainly Clayton's family had distinguished itself. His mother, Sally Tsosie, was a teacher of the Navajo language in Tuba City, Arizona. She, along with Clayton's aunt, Louise Benally, and his grandmother, Alice Benally, were deeply involved in the struggle to prevent the forced relocation of the Navajos from the Joint Use Area (JUA) of Arizona. A great-uncle, Corporal Mitchell Red Cloud, had earned the highest award the U.S. can confer, the Congressional Medal of Honor, for bravery in Korea. Clayton's grandfather, Samuel Lonetree, is a revered Winnebago holy man and peacemaker.

Clayton, too, dreamed of doing something big.

Clayton Lonetree entered the Marine Corps on July 29, 1980, two months after graduation from Johnson High School in St. Paul, Minnesota. After boot camp in San Diego and Infantry Training School at Camp Pendleton, he served a year at the Marine Barracks, Guantanamo Bay, Cuba, before being reassigned to the First Marine Division at Pendleton, where he remained until August 3, 1984. He then volunteered for, and was accepted by, the Marine Security Guard Battalion at Quantico, Virginia, following which he was assigned to the U.S. Embassy in Moscow.

Clayton had been a model marine. "His Military Occupational Specialty (MOS) was rifleman," and along with promotion through the ranks to sergeant, he earned the Sea Service Development Ribbon, and the Good Conduct Medal twice. His fellow marines liked and respected him.

But someone messed up assigning Clayton to the Marine Security Guard Battalion. The young man was a loner, a dreamer. Later, in the USSR, after meeting a KGB agent, he became obsessed with spy literature. He dreamed of himself as a spy. Enamored especially of the spy books of John Barron, he fantasized performing great deeds of derring-do for his country.

In September, 1985, a "chance" meeting while riding Moscow's Public Metro Train System (subway) changed Lonetree's life. He met Violetta Sanni, a translator at the U.S. Embassy, a beautiful young woman with whom he struck up a conversation. Violetta was almost surely an operative of the KGB, but Lonetree didn't suspect. He fell head over heels in love. What seemed an idyllic love affair—long talks, walks through Moscow parks, movies, candlelight dinners—soon became sexual. The love affair, between the young, introverted marine and the lovely Soviet translator was typical of the widespread KGB practice of employing female agents to compromise foreigners.

I learned from our client what happened next:

> During a meeting with Violetta in late January, 1986, she indicated that her Uncle Sasha wanted to meet Lonetree. At this time he was not aware Violetta had an uncle, and he asked her why he wanted to see him. She simply indicated he wanted to meet Clayton.
>
> The entire thing seemed innocent, so Lonetree agreed to meet her uncle. Not long after this discussion, Violetta arranged the meeting. They met at a Metro station and proceeded to Uncle Sasha's residence by bus. Violetta asked Lonetree not to mention

to Sasha that he had met her father. She explained that her mother and father were divorced, that Sasha was her mother's brother, and that as a result of the divorce, Sasha didn't like her father.

During this meeting with Sasha, Violetta was in the room and served as translator, though Sasha spoke some English. He was 6'4" tall, in his mid-30s to early 40s, had a clear complexion, with brownish-gray hair styled straight and worn combed back. He was single, but engaged to a woman called Katya who lived in Suchi, a resort on the Black Sea.

At their first meeting Sasha did not explain the purpose of the meeting. Lonetree guessed he just wanted to know what he looked like. He talked to Clayton about life in America, and general topics such as food, salaries, etc.

Lonetree asked Sasha what he did for a living, and was told he was a lawyer. They talked about salaries and after Lonetree revealed how much he earned, Sasha said he himself earned more.

Sasha's home was well kept, and he explained he was a member of the upper class. He asked questions about how Clayton was enjoying Moscow and life in America. Sasha did not have any children, and he seemed to treat Violetta as his daughter.

Sasha also asked questions about Clayton Lonetree's family. They watched t.v. for a while as they talked. Sasha told Clayton he had traveled abroad, but never to America. Sasha also told him he had friends in the Central Committee that helped him to travel.

At this meeting Sasha never asked questions about Lonetree's job or things about people or events at the embassy. Lonetree never reported his contact with Sasha because he thought there was no harm in the meeting.

In early February, 1986, Violetta told the sergeant Uncle Sasha wanted to see him again. Lonetree was curious about this but agreed.

At no time during any of the meetings with Sasha did Clayton use countersurveillance.

During this second meeting Sasha spoke better English. He again offered food and drinks.

Sasha didn't really say why he wanted to meet Lonetree again, only that he thought Lonetree was a good guy and that he should cooperate. He said this would help Violetta. The sergeant asked how it was going to help her. Sasha explained that it would mean helping a friend, but it would also be helping the Soviet people. At that time he began asking a series of questions which were written on a list he held on his lap. He said the list had been prepared by a friend of his who was a general in the KGB and also a member of the Soviet Central Committee.

At this point Clayton Lonetree made one of his biggest mistakes. He became a spy buff, reading everything he could get, and tried to out-KGB the KGB; but the man he dealt with, Uncle Sasha, ranked as a master of espionage. Sasha, in fact, had since 1983 been meeting with the embassy's top "political officer," Shaun Byrnes. I would see cables Byrnes sent to the State Department, based on information obtained from Uncle Sasha. Included were the names of high Soviet officials who supported Mikhail Gorbachev and Glasnost, and those officials who opposed the general secretary and his avowed program of openness.

On March 10, 1986, six months after he met Violetta, Clayton was transferred to the U.S. Embassy in Vienna, Austria. Here, as in Moscow, a number of cloak-and-dagger meetings took place between him and Uncle Sasha. Clayton had devised the plan of winning Sasha's confidence, thus putting himself into position to become a valuable double agent. Indeed, the information he provided was of *no value at all* to Sasha.

Lonetree's actions would be comic if they hadn't proved so personally tragic. Among his plans was a complicated scheme to ensnare the KGB man in a sexual liaison with an Austrian prostitute, thereby compromising the Soviet and placing him at Lonetree's mercy.

Throughout all of this, Violetta and Clayton exchanged love letters. Never for a second did he believe the Soviet woman loved him any less than he loved her. Probably the most heartbreaking moment for him—he broke down and wept unashamedly—came when his illusions were shattered; shattered by the man he admired perhaps above all others, the writer John Barron.

On December 14, 1986, Clayton Lonetree *voluntarily* (he had never been under suspicion, and probably never would have been) approached a U.S. government intelligence agent, aka Big John, because revealing his real name would compromise the Central Intelligence Agency; or so Military Judge Roberts ruled. In fact, Roberts said at the court-martial that the defense would be committing *a crime* if it even mentioned the CIA.

Lonetree's plan, he told Big John, was to become a double agent; specifically, Lonetree thought he could help get Ed Howard, a defected CIA agent, out of the Soviet Union. Incredibly, debate raged for some time in the State Department and various intelligence agencies over whether to take Lonetree up on his offer. Of course, *if* he had been used as a double agent, there never would have been a punishment or a court-martial. In the end Lonetree wasn't used as a double agent, but as a scapegoat.

While Lonetree thought he could help his country, Big John had something else in mind. Big John told the young marine to tell no one else about what he'd done, thus ensuring that a fair-minded individual wouldn't stop the subsequent chain of Lonetree's disclosures by advising him to obtain legal counsel, or to remain silent.

Big John sought information about the "classic vulnerabilities, drugs, alcohol, sex, and money." Lonetree told him no classified information had been passed to the Soviets.

Big John then set up the first of several meetings with his colleague Little John, a specialist in counterintelligence and a member of the same Certain Intelligence Agency (the phrase

we used during the court-martial) that employed Big John.
Little John also was an officer and ostensible employee of the
U.S. Department of State, with duties and responsibilities
connected with his cover position at the Vienna Embassy.

Little John, pretending to be a friend, induced Lonetree to
continue his disclosures. He told Lonetree it could not possibly hurt him to be as truthful and forthcoming as possible. He
told Lonetree the disclosures were "confidential." He told
Lonetree he would not be hurt in any way by cooperating. He
discussed in a positive fashion the possibility of Lonetree
becoming a double agent operating under the direction of a
Certain Intelligence Agency of the United States.

Little John admitted under oath during the court-martial
that he intentionally used language to imply to Sergeant Lonetree that his best interests involved continuing with his brief-
ings unaided by independent advice. Little John conceded that
he knew of and exploited Lonetree's trust in his advice, and
that the Native American was "passive," "docile," and "easily
pressured and manipulated" by others in the name of friendship.

No *Miranda, Tempia,* or Article 31 warnings were ever
given to Lonetree by Big John or Little John. This foolish
young man, thinking he was helping his government, was in
reality being set up for serious criminal charges. An interroga-
tor from the NIS, introduced to Lonetree as a "colleague,"
urged the marine "to just tell us something—tell us a lie."

15

THE LONETREE COURT-MARTIAL

In a compassionate world the court-martial never would have taken place. Had we been wise and just, we all would have just gone home.

The decision to prosecute Lonetree, rather than reward him with a career advancement, came with a blare of trumpets. Suddenly this lone marine became the focus of American embassy security ills that had begun to gather ominously into a dark cloud of scandal. Perhaps others could be spared with a Lonetree sacrifice.

The deepest secrets of the U.S. Embassy in Moscow *had been* vulnerable to the Soviets, but not because of Clayton Lonetree. The State Department's Foreign Building Office (FBO) had allowed the *Soviets* to draw up the final plans for the embassy. Fundamental components of the building were prefabricated by the Soviets far away from the construction site, allowing the KGB to embed hundreds of listening devices into the skeletal parts of the embassy. Even whispers could be overheard by Soviet listeners.

But it was even worse. As reported in *Reader's Digest* by John Barron, "The entire building [became] the equivalent of a microphone. . . . One steel girder turned out to be, in effect, a giant antenna. The Soviets had dug tunnels [underneath the embassy] that could be used for surreptitious entry. . . ."

To add insult to injury, the Soviets proved expert at the old defense-contractor ploy of cost overruns. The original estimate of the embassy's cost was $85 million, but Congress has since been forced to appropriate $192 million. But this wasn't the only scandal the government feared.

My investigation revealed that trading on the black market and currency violations were common practices among U.S. Embassy personnel in Moscow, from the lowest clerk to the highest echelons of command. Many more rubles could be obtained for the dollar in street-corner deals than on the official exchange. People could and did become rich.

Jeans, stereos, even a Corvette automobile were sold on the black market. U.S. Embassy employees often more resembled sidewalk hustlers than diplomats as they grabbed whatever they could.

How convenient for these, and for the currency violators, and for others with vested interests in rekindling the cold war, that a lone marine gather the full glare of publicity. No matter that his motives were pure, that he gave away nothing of value, and that he came forward of his own accord, believing he could help his country.

Comments by government officials didn't help our defense efforts. Secretary of Defense Caspar Weinberger, questioned during a press conference several weeks after the arrest, said, "He should be hung, but I guess these days we just shoot them."

The name of the key prosecution witness in the court-martial of Sgt. Clayton John Lonetree remains unknown to those of us who composed his defense team. In fact there is hardly anything we do know about the man. We were not permitted, either in pretrial deposition or during his two-hour appearance on the stand, to question him on his professional background or in any way to test his credibility as a witness.

As William Kunstler, Lonetree's civilian co–defense counsel, incredulously pointed out, this was the first time in the history of U.S. criminal law that a witness testified in a major court case without giving his name and without the accused being given the right, granted by the Sixth Amendment to the U.S. Constitution, "to confront the witnesses against him." It was a right that thousands of courts before this one had interpreted as allowing the accused to establish the identity and credentials of his accusers, and to cross-examine them as to the veracity of their testimony.

There was no way for us to show whether this court-declared "John Doe" was lying or was simply an out-and-out fraud.

I conducted a pretrial interview of John Doe. In his late fifties, six feet tall, heavy-set with a puffy face, small hands, and gray hair not quite long enough to give him a hippyish look, he sat across from me in a Quantico office flanked by CIA and state department lawyers.

I asked him: "Are you told during your training that at certain times you must lie?"

"Yes."

"Under oath?"

"Sometimes."

"How do we know you'll tell the truth during this court-martial?"

"Well, I will."

"But you've been told there are times for you to lie under oath?"

"Yes."

"But you'll tell the truth at the court-martial?"

"Yes."

"How can I be sure?"

"Because I'm telling you."

"But you could have been told to lie to *me?*"

"Yes."

"How am I supposed to know when you tell the truth?"

"Because I'm telling you."

"But you might lie about that?"

"Yes."

Doe was admitting he *might* lie while saying that he *would* tell the truth. Which itself might be a lie. Alice in Wonderland, yet another charade in a trial that became a travesty of justice.

No reporters were allowed to witness the court-martial. Even the transcript of the proceedings was censored. In addition, we were told we would be jailed if we used the phrase Central Intelligence Agency. It was a travesty. John Doe was a CIA operative, but we couldn't bring this out.

William Kunstler and Mike Stuhff did everything they could to avert what they feared would be a sentencing tragedy. Both were men I held in the highest regard. I'd worked with Kunstler previously at Wounded Knee, and with Stuhff on dozens of Native American cases.

Kunstler is indeed a remarkable American. He has a B.A. from Yale and a law degree from Columbia. He was a World War II hero, and had been a teacher at Columbia, New York University, Pace College, and the New School for Social Research. Books he had authored filled an entire bookcase, not only works dealing with his wide-ranging legal career—including *First Degree* (1961), *The Minister and the Choir Singer* (1964), and *the Hall-Mills Murder Case* (1981)—but also collections of his poetry and essays. A Phi Beta Kappa, Kunstler had published in the *Columbia Law Review,* the *Yale Law Review,* and virtually every magazine and newspaper of major size in the country.

Kunstler was the virtual embodiment of the modern civil-rights era, as proven by the cases he handled: *Hobson v. Hansen,* a landmark civil-rights case; *Mississippi v. Thomas,* the famous 1961 Freedom Rider case; his representation of David Dellinger in the Chicago Eight conspiracy trial; of Adam Clayton Powell, Jr., in his reinstatement to Congress; of Martin Luther King, Jr.; of Daniel Berrigan, accused of destroying draft records in Catonsville, Maryland; and, more recently, of Leonard Peltier, wrongly convicted for the murder of two FBI agents on the Pine Ridge Indian Reservation in South Dakota.

If I needed confirmation of Kunstler's worth, I got it one day during a break in the actual court-martial. "Lake," he said, taking me by the arm, "I want to introduce you to General Petersen."

"Sure you do," I said.

Kunstler enjoyed practical jokes, and this surely ranked as one. Quantico Commanding General Petersen was the convening authority for Clayton's court-martial, and I didn't consider him a friend of the defense.

"I'm serious," Kunstler said. "He wants to meet you. Come on. He's in the barber shop."

The much-decorated black general was indeed in a barber chair, from which he rose to greet me with a warm smile and a firm hand.

"I was a youngster in Topeka, Kansas," General Petersen said, "when Mr. Kunstler came to my school and talked about Brown. He's one of my gods."

The Brown the general referred to was Linda Brown of *Brown v. the Board of Education of Topeka,* one of the nation's great civil-rights cases. The respect General Peterson held for Kunstler, whom he had listened to as a grade-school student three and a half decades earlier, gleamed on his face.

"How is the case going?" Petersen asked.

He knew very well how the case was progressing. "Your guards say my hair is too long," I answered.

"Lake, your hair is just perfect," Petersen said.

Later I thought about the irony of that meeting, the fate of Kunstler's client in this major case being largely in the hands of a man who had listened to the great civil-rights lawyer as a black schoolchild that long-past day, his chances of becoming, say, a Marine Corps general greatly enhanced by the landmark case Kunstler himself had lectured about.

In a sense, I knew, the Marine Corps didn't stand as the major villain here. In fact, the case embarrassed the corps. Someone as astute as General Petersen had to know that.

The Marine Corps, specifically the Moscow Marine Guards, had been scapegoated. *All* had been relieved of their Soviet posts. And, more specifically, Marine Sgt. Clayton Lonetree had been scapegoated to protect the higher-ranking civilians actually responsible for the embassy fiasco.

I didn't need Kunstler to tell me that General Petersen loved the Marine Corps. You aren't promoted to general if you don't. Seeing what was going on had to be cutting him to the quick.

And not just General Petersen. Especially sympathetic to Clayton throughout the ordeal were the marine guards he'd worked with in Moscow. They remembered him as quiet, pleasant, eager to help out—hardly a potential spy. And of course, when push came to shove, they saw firsthand how easily one of their own could be sacrificed.

I talked to many of these marine guards. They told of how the NIS had tried to implicate them—since clearly Clayton couldn't have acted on his own. The fact is, he hadn't acted at all, except in his own mind as a double agent.

My investigation uncovered that Lonetree, when he couldn't think of anything else to say, had been told by the NIS "to say anything, to lie," to keep the information flowing. Whereupon the ever-polite Clayton, always willing to please, did indeed lie.

It would have been funny if Clayton hadn't faced the death

penalty. The NIS was taking a confession from him. *He thought he was being briefed for work as a double agent.*

Increasingly, my investigation began to zero in on Shaun Byrnes, a foreign-service officer in Moscow employed by the State Department. I became convinced that Byrnes held the key to the entire MSG "scandal."

Byrnes, I had discovered, had been meeting for approximately two years, on a regular basis, before and after Clayton's arrest, with Uncle Sasha. Byrnes had been cabling all sorts of information gathered from Sasha—the state of Gorbachev's health, the key groupings within the Soviet Central Committee—to the State Department in Washington.

But the story went deeper. For four additional years, Byrnes's predecessor, and *his* predecessor, had met regularly with Sasha. The meetings were quite cordial. Gifts were exchanged.

"Who paid the restaurant tab?" I asked in my pretrial interview. (Byrnes had also been trained to lie, under oath if necessary.)

"Sometimes I did," Byrnes answered. "Sometimes Sasha did."

It was like extracting teeth—the man didn't want to give up anything—but I managed to get out of him a very curious admission: he had seen Clayton on several occasions exiting the Metro and entering Byrnes's own apartment building to visit an American friend from the embassy.

What made this admission curious was something Clayton told us he had learned from Violetta just before he'd left Moscow: that Byrnes, a man she didn't know, had called her three times at the Irish Embassy (where she'd also worked occasionally) and had once invited her to his home for dinner. Why had he been so eager to meet her?

Byrnes, off his admission to me, had observed Clayton getting off the Metro, the same Metro Violetta had ridden the day of her first meeting with Clayton. Could not, I suspected, Byrnes have told Sasha just where in the train to situate Violetta so she would meet the young Indian . . . and then try to confirm this directly with Violetta?

Why?

Because the scandal of the new embassy was about to erupt. Sasha could have been doing a favor for his friend Shaun Byrnes, offering Violetta by way of setting up a distraction from—perhaps a scapegoat for—the Moscow mess that Byrnes, as a State Department official, had to know was impending.

By the time of Clayton's trial, the full extent of that Moscow farce had become public. Its foundations were laid in 1972 when President Nixon and the Soviets agreed that each could build a new embassy in the other's capital: the Soviets had to use an American contractor; the Americans, a Soviet one. Each side had the right to inspect what the other did. As *Newsweek,* April 20, 1987, observed, "Fifteen years later the Soviets have a spanking new compound on the site of a former Veterans Administration hospital in northwest Washington—a site that happens to be ideal for intercepting microwave communications across the city, as many security experts have warned. The United States, on the other hand, chose to locate its new embassy on the bottomlands near the Moscow River. The new chancery building is surrounded on four sides by taller Soviet buildings. . . ."

Construction on the U.S. Embassy in Moscow started in 1979. The Soviet contractor used prefabricated building components, while the Soviets had insisted on solid, rather than hollow, concrete blocks on their own embassy in Washington, D.C. In addition, they had refused to accept any concrete slabs that had been cast off-site.

The Soviet inspectors, of course, carefully inspected everything that went into their Washington embassy. Said *News-*

week about the embassy in Moscow: "Although U.S. experts were present at all times, sources say security supervision was poorly coordinated, and U.S. counterspooks did not inspect the plant where the concrete beams and panels were being poured."

The listening devices implanted in the U.S. Embassy were reportedly so numerous that when Rep. Dan Mica visited the building he held up a Magic Slate, the kind kids use, and asked, "We'll have to write down everything we want to say on these scribble pads?" And when George Shultz visited Moscow in 1987, political wags joked that he'd have to conduct business while being driven around the city in a Winnebago.

Whenever the defense tried to pursue a Violetta-Byrnes connection, Judge Roberts cut us off, claiming irrelevance. Byrnes testified as a prosecution witness—the only government witness to have had direct contact with Uncle Sasha—in the prosecution's attempt to confirm the relationship between Sasha and Clayton.

Kunstler, during cross-examination, uncovered twenty-two meetings of Byrnes with Sasha—who was described by Byrnes as one of the "sharpest, toughest Soviets" he'd ever met—and countless meetings of Sasha with Byrnes's predecessors. Cozy dinners. Presents exchanged. Then, suddenly, Sasha, a person important enough to have the ear of the Central Committee, appears to corrupt an American Indian noncom. Why should Sasha have risked such a compromise of his relationship with Byrnes?

But everything made sense if Byrnes, acting under orders from some higher-up, had asked a favor from Sasha: the favor of setting up Sgt. Clayton Lonetree with his "niece" Violetta, shortly before the security fiasco of the new embassy building was likely to come to light.

The next witness after Byrnes was a superstar in the cloak-

and-dagger community. Gartner "Gus" Hathaway, "chief of the counterintelligence staff of the CIA," had been with "the Company" for thirty-five years. He had been a close personal friend and confidant of William Casey's.

I suspected Hathaway, whose service dated back to Wild Bill Donovan's time, made the final decision *not* to use Clayton as a double agent after Sasha's little present to his friend Shaun Byrnes had netted not only a scapegoat but a young man who himself wanted to burn the espionage candle at both ends (when CIA telegrams were flying back and forth between Vienna and Langley over Clayton's plan to get Edward Lee Howard out of Russia). Too bad for the young Indian. Clayton's fate had hung for a while on either being a prized double agent or facing the death penalty.

The transcript of Hathaway's testimony contains mostly blank spaces, though it really needn't have. It amounted to nothing. Mainly, Hathaway pontificated about the dangers an amateur spy *might* pose. But nothing Hathaway said indicated that Clayton had caused any damage.

The defense interpreted the calling of this old war-horse, who had seen it all, as an act to impress trial members with the gravity of Clayton's case. The mere fact of Hathaway's showing up had to underscore the seriousness of Clayton's "crimes."

Clayton was accused of fraternizing with a Soviet citizen—but virtually every American at the Moscow embassy could have been put on trial for that "offense." Worse than that, I discovered that a Soviet citizen named Raya—who worked in the embassy—was in reality a KGB colonel. President Reagan, I also learned, was told of Raya's identity, and ordered her dismissed at once. Only it didn't happen. This KGB colonel continued to work in sensitive positions.

Where were the charges against higher-ups? I produced a

photo of two embassy employees, at a party, one with his arms around Raya.

One of the more extraordinary diversions of the entire court-martial proceedings occurred when the venerable Sam Lonetree, Clayton's grandfather, showed up at the trial. Though not a witness, Sam had come to make a statement.

Sam barged right into the courtroom wearing full head-dress, a complete medicine-man outfit, carrying rattles and a peace pipe. The court could only look on in shock. Very dignified, Sam faced north, south, east, west, all the time chanting a prayer. Then he walked over and brushed Clayton with an eagle feather (the eagle is a symbol of the Great Spirit to many Native Americans) before leaving and setting himself up outside the courtroom to denounce the trial to the press.

By then some twenty-five members of the American Indian Movement (AIM) had gathered outside the Quantico head-quarters building to protest the court-martial. They claimed—and who could contradict them?—that the land on which the trial was being held legally belonged to Native Americans, and that if they, its rightful owners, had control, there would be no court-martial.

The government's reaction to the AIM demonstration was to post a sign specifically forbidding "the beating of drums" outside the courtroom.

The court-martial panel consisted of ten officers. They were the equivalent of a civilian jury, except they decided not only guilt or innocence but also the penalty. I was not especially confident of Clayton's chances with this all-officer jury. Why not some noncoms, or even enlisted men? These were Clay-ton's peers. But my worst fear was that these officers knew what higher-ups expected of them. Their own boss, Defense Secretary Weinberger, had already announced his verdict—and the sentence he would want, death by hanging. It would take a very brave officer to hold out for acquittal.

Stuhff gave an impassioned closing argument, and then came Kunstler, the master. If anyone could reach these officers' hearts, it was he, a war hero, owner of the Bronze Star and *four* Purple Hearts:

> You must decide whether Clayton had the requisite intent to commit a crime, or whether he was a foolish young man who thought he could do what . . . you can't do, he could expose Sasha. He could expose the KGB.
>
> Take into consideration that he came forward, no one had to catch him and, if he hadn't come forward, Sasha might be out there yet with other Marines, other Americans, other foreigners in Moscow. He's been exposed and Sergeant Lonetree did that.
>
> I'll tell you this, it took a lot of courage to do. If he had shut his mouth, never tugged at Big John's sleeve at that party on December 14th, and just said, I'm going to put in for transfer, I'm going to get out of here, leave the KGB, leave all this behind, we wouldn't be here today. You never would have known, the prosecution wouldn't have known, the judge wouldn't have known, no intelligence agency would have known.
>
> It was wrong for him not to report, but I submit to you he did not have the specific intent to commit the crimes, except not reporting, that are charged against him.
>
> I think you have to put aside all of the feelings about the cold war, or whatever type of war we are in now with the Soviet Union. You have to put aside all of the stereotypes about that country or this country. You have to do what Sergeant Lonetree told one of his fellow Marines . . . you have to try to understand that only by some mutual understanding can we insure our children and grandchildren life itself on this planet, which is in such grave jeopardy.
>
> If you decide this case on any ground but that you are convinced beyond a reasonable doubt that every element, every material element of each specific crime has been proved beyond a reasonable doubt, if you decide on any other aspect but that,

which is the legal standard, then I tell you that some night, somewhere, sometime, you will wake up screaming.

Thank you.

The court-martial panel had to decide Lonetree's guilt or innocence on the following charges:

1. Clayton gathered names and photographs of covert agents, and turned them over to Sasha.
2. Clayton had meetings with Violetta, Sasha, and Sasha's KGB friend George.
3. Clayton failed to report telephonic and personal contacts with Sasha and Violetta while in Moscow.
4. The same as number 3, for Sasha in Vienna, plus contact by mail.
5. Clayton identified covert agents for Sasha.
6. Clayton discussed "national defense information" with Sasha and Violetta, and "did agree to obtain, or attempt to obtain, floor plans to the United States Embassy, Moscow."
7. Clayton wrongfully revealed to Sasha the "identities, addresses, and phone numbers" of covert agents.
8. Clayton secreted a list of covert agents in his room.

The following, point-by-point, represents the defense's assessment of the charges:

1. Yes, Clayton gave three photos to Sasha. Two were of agents already transferred, and *all* the covert agents were already known to the Soviets. Clayton turned the pictures over figuring them harmless, and believing in his double-agent-obsessed mind that they might help him help the U.S. Certainly he made a mistake in judgment, but no damage was done.
2. Yes, Clayton had meetings with Violetta, Sasha, and George. Basically, this was a fraternization offense, and we could show that hardly *anyone* in the Moscow or Vienna embassies remained free of this taint.
3. "Failure to report" contacts. Okay. But hardly a major offense. And eventually he *did* report them.

4. The "mail contact" involved love letters from Violetta.

5. This offense involved pairing the right husband with the right wife. They were photos Sasha had. Lonetree had not brought them to the Soviets.

6. The "national defense information" Clayton and Sasha discussed involved conversation any two people might have about, say, U.S. and Soviet policy in the Middle East. Clayton gave away no secrets. He did not give away actual floor plans to the embassy in Moscow. He had stalled Sasha on that, knowing he'd soon leave Moscow.

7. As for "identities, addresses, and phone numbers" of covert agents, Clayton had simply turned over an unclassified embassy phone book easily accessible to anyone.

8. Possession of a list of covert agents is no crime. And as the prosecution itself allowed, Clayton didn't turn his list over to Sasha or anyone else. In short, this "crime" wasn't a crime.

Clayton lost. The officer jury found him guilty on all counts except one. The only not-guilty involved the charge that Clayton had talked to the KGB over the phone, when in reality he had spoken to someone else. They even found him guilty of the noncrime of possessing a list.

Hearing guilty, guilty, guilty shook Clayton, despite his fatalistic expectations. Grimness was written all over the young Indian's face.

But outside, a few minutes later, as he was being led to the brig, he smiled as he passed his mother, Sally Tsosie. This angry, courageous Native American woman was clutching an eagle feather in her hand and shouting "Innocent!" as Clayton looked into her eyes.

What burns away inside me is the injustice, making that kid— and that's what he was—a scapegoat for the sins of powerful superiors. If anyone was prosecuted for the boondoggle construction of the U.S. Embassy in Moscow, costing taxpayers tens of millions of dollars, I never heard of it.

Whatever, the terrible punishment is printed forever in shame on page 1,995 of the cold court-martial transcript:

- Reduced to the grade of E-1
- Fined $5,000
- Forfeit all pay and allowances
- Dishonorable discharge
- Confinement for 30 years

Without some sort of intervention, this gentle Native American, who all of us came to know as a friend, will be more than fifty years old when he is released, "his life," as Kunstler put it, "effectively ruined."

16

THE HIT MAN

Back in the early days of television—before computer chips, compact discs, VCRs, movie rentals, cable, and satellite dishes made the average American home look like a sales floor at Circuit City or Radio Shack—families gathered in the living room around the only set in the house, usually a Zenith or Motorola, and delighted in what we now consider poor reception to "relive those thrilling days of yesteryear" in weekly western dramas. We helped the Lone Ranger and Tonto outsmart the bad guys, held our breath through "Gunsmoke" until Matt Dillon and Chester removed the lawless from the streets of Dodge, ate trail dust with Ward Bond and the "Wagon Train" pioneers, drove cattle on "Rawhide," played it close to the vest with Bret and Bart Maverick, and labored with Ben Cartwright and his boys building the Ponderosa.

One of my all-time favorites was "Have Gun Will Travel." Little did I realize then, as I vicariously packed Paladin's saddlebags, mounted up and headed off with him to answer yet another request for help, that one day I too would enjoy the luxury of a career that satisfied my wanderlust and earned enough money, some of the time, to pay the bills.

Like my granite-faced hero, I lived only a spit shine on my basic-black Tony Lama boots away from zipping my standby wardrobe—two pairs of laundered jeans, a couple of starched dress shirts and, if the climate required it, my old reliable, go-anywhere tan corduroy sportcoat—into a carryall and catching the next flight out.

Such was somewhat still the case in February, 1989, when I heard a voice on the phone say, "How would you like to find Jimmy Hoffa?"

I recognized Bill Helmer's Texan drawl. Helmer and I went back fifteen years to when he was a senior editor at *Playboy* magazine in charge of the "Forum" section, and I was facing two life terms at Red Lodge. At that time the Playboy Foundation was a leading contributor to various causes; civil rights, prison reform; that sort of thing. Helmer was the magazine's representative to the Playboy Foundation. Bill Helmer could and did introduce projects in which I was involved to the foundation and received financial as well as editorial support in *Playboy.*

Bill and I had become close over those years. Real close. He's been to my house and I've been to his. Helmer knows and likes my three sons and I know and like his kids. We're so well acquainted we know each other's ex-wives.

After unexpected brain surgery felled him a few years back, and he was forced to undergo a tumor operation with a complicated recovery, Bill became semiretired. Now he continues to contribute to *Playboy,* working at his apartment in company with his cat Floozy.

Helmer has written or contributed to several books, most notably his *The Gun that Made the Twenties Roar,* the authoritative text on the Thompson submachine gun. Helmer is also an avid John Dillinger historian, and organized and publicized the John Dillinger Died for You Society, a put-on club of tongue-in-cheek Dillinger buffs. His book *Dillinger: The*

Untold Story, is scheduled for publication in 1994.

Reared in a south Texas truck stop, Helmer exhibits the culinary tastes acquired at his father's greasy spoon. A liking for ketchup on filet mignon, chicken fried steak, and Tex-Mex caused Bill's ex-wife Jean to dub him "a food bigot." The name stuck and so did the weird eating habits.

I hadn't heard from my friend for a long time and was surprised, very pleasantly, by his February, 1989, call.

"What's this find Hoffa shit, Buddy?" I asked, knowing there was a real reason for this midafternoon call.

"Lake, I went downtown to the magazine today and ran into Peter Moore. He's an articles editor at *Playboy.*"

"Yeah, I remember Peter."

"Well, Peter told me he's been getting calls from a guy who claims to know who killed Jimmy Hoffa, how they killed him, and where the body's buried."

"If true," I said, "that's the story of the decade, no foolin'."

"The problem is this. Moore is salivating at the prospect of a Hoffa scoop, but he's totally out of his element with this guy. Peter's a good articles editor, but he doesn't know shit about gangster stuff. I told him to call and have you check this guy out. *Playboy* gets hundreds of crank calls a year. Almost always they're nothing. But the point here is, the story value— Hoffa and all that—makes checking it out worthwhile. Anyway, Peter agreed you should handle it and said he'd call you today."

I can't say I wasn't intrigued or interested. I was. But as a private investigator for more than thirty years, meeting criminals and hustlers of every stripe, I'd become a skeptical, cynical, doubting Thomas. You had to show me. I'm willing to listen, especially with bait as attractive as the story of, and the solution to, Jimmy Hoffa's murder.

"Did Peter tell you this guy's name?" I asked. "I gotta start somewhere."

"He didn't give me his name, because he didn't get it. The guy will only tell Peter his initials, D.F., and his number, and that he's in the Federal Witness Protection Program." He sighed. "It'll probably come to nothing." Helmer was about as excited as Helmer gets. Thirty years in the publishing business had provided him with the same skepticism I had.

I knew everything connected to the Federal Witness Protection Program was supersecret. Run by U.S. marshals, this program got established to provide a haven for government witnesses, rats, informants, snitches, and finks. In my years of criminal defense investigation I have encountered many, many informants. Most, if not all, criminal cases feature an informant. These "rats" are coddled, catered to, rewarded, and in many cases allowed to continue committing crimes. When I was a detective in Las Vegas assigned to the sheriff's narcotics squad, we had plenty of informants. We just didn't have a program.

I frequently told informants, "Do what you have to do, just don't tell us about it." Or, "Remember the only thing we can't fix for you is if you kill a police officer and get caught." Those words of advice are still operable.

The big difference in law enforcement between back then and today is money. Before the federal funds made available through the Law Enforcement Assistance Administration (LEAA), there simply wasn't money in a local police department or sheriff's office to pay informants. Our informants had to settle for a twenty-dollar bill out of *our* pockets and a promise to look the other way, or "turn left" as it's called in the trade. All of that still applies, but now the feds pay big figures to their snitches. They call it "immunity from prosecution" and/or "in the interests of justice."

A fix is a fix is a fix. We could only give our snitches a local "pass." Now the feds give their informants immunity from everything, up to and including murder, and pay them hand-somely, too.

Case-in-point, Jimmy "The Weasel" Fratianno, govern-ment informant, was handed immunity from prosecution for eight murders he admitted committing. "The Weasel" went into the Federal Witness Protection Program, testified numer-ous times for government prosecutors, and wrote a bestselling book, *The Last Mafioso*.

Not bad for a former Mafia kingpin turned snitch. Of course, the most visible flaw in the program is the system of rewards: the government pays for good information, but it pays more for *better* information, so the temptation to elabo-rate, exaggerate, and lie is often impossible for the prospective witness to resist. Many informants I know could teach courses in creative writing at the university level. Thus, when I heard that a government informant, a member of the Witness Pro-tection Program, wanted to tell a story of the magnitude of the Hoffa murder to a national magazine, I had many doubts.

"What else can you tell me?" I asked Helmer, who'd gone silent on the line.

"Nothing. I've told you the sum of my knowledge to this point."

"Well, I'll call after I hear from Peter Moore."

Placing the receiver back on its cradle, I picked up my yellow striped cat, Oliver, a loyal friend dating back to the Bolles case, and gently persuaded him to sit while I scratched behind his ears. Oliver and I had been together for more than ten years. A lot, considering I never had a marriage that lasted as long, and I'd tried three of them.

"The story might prove interesting, old guy, but if there's anything to it, I'll have to do a lot of traveling. But don't worry; Lake III will be here. He always takes good care of you."

I enjoyed being with my family of three sons, my daughter-in-law Tammy, my new grandson, and my friends. Thirty-three years in Las Vegas had given me a sort of "old timer" position and helped soften some of the bitter cases I'd worked. I was happy in my little house that functioned as a command center as well, and happy working on some cases for a limited number of defense lawyers who were my close and dear old friends. But even these cases often involved travel.

When Peter Moore's phone call came he told me the story briefly and exactly, sounding very much the *Playboy* senior editor, even more the articles editor, a high-level position in the publishing world.

"I've talked to this guy several times in the past few days," Peter told me. "All he'll say is that his initials are D.F., his number is 1385-066, and he has a New York attorney named Julia Heit. He's doing life for a murder-for-hire killing in New York. He's in the Witness Protection Program and is sick of it. That's about all I know. I don't understand much of what he says, but he claims to know, firsthand, all about Hoffa. Would you check him out and see if he's for real?"

"There's not much to go on, but I'd like to try. Let's start by you putting me in touch with him direct. Just give him my number, the one you just called, and tell him I'm *Playboy*'s investigator. If he calls me, I'll see what I can learn and get back to you."

I thought for a moment, then phoned Terri Lee, my research assistant. Previously she'd been much more, including my wife. I'd have died in that arson fire in Phoenix if she hadn't rushed back into our blazing apartment and saved my life. Anyway, Terri is the best I know at records—library files, newspaper morgues, court documents—and extracting exact kernels of data that make or break an investigation. She was tall, thin, very pretty, with brown hair that changed color with the seasons. I would have hired her full-time, but I couldn't match her earnings as a first-class cocktail waitress.

"Hi, hon, did I wake you up?" I asked.

"Since when did that make any difference?" she snarled, telling me I had.

"You want to do some digging on what might be my biggest case to date? Or do you want to go back to sleep?"

"I can sleep any time, any place, and you know it. And save that biggest case garbage, too. Whatever you're working on you say is your biggest case."

She'd made the observation before, and maybe it was true. Whatever, I related the highlights of my conversation with Peter Moore. She said, "Okay, shoot. Whatcha need?"

"Call the U.S. marshals. The Justice Department. The FBI. Ask them for any statistics they have on the Federal Witness Protection Program. Use your maiden name; tell them you're Terri Yoder, a political science student at Las Vegas City College doing a paper on the Witness Program. Check the reference desk at the public library while you're at it."

"Got it." She hesitated. "I'll let you know what I learn." Another hesitation. "And I love you, Lake."

"I love you, too."

Terri Lee is really great.

I spent the rest of the day thinking. From the smattering of Hoffa history I recalled, I considered it a foregone conclusion that he had run afoul of organized crime. It was no secret to law enforcement—even thirty years ago when I'd been a cop—that the Teamsters Union had been largely under the control of one or more of the New York crime families. Either Jimmy Hoffa did business with the mob, or it was a coincidence of astounding magnitude that so many Teamster locals featured button men, soldiers, and even captains in key union roles.

And hadn't Hoffa gone to that Detroit restaurant, Machus Red Fox, on what surely was the last day of his life, to meet with Tony Giacalone and Tony Provenzano? Some things are too obvious to ignore. Of course the mob killed Hoffa—which made me think some more.

Stirring up the Hoffa murder would irritate the people responsible for that murder. In addition, I foresaw a risk from government agencies and agents.

Would the government encourage the reopening of the Hoffa murder by a national magazine in the person of a meddlesome p.i. with a history of "interfering" in high-profile cases?

I think I knew the answer to that question, but just to be sure I asked an old friend to drop over soon as he could. I'd known this man almost thirty-five years and respected his judgment highly. I told him about D.F., Peter Moore, and *Playboy,* and waited for a reaction. It wasn't long in coming.

"This," he said, "is the height of folly."

Height of folly was familiar territory to me. I'd climbed that mountain several times.

"I mean, you've gone nuts. If this turns into anything, and I'll pray that it doesn't, you're about to piss off the two biggest mobs in the country: the Italians and the FBI. Since you asked my opinion, this makes you stark fucking mad."

"I take it you don't like the idea."

"You've got plenty of lawyer friends who will let you serve divorce papers. Pick up a few easy bucks and enjoy a comfortable semiretirement."

"I'm not ready for that."

"Are you ready for the Detroit mob? They're nothing to fuck with. And the FBI, I guess you know you've been on their hit parade ever since you arrested those agents at Wounded Knee? They loved you even more after that SLA business. Lake, don't you ever think? Are you oblivious to everything?"

Before I could come up with an answer, my friend headed

for the door. He knew how to disconnect from a tacky situation. But, of course, when he reached his Mercedes, he turned and smiled. He was a person who recognized danger but couldn't stay away from it. He'd be back, I knew, for updates.

The next morning I heard from Terri Lee. "This Witness Program you asked me to check out," she said. "I called the FBI and talked with an agent. He said he couldn't discuss it because the U.S. marshals run the program. I called the marshals' office. One of them said the program is very secret and he couldn't talk about it. He suggested I pick another subject to write my paper on. I thanked him and called the justice department who referred me back to the U.S. marshals."

"What about the library?"

"Mrs. Kline at the reference desk ran the Witness Protection Program through her computer and drew a blank. They have zero at the library."

"If that's what you got, I guess that's what we'll have to go with."

"I'm sorry, Lake."

"Me too," I said, but a few minutes later the phone in the living room rattled out a ring. So did the one in the kitchen, the bedroom, and the portable cordless on the hall wall charging its batteries. Since a big part of my business is done by telephone, I make sure I can answer quickly.

"This is the operator. I have a collect call from D.F. in a federal correction institution. Will you accept the charges?"

"Yes, I will."

"Go ahead, please."

And go ahead I did, taking the first step on a path through one of the most important cases of my career. My guide on this path would become my client, my teacher, and my friend. Donald Gus Frankos, contract killer, was waiting on the other end of the line. But at this point, and for the next few weeks, I knew him only as D.F.

"Hello, this is D.F. I'm trying to reach Mr. Headley. Is he there?"

As if sent from central casting to audition for a godfather part, the voice was low and well modulated, heavy with the New York street, raspy, harsh, throaty, and more.

"This is Lake Headley. I've been expecting your call. Peter Moore at *Playboy* said I should see if we could work something out." I was trying to keep it vague enough not to alarm him, but explicit enough so he'd know he was dealing with *Playboy* through me. "I understand from Peter you have a story *Playboy* might be interested in."

"Yeah, here it is. I know who killed Jimmy Hoffa, how and why he was killed, and where the body is buried."

The guy didn't fool around.

"If we can work out some details," he continued, "I'll give *Playboy* the story from beginning to end. I won't hold nothing back. But right now I can't tell you my name or where I'm located. I can say I'm in the Witness Protection Program and have been for about three years. I can also tell you that my lawyer is Julia Heit from New York City. She's working on a motion for a new trial for me. I'm doing twenty-five to life for the murder of a black drug dealer in 1981. But I guess you want to hear about the Hoffa killing."

"What is it you want from *Playboy* in exchange for this story?"

"I want to get my story out. My story *and* the story of this fucking Witness Protection Program. How the feds promise the moon and then when they get the information they're after, all they got for their rats is a rotten jail cell. I've had three fucking years of solitary confinement. My only visitors have been FBI agents and U.S. attorneys. No friends or family. Only Julia Heit, my attorney; and I can't see her much because she's in New York and I'm in the midwest. Anyway, I think *Playboy* is the best place to tell my story."

"So you want two stories," I said.

"One about Hoffa: who, why, where, when, and how. The other about this fucking Witness Protection Program. I want to let people know how their money's being spent. You wouldn't believe it."

I thought I would. At least the Witness Protection part of his story. From my experience dealing with rats, I suspected the program was at least a partial boondoggle, with the government coddling snitches at considerable expense. Besides, having worked the defense end of criminal law for thirty years—after seeing Adamson frame Robison and Dunlap in the Bolles murder—I didn't like prosecutors using criminals (who had a lot to gain by lying) to help jail defendants. Yes, I suspected I'd believe, and be able to prove, that abuses were rife in the witness program.

The Hoffa murder? Well, I thought, keep an open mind. *Check it out.*

And check out something else, I reminded myself: getting paid. I've been known to forget a vital part of any case, the fee. Consequently, I've probably done more *pro bono* investigations than any p.i. in history. At least my banker and accountant thought so.

Lawyers have a saying: "I'm waiting for a critical witness to come in; Mr. Green has not shown up yet." I've heard numerous lawyers use precisely that language to obtain a continuance from a judge.

"Mr. Green" is money: the fee. Judges, knowing the translation, almost always granted the request for continuance.

When I expressed surprise, a veteran attorney said, "Don't forget, judges were lawyers first. Most of them will be lawyers again, after they leave the bench. This is their way of sticking together."

Anyway, I didn't intend to forget Mr. Green with this investigation. After I hung up with D.F., I called Peter Moore at

Playboy. He said he had spoken with Arthur Kretchmer, *Playboy*'s editorial director and the magazine's boss. "Arthur," said Peter Moore, "is excited about this Hoffa thing. He says a story of this magnitude would fit in fine with plans of changing the *Playboy* image from a first-rate, classy girlie magazine to a more visible editorial policy. Sort of a monthly *Time* or *Newsweek.* With girls, of course."

I told Peter Moore about my conversation with D.F. Moore said, "Arthur wants you to check this guy out good. I know his being in the Witness Program won't make your job any easier. You got any ideas on how to proceed?"

"The first, and possibly only, thing I can do right now is call his lawyer."

I phoned the New York City law firm of Heit and Grant. By mentioning D.F.'s initials to the receptionist, I was put through to Julia Heit without delay. I introduced myself and explained the D.F./*Playboy* connection.

"Well, Mr. Headley," she said, "I must say this is a surprise to me. I know who you mean when you speak of D.F. and, yes, he's my client. I can't go into the facts of this case now, but I can say I'm preparing a motion for a new trial for him. I don't know why he wants to tell his story to *Playboy,* but I am sure he is what he says he is. I get calls from prosecutors all over the country wanting to talk to him. I've heard the Hoffa story from him and I tend to believe it. He ought to know, he was right there with all of them during the seventies. I'm sure you know by now that D.F. is, or was, a hit man, a free-lance contract killer. By free-lance I mean he worked for anyone who could and would pay."

She seemed tired, as if she had gone over D.F.'s story many times.

"Like I said," Julia Heit concluded, "I don't know why he wants to talk to *Playboy.* But if that's what he wants, I don't care. In fact, if there's anything I can do to help, please call me."

There was something she could do, but I didn't bring it up at the time. I needed to see D.F., visit him in person, and I figured a ploy I'd used often in the past would work here: I'd ask Julia Heit to hire me as her defense investigator; then, as part of the defense team, I *couldn't* be denied access to my client.

That's how it worked out. I sent my resumé to her by overnight mail (using Bill Kunstler as a reference impressed her), and she saw advantages for both of us. I'd serve as her liaison with D.F., do needed investigative work on the appeal, all *for free,* and *I'd* gain access to the sine qua non source for the articles. She told me she'd write the needed letters to government officials, and I should call them in a few days.

D.F. called at least twice a day and we began to get to know each other. He told me his name—Donald Gus Frankos—and his location: the federal correctional institution at Sandstone, Minnesota.

One of the people I needed to talk to was Alan Cohen, an Assistant U.S. Attorney for the Southern District of New York. Frankos had told me he'd "saved Cohen's life" by exposing a murder plot aimed at the prosecutor. This, I later learned, was true, but when I phoned him, Cohen didn't seem filled with gratitude. I guessed that D.F. had asked him for favors in the past, and he'd gotten exasperated trying to grant them.

Chilly reluctance best describes the attitude Cohen presented to me. He was cold and impersonal, clearly not happy with the idea of my becoming involved. "Of course," he said, "you'll have to be checked out and cleared before any visits can occur."

He sounded as if he pinned heartfelt hope on my being

unable to pass a background check, so I couldn't resist telling him that I'd recently been cleared by the Marine Corps and the State Department to attend the ultrasecret court-martial of Clayton Lonetree. "I'll be happy," I said, "to provide you with my date of birth and Social Security number to facilitate the background investigation."

"That won't be necessary," he said curtly.

I figured from his answer that he already had my identifiers. It also suggested that he rested uneasily on the horns of a dilemma. On the one hand, he didn't want me anywhere near Frankos; on the other, he didn't want to provoke the government's star witness by denying me access.

I didn't think he could keep me away from Frankos. I'm "clean," as the cops say, no felony convictions ever, and since I was part of the defense team, the feds *couldn't* deny me visits with my client.

I first met Donald Frankos early in April, 1989, at the federal prison in Sandstone. To reach this remote place you need only to make two right turns out of the Minneapolis airport, one at the end of the access road, a second onto 43 North. A hundred miles of pretty scenery later you'll hit Sandstone.

I stayed at the Twin Pines Motel and the next morning, headed out to visit Frankos, I noticed a white Chrysler with New York plates parked four places down from my rented Mustang. *Get a grip on yourself,* I thought. If the Mob had been tipped off, they would have flown to Minnesota and rented a car, just as I had. The same applied to government agents.

I made my way without difficulty to the prison, a multilevel institution surrounded by a ten-foot-high chain-link fence topped by menacing rolls of razor wire. I drove along a black-top road to a sign that said STOP. I stopped. I saw another sign, smaller than the first: PICK UP PHONE. I picked up the phone. A still smaller sign said DIAL 376.

"Guard tower. State your business."

I felt like saying, "Avon calling," but I didn't want a hassle. "I'm here for a visit with D.F.," I said instead. "He's Number 1385-066. This visit is approved by Mr. Franklin."

"Please stand by while I verify."

It didn't take long for the voice to return to the line.

"Do you have any weapons with you?" he asked. "Any drugs, tape recorders, or cameras?"

"No, I don't," I said.

"When I raise the arm, follow the road to the gate and park facing the fence. Wait in your vehicle until someone comes out to get you."

"I sure will," I said.

I hadn't finished my Benson and Hedges, Deluxe Ultra Light, when a man in a blue shirt and black tie came out of the prison and headed for my car.

"You must be Lake," he said. "I'm Ben Franklin. Actually, my name's Bernard, but everyone calls me Ben."

I followed him into the prison. "You're from Las Vegas," he said. "My wife and I used to go there when I was stationed at Lompoc up by San Francisco. We haven't been back in seven or eight years."

"You should visit again. The town is growing like crazy."

"Have you lived there long?" I figured he was just making conversation. Surely he'd read the background check the government had done, and knew all about me.

"Thirty-three years," I said. "Off and on. Ever since I went to work for the sheriff's department." It never hurt to let a cop know I had been a fraternity brother at one time.

Franklin left me in a room that was maybe twice the size of an average living room. Chairs lined the wall on one side, under barred windows. Several paintings done by inmates hung on the gray walls. The room boasted what appeared to be a small altar, the project of someone with a lot of time to kill.

I ambled around, checking for bugs, not the crawly kind but electronic listening devices. I found neither, but I did come across a big picture puzzle depicting Jesus kneeling in the dirt. The picture seemed to speak to all the lonely days and nights, the unending boredom of doing time, much more eloquently than the wall, the hacks, the courts, and the judges. I wondered which took longer, the completion of this large, intricate puzzle or the help from Jesus it so obviously implored.

"Clear those halls!" I heard someone yell.

I figured I was minutes away from meeting the self-confessed hit man.

"Are those halls clear?" the voice boomed again, several minutes later.

"Okay," shouted another voice. "Bring him down."

I can't say what I expected to encounter when I met Donald Frankos. Some combination of Hulk Hogan, Godzilla, and Count Dracula, I guess. Instead I met a man of medium height, handsome, with graying temples around a balding crown, dressed in tan slacks, striped polo shirt, and sneakers. "You gotta be Lake," he said, sticking out his hand to shake. "I'm glad to meet you. I'm Donald Frankos; that is, in here I am. On the street I'm Tony the Greek."

We sat at a desk atop which sat a phone. I asked about his background and he wanted to know mine. It turned out we shared an admiration for Bill Kunstler, who had represented him briefly on one of Frankos's many cases.

My first impression was of a guy I'd be happy to sit next to on a long flight. Articulate and humorous, he was—on the surface—a real charmer. He had the been-down-the-road, rugged countenance that carried the scars befitting an ex-boxer or street fighter. About fifty years old, Frankos had a fighter's build he'd kept in shape despite, or maybe because of, long

periods of confinement. Just shy of six feet, weighing about
165, he looked as though he'd been a ladies' man in his youth.

Frankos told me that he liked all sports and had, in his
youth, excelled in football, boxing, and swimming. He talked,
without a trace of self-pity, about his wretched childhood.
Raised by a vicious uncle who molested Frankos's sister,
Frankos committed his first murder before age twenty—more
than forty others would follow.

Frankos told me about the murder for which he currently
was serving twenty-five-to-life—for which he claimed innocence—the contract murder of a black basketball-star-turned-
drug-dealer named Clarence Jones. He told me of brutal,
inhuman beatings he and his codefendant had received from
guards at the Westchester County Jail in New York. He said
he had been beaten, bitten, and burned with cigarettes, then
forced to stand trial, bloody and battered. These circumstances formed the basis for the new trial motion Julia Heit
was preparing. I was able to verify everything Frankos told
me about his treatment in Westchester, but in the end the
judge ruled against him. I think the Greek had an idea this
would happen, that despite the fact that he was *entitled* to a
new trial, the system would not grant one to such as he.

Frankos was at his most emotional when he talked about
the Federal Witness Protection Program and his "sellout" to
the program. "All my life I've hated rats," he said. "And
that's what they made me into, a rat. I can't believe I went for
it. I wake up at night in my cell and think I'm a fucking rat,
that's what I am, a fucking rat. That's what bothers me more
than any other thing I've done in my life. I let them take away
my manhood, my self-respect. I went for their bullshit. Me,
the wiseguy, went for it like a stone sucker. I guess I'm sorry
for all the guys I killed, but for the most part they were
scumbags. Mostly rats, like I've become because I was weak.
I take pride in the fact that I never killed anybody that didn't

deserve it, and I never killed a woman or kid. Now John Gotti, who I've known for a long time, done time with, worked with and did hits for, John's offered three hundred thousand dollars to anyone who gets the Greek. It makes me more sad than scared. My old friends, gone, my self-respect gone, my manhood gone."

"I know it's not easy for you," I said, knowing the response was inadequate. Here was a rat who was sorry he'd become a rat, and I sympathized with him.

I asked Frankos to go on, and he did. He went on and on. He told me how he had gotten close to Jimmy Coonan, the head of the infamous Irish gang called the Westies that specialized in murder and dismembering bodies.

Frankos spoke with admiration of his longtime friend and partner in numerous murders, Joe Sullivan, known as Mad Dog. The son of a New York City policeman, a gold-shield detective who retired with honors, Joe followed a different path. Besides becoming one of the most prolific murderers in American history, Sullivan attained fame as the only prisoner ever to escape from Attica. Frankos suddenly stopped in the middle of his narration and said, "I hope I'm not boring you with all this shit, but you got to understand me in order to understand how the Hoffa hit came about and how and why I was involved."

I assured Frankos I wasn't bored. On the other hand, I wanted to hear about Hoffa. That's why I'd come. I was here legally, and legally I could come back, but I didn't trust authorities always to obey the law. If they forbade further visits, I could file lawsuits from now till the end of time, but they might not do any good.

"Maybe you should tell me about Hoffa," I said. "We can get to the rest later."

"Right. I know that's why you came here. To make a deal

for *Playboy*. And we can and will make a deal. You know why? Because I don't give a shit about the money. Sure, I like money, but what the fuck can I spend it on in here? What I want is to get the story out about this fucking witness program. If I let people on the outside know what bullshit it is, maybe I can keep the next sucker from falling for it. That's my main motive. So let's talk about Hoffa."

"First . . ."

"Let me say something first. But I gotta know, you won't repeat it to anybody." (He later authorized me and Bill Hoffman to make this information public in the book we wrote about him.)

"If that's what you want, that's what you get. I'm working for you. I'm part of your defense team. I *can't* reveal privileged communications. I never have and never will."

"Yeah." He thought this over. The law and ethics were two things—and they said I couldn't reveal privileged communications—but reality was another. Could he trust me?

"I think you're a straight shooter," he said, "so I'm gonna tell you this. I don't want nobody else to know."

I waited. Telling him *again* that I wouldn't break a confidence would cut no ice at all.

"I know you're gonna look closely into this Hoffa business," he said. "What I'm gonna tell you is the absolute truth. How do I know? Because I was there when he got killed. *I killed Jimmy Hoffa.*"

Jesus Christ. I just sat and looked at him.

"I want you to know that," he said. "Later on, when I give you the whole story, you'll understand."

And I did understand, as weeks of dealing with Frankos turned into months and then into three years. He didn't want to name himself as the killer because Michigan had the death penalty; more important by far to him, he didn't think the other conspirators in the murder could possibly be convicted on his word alone and, make no mistake, he didn't want to be a rat again.

Interviewing Frankos, in a courtroom, various prisons, and hundreds of times over the telephone, and checking out his story, became an obsession with me. I logged some 50,000 miles in this quest; put another way, around the world twice.

This was the most important investigation I'd ever handled, and I didn't want to come up short. I remembered a guy Muhammad Ali had knocked out saying, "I guess I just couldn't get myself up for this one."

I felt like saying, "If you can't get up for Ali, what in life will ever motivate you?"

Playboy turned loose its own excellent research staff, and working separately and together we tried to disprove what Frankos told us about the Hoffa murder. As the saying goes, we couldn't put even a nick in his story.

We tried. That was the goal. Finding he had lied to us and going on to something else.

A *Playboy* story and interview with Frankos appeared in the magazine's November, 1989, issue. Except for Frankos admitting that he had killed Hoffa, and giving the exact location of the body, everything *Playboy* ran was as true as human research could make it.

But my job was far from over. The *Playboy* story covered only the Hoffa murder, but there was much more to Frankos's life than that. I got hold of my writer friend Bill Hoffman, and we contracted to do a book on Frankos, which we would call *Contract Killer*. Again, our goal was to *disprove what he told us,* looking not only at the Hoffa murder but at Frankos's entire life. Ever since I'd left Papa Ralph Thorson in Los Angeles, I'd tried always to act ethically, always to find the truth no matter where it led, and I took pride in the career I'd built. I knew Hoffman felt the same way. He had written thirty-seven nonfiction books, and he didn't intend to tarnish that accomplishment with a story that wasn't true in every respect.

For the next eighteen months Hoffman and I researched and wrote the Greek's story (research consumed much more time than writing). Some of the things he told us were simply incredible—for example, that he'd been able to buy furloughs and leave prison to commit murders—but they turned out to be true.

I visited Joe Sullivan at the New York prison where he was doing life, and this player in the Hoffa killing (and the Greek's confidant) confirmed everything Frankos had said about the Teamster leader's murder; I interviewed Bobby English, a former Westie; Frank Sacco, a reputed mobster linked to the Lucchese crime family; and Joe Kersch, the Greek's codefendant in the Clarence Jones murder.

All of these people had a reason to hurt Frankos. The Greek was a rat, and they would win no points confirming what he told us. But confirm him they did.

I visited Joe Sullivan's wife, Gail. She had known Frankos very well through her husband. Gail's concern was with Frankos digging up so much dirt from the past.

I also interviewed numerous law enforcement officials. *Everyone* I talked to confirmed the area in which they knew the Greek. A comment common to *all* the people I interviewed: "Don't worry about Frankos. He's everything he says he is."

I did break my promise to Frankos in one respect, and I hope he'll understand. I confided to my son Lake III that the Greek had told me he'd been the one who'd fired the fatal bullets into Hoffa. I rationalized that Lake III was part of the defense team (he'd been with me on *every* case for more than fifteen years), but I also knew this might become important later. I anticipated that the Greek might change his mind later, confess his own role—as he has—and I wanted him to have backup in case that eventually occurred. If he didn't change his mind, I knew his secret was as safe with Lake III as it was with me.

I worked full-time on the Frankos investigation as long as I could; but something intervened: the doctors told me I was going to die.

We'll see about that, I thought. I continued to work on Frankos, but at a slightly slower pace.

17

THE UNWINNABLE CASE

I started experiencing cramps in my legs and twitches in my arms in June, 1989, but I ignored them as long as I could. In October, 1990, I went to a general practitioner and he prescribed quinine.

My condition grew worse. Periodically my whole body twitched. My friend Nick Behnen, a wealthy Vegas real-estate developer, insisted that I call on a neurologist friend of his, Dr. Gerald Dunn.

"I can't afford to see Dr. Gerald Dunn," I said. It was unbelievable to me that my book about Donald Frankos with Bill Hoffman had been rejected by its original publisher (I suspected the government's hand in this), but that's what had happened. Hoffman was looking for a new publisher. I was broke. It was March, 1991, and money I had counted on for more than two years of work had just disappeared.

"Go see Dunn," Behnen demanded. "You can't afford it, but *I* can."

4-20-91

Dear Bill and Judy,

Well, my dear friends, the results are in. I have ALS, also known as Lou Gehrig's disease. I'm enclosing some literature on this thing so you can see what the doctors think of my chances. Looks like we better not waste any time with *Vegas P.I.*—you can see that time has suddenly become a serious consideration.

I hope a publisher wants it. I need the money now as I don't know how long I'll be able to work. My doctor gives me two years, at the outside, to live, with gradual deterioration that has already begun. You can probably tell by my handwriting. And my speech. I sound like I'm about half drunk, especially when I'm a little tired. The doctor says this will become more pronounced as time passes. I've had every test known to the medical profession and it's absolutely sure that the diagnosis is correct. So what can you do? Since it is inevitable, I'm going to try to relax and, if not enjoy it, at least accept it. After all, nobody gets out of this mess alive. What can you do? The answer is nothing.

4-22-91

Dear Bill and Judy,

I've decided to treat my diagnosis as a criminal indictment. I intend to conduct a most thorough investigation seeking alternate treatments and hopefully a cure. To finance a quest, equal to the quest for the Holy Grail, for a cure for ALS, I intend to hold one or more fundraisers. I'll keep you posted as to the details of fundraising. Treating my disease as an indictment allows me a path of resistance that accepting precludes. Sort of like pleading guilty. I can't bring myself to throw in the towel. I know for sure that you fully understand my position.

Telling Lake III was the hardest part. We sat in our living room, me in my favorite chair, he on the sofa, surrounded by Native American artifacts. "I went to the doctor today," I said. "He gave me the results of the tests and I have arterial lateral sclerosis. That's Lou Gehrig's disease."

I saw Lake III didn't understand, so I handed him a medical journal article on ALS. "Read this."

"This is very bleak," he said when he'd finished reading it. "What are we going to do about it?"

"I'm going to fight. Like I'd fight anything else. I'm going to treat this like it's my death-penalty case. I won a few of those, you know."

"I'll do whatever I can to help, Dad," he said.

I knew he would. From SLA to Red Lodge, from Bolles to Frankos, I could always count on him.

I talked about how this was just one doctor's opinion, that there were many avenues to explore—and I'd explore them all.

5-1-91

Dear Bill and Judy,

I just got information that I have an appointment with Dr. King Engle, the head of the Jerry Lewis ALS Clinic at USC in L.A. next Wednesday and Thursday (May 8 and 9). This appointment was made for me by Jerry Lewis at the insistence of Dominic Gentile, my lawyer friend here in Vegas. The news is good in the respect that there's a six month waiting list just to get in this clinic. Jerry Lewis was able to circumvent the waiting period.

I don't really expect a different diagnosis, but I feel there's therapy available that I don't know about. Ways to prolong the quality of life, if not the quantity. So I'm going to take a look. Dr. King Engle is the leading authority on ALS in this country, and I feel lucky to have friends like Gentile that can make it possible for me to get in there.

ALS sure makes one think. Especially when *this* one has no money, no insurance, and no way to make a living in the ensuing months of predictable life. So many things to do, so little time to do them. There's a saying among ALS patients:

"If you like a challenge, you'll love ALS." I suspect that is right on point.

About all I know of this situation so far is that there is always a great concern that an ALS victim will commit suicide. I guess there's a high rate of this course of action. While I have not thought of this way out too seriously at this point, I've not ruled it out totally either. I'm not too sure I'd settle for "life as a vegetable." But that decision is down the road a piece, so I don't dwell on it. Not much anyway.

One thing I should tell you, a little cheerier, too. Since I received the diagnosis, I've been told "I love you" by more men and women together and separately than all the rest of my life combined. I've also seen more adults, men and women, cry than the rest of my life.

Maybe you'll want to explore this in *Vegas P.I.,* maybe devote one chapter to death or the prospect of death, more accurately, as an aphrodisiac. More good looking women have made offers than all the other 60 years produced. And this is just 10 days to two weeks old. I guess I ought to take 'em up and try to check out that way. Neat form of suicide, huh?

5-11-91

Dear Bill and Judy,

I just got back from the Jerry Lewis ALS Clinic in L.A. Quite an experience! If they had done to me, in a jail, what was done in that hospital, it would have been a clear case of cruel and unusual punishment. I told Lake III when I got back that I'd been hurt worse in the name of medicine than I'd been hurt in shootouts that I've been in and gotten hit.

Three days of continual testing. Such fun things as the EMG, where two-inch needles are inserted into muscles of the arms and legs and then electric current induced into these needles to measure the reaction of the muscles. This lasted for about 90 minutes. All without the benefit of painkillers of any type. And the bone marrow test where a hole is drilled into the pelvis from the back and a plug of bone marrow is removed. The spinal tap, a hole in the spine to drain off a sample of spinal fluid. But maybe the most insidious test I was the victim of was the muscle biopsy. This little honey took two hours on the operating table (in surgery). The procedure is to open up my left thigh and secure a sample of the muscle tissue to determine the amount of deterioration of that muscle. This has to be done without anesthetic in order to avoid contamination of the tissue (at least that's what the surgeon told me). As they were finishing the job, I asked how many stitches it took to close the hole they had made. The doctor said he hadn't counted, but he thought about 35 or 40. Judging from the pain, every fucking one was needed. I'm sitting in a chair with an ice pack on the incision as I write this. The ice helps, but walking is extremely difficult.

I'm supposed to get the results of these tests Tuesday, but ALS seems to be a foregone conclusion among the highly qualified doctors at the Jerry Lewis ALS Clinic. So I wait. But enough of my written snivel.

5-20-91

Dear Bill and Judy,

I have run up some absolutely staggering doctor, hospital, and lab bills in the past two to three weeks. I have become an absolute expert on "the high cost of dieing"—I can't spell it, let alone pay for it. So far my costs are about $25,000 and go up with every series of tests.

Last week at the Jerry Lewis Clinic in L.A., they told me (they being Dr. King Engle, the head of the clinic) that there was a ten percent chance that I had a blood cancer called IGG-Kappa which could be producing the ALS syndrome symptoms. Since ALS is *not* treatable and the blood cancer is treatable, they want me to undergo a treatment that includes chemotherapy and a process called homophoresis which is like dialysis. The blood is removed, cleaned up, and replaced. This process is done twice a week for four weeks, and then I'll be reevaluated to see if I have ALS or if it's blood cancer. Big choice, right? Two fatal diseases in one old worn out body. I always get more than my share.

The kicker is that these treatments cost $1,000 each, or $8,000 total, in front. Seems like all the doctors want money in front once a patient is found to have a fatal disease. Can't blame them though. Long payment schedules are out of the question for someone like me.

I hope it's not because I'm ill, but I learned that I've been voted Outstanding Investigator of the Year by the International Society of Private Investigators (I-SPI). They have some good people in the organization. I feel honored.

I've also learned that the homophoresis is a longer shot than I thought. The odds are ten to one against my having blood cancer instead of ALS. If I have blood cancer—and that would be *good* news—the odds are ten to one against its being treatable. I asked an old crossroader friend what that made the total odds. He said one hundred to one.

It's all academic. I can't afford the treatment. Then again (shades of Papa Thorson, Richard, and me tied up in the Mexican basement), neither will I sit quietly and wait to be killed without putting up a fight. What I can do is pursue alternatives, and that's my plan.

6-3-91

Dear Bill and Judy,

I spoke to Eric Protter three times over the weekend. He's primarily interested in me contacting a "healer" in L.A. in order for me to seek treatment through alternative medicine for this ALS thing. I did contact Eric's friend who told me he was researching the possibilities of treatment for ALS at a clinic in Tijuana. I think this is the same clinic Eric took his wife to before she died. Eric spoke to us about this place when we all got together in New York. As I recall, he wanted you to do a book about the clinic.

Anyway, I called and spoke to Carlos Sebastian in L.A. and then called Eric and told him what Carlos said. Eric was happy that I called and wants to go with me to Tijuana when the time comes. Okay with me, of course. We'll see what Carlos comes up with although I have to tell you, I feel a little bit like a high school kid seeking an abortionist. Maybe this is an answer not available through the AMA which admittedly knows no more about ALS now than they did 110 years ago when the disease was first discovered.

I think I should tell you about a phenomenon that has surfaced since my recent diagnosis with ALS. Might be good material for *Vegas P.I.* Bill, you wouldn't believe the number of my friends from all over the country who call me with suggestions for treatment of this ALS. Alternative medicine, metaphysics, crystals, tarot cards, fruit and vegetable juice diets, ginseng, acupuncture, magnets, God, love, to name just a few that come to mind easily. This goes on at the rate of four to five calls and/or letters weekly. I truly appreciate the thoughts behind this, the interest in my welfare, and of course the love of these people. I thought you would appreciate this too, hence the story. Lots of strange things connected with having a fatal disease.

I tried other treatments, and looked into still others. I went to an acupuncturist who said he could "cure" me—"just five hundred dollars a week"—but I decided to look elsewhere. I explored herbology. The woman friend of mine who recommended it said she had cured certain nerve disorders with herbs, and she had a long list of patients who swore by her. I started taking herbs.

Another friend of mine recommended the "black salve." It looked like mud, but it was really herbs mashed together. The herbs came from Wyoming and had been developed by an old Indian who claimed to have cured cancer in cattle. I started using the black salve after my friend produced a *human* who swore he'd been cured of stomach cancer by the concoction.

I heard about an experimental treatment for neuromuscular diseases that involved ingesting cobra venom. I was already taking herbs and the black salve, so why not cobra venom? I launched a search to find the individual with this treatment, but wasn't successful.

What I really had hope for was help from my dear friend Carter Camp, chief of AIM's Warrior Society. The American Medical Association would scoff, but I knew firsthand that Native Americans could deal with certain illnesses far better than any traditional doctor. I finally found Carter in Oklahoma and called him.

"Carter, how you doing?"

"Lots of things going on, brother," he said.

Being called "brother" by Carter Camp ranked at the top of any honors I could imagine. I knew the word was never used lightly by Native Americans.

"How are things going with you, brother?" he asked.

"Not good, my friend. I have Lou Gehrig's disease."

"That's fatal, isn't it?"

"Yes."

"You know," Carter Camp said, "that my people have cured many things, and I think we can cure this."

"I'd appreciate anything you can do."

"I need to do some checking around. There are some things I'll have to gather."

Exactly what he had in mind I didn't know. I figured there would be a pipe involved, and ceremonies that needed to be performed. Probably a sweat lodge would be involved, and maybe the euweepe (offering of flesh) and peyote rites.

"I'll wait to hear from you," I said.

Carter called a few days later and said that Black Elk was the man to see. Black Elk, he said, was currently in Europe, but he would arrange things as soon as he could.

Black Elk was one of the best, I knew, right up there with Leonard Crow Dog. The AMA might laugh at Black Elk and Crow Dog, but I knew of many people they'd helped that the medical establishment couldn't. I also knew they wouldn't charge an arm and a leg—they wouldn't charge anything—for treatment.

6-15-91

Dear Bill and Judy,

Bill, I feel that I must tell you something I've told no one else, not even Lake III. And that is this ALS thing is progressing much faster than I have been led to expect. Although that may have been wishful thinking on my part. They told me in L.A. that I probably had one to three years. I think we can count on being closer to one than three. It's a pain in the ass to watch one's body fail to function in such basics as speech, hand movements, walking, etc. But that's what's happening, at a faster rate than I expected. Also you should know that I have no intention of becoming a total vegetable or anything approaching that condition. I know how to take control of that destiny and I fear disability far worse than I fear death. This is not meant as a snivel or bitch, just as accurate an appraisal as I can make to you. I'm not shy about telling you these things because I know in my heart that you not only understand but that you certainly agree with me. I *know* that you love me and wouldn't want me to just hang on while becoming totally incapacitated. Who knows what lies on the next level, if there is one?

I would love to do *Vegas P.I.* with you both for the legacy and the bucks. I know you could make my life sound and read as if it were truly worthwhile. . . . But it would be great fun to just get together with you and put it together. Great for my kids, too. This is much harder for them than for me, and this book would be eternally theirs as an explanation of their father's life. So I hope we get it together soon.

My friend, you have taught me so very much over the years, and I'll always be grateful to Eric for putting us together. Without you, my meager accomplishments would have gone unheralded and unacknowledged (if only we'd have had time for you to teach me spelling and grammar—too late in the game now). I thank you and I'll continue to thank you as long as I live. That's almost funny in view of my situation, but you know I'm being very sincere when I say thank you from my heart.

Bill, I've said before, but I'll say again, do anything you think is right in relation to our books and I'll go along with what you decide. You have now and always have had carte blanche in that department as far as I'm concerned. Don't let this fucking disease fuck that up. Just do what you think is right and it will be right. And let me know what you need me to do and I'll do it as long as I am able. When it's over, it's over. Remember, my friend, I had a hell of a ride this time around.

6-22-91

Dear Bill and Judy,

I have to apologize to you for the condition of my speech this morning when we talked. It comes and goes. Sometimes it is much clearer than this a.m. Sometimes a little worse. I told you the symptoms are worsening, including the speech problem. My hands, arms, and legs are becoming weaker, too. I guess that is to be expected with this damned disease, but that knowledge doesn't make it a whole lot easier to accept or deal with. But it does have the sobering effect of shattering the illusion of immortality that we all cloak ourselves in. To me, sickness and death are no longer something that happens only to others. Both have taken on newer and more personal definitions now that I'm face to face with these dark spectors. It's only the support, love, and consideration of friends like you that allows me to continue. And continue I shall, as long as possible. But my dear friend, death is no longer an abstract concept, but a foreseeable realism that is most probably not a hell of a long way off. So I try to make it a day to day thing. Like the t.v. show—One Day At A Time.

It became like the TV show "This Is Your Life," and I loved it. Friends from near and far came to visit. Bill Rittenberg, the civil-rights lawyer who got involved in the Red Lodge case, came from New Orleans along with his wife, Paulette, to visit me. Bill told me his father died of ALS, but we laughed about past battles we'd fought. I know he thinks he's paying his last respects, but *I* haven't conceded anything.

Playboy's Bill Helmer flew in from Chicago. He can't believe we haven't yet found a publisher for the Frankos book. I'm lucky to have had people in my life like Helmer.

Jon and Glynna Robinson came to see me from my hometown of Goshen, Indiana. I think I want to go back there.

George Vlassis, from Phoenix, my oldest friend. George accomplished more for Native Americans than any white man who ever lived. He has helped right many wrongs. He'd been instrumental in negotiating a contract with Peabody Coal—which previously paid the Navajos a paltry five cents per ton for coal mined on the reservation—whereby the Indians became equal partners. A sizable chunk of the electrical power for Los Angeles came from energy generated on the massive Navajo reservation, and George secured them a cut of this income, too.

It was pleasant reminiscing about our Indiana childhoods. George and I played both ways as guards for the Goshen High School football team, on a line featuring center Doug Weaver, now athletic director at Michigan State, and Ken LaRue, business manager for the Los Angeles Raiders.

So many people kept coming: Pody Poe, a legendary casino owner; Shirley Sutherland, Donald's wife—Shirley had contributed money to help keep the SLA investigation going; and Ralph Lamb, the crusty ex-sheriff.

Harry Claiborne stopped by. He looked good.

And my wives and former girlfriends. There was Evelyn, the mother of my three kids; Margie; Terri Lee—geesus, I'd blown it with a lot of good women. One of my favorites—I *wanted* to marry her—rode all the way from Chicago to Las Vegas on her motorcycle. This was Victoria Cerenich, Vicki, one of the first women cops in macho Chicago.

Nick Behnen stopped over almost every day. When he wasn't cooking his delicious lemon chicken, Terri Lee was the chef.

Best of all were the regular visits from my sons Rod and Anthony (Lake III lived with me) and my daughter-in-law Tammy and grandson Matthew.

John Soares, the old crossroader, came by. "If there's anything I can do to help you or your family, just name it," he said.

Mike Stuhff, his wife Sandy, and their children showed up almost every day. I'd done more cases with Mike than anyone else.

Mike Wysocki, a great p.i., visited whenever he could.

Those who couldn't make it, called: Donald Freed; Don Devereux; Jim Robison; Max Dunlap; Molly Ivins; David Kennedy; Michael Kennedy; Bill Kunstler; Jerry Shields; so many others.

7-6-91

Dear Bill and Judy,

I think I should update you on my progress, or rather the progress of Lou Gehrig's disease. As you can probably discern my speech is becoming more slurred. There's nothing can be done about it and according to the doctors it will continue to worsen. I'm not too sure what the final outcome in the speech department is going to be. I haven't asked, probably because I'm not sure I want to know. I'm sure it's not a pretty picture.

Also my hands are weakening at a rate more rapid than I had anticipated (or maybe hoped). Even more alarming to me is that the disease is starting to have a marked effect on my legs now. I took a short walk, less than one half mile yesterday, and I had to come home. It felt like my legs weren't mine. I became concerned that I wouldn't be able to walk and would be found *helpless in the park* where I was walking. (Great title, Helpless in the Park, huh?) Also, as if the above is not enough, I'm having increasing difficulty swallowing. That is one of the symptoms the doctors predicted. Also a certain amount of choking goes with it. That's how they said it will end. Either through suffocation or strangulation or both. I told you this is not a pretty picture.

Bill, I don't intend this as a snivel but rather as a progress, or lack of progress, report.

I like to think I'm mentally prepared for this shit, and to a certain degree I am. What I mean is I'm not afraid of death, but I am afraid of disability. I'm not too sure I can handle disability to the degree that I'm certain to be facing. I think you know that I've spent my entire life as a warrior. Now to be faced with the prospect of becoming a totally dependent slug is a frightening and depressing future. All my life I was sure death would come to me out of the end of a barrel in a bright orange flash, not the inch at a time kind of thing fate had in store.

Bill, I really don't mean to make my problems your problems, and I know there's nothing you or anyone else can do about this insidious fucking sickness. I haven't told anyone else what I've told you here in this letter. I probably wouldn't *tell* you if you were here, too tough to say, but it's more abstract to write it. Thanks for listening, my friend. Maybe some of it can go in the book.

Two good things happened in July. A lawyer friend of mine, Gene Porter, has arranged for me to get those homophoresis treatments: I figure maybe I'll get lucky, hit that hundred-to-one shot. Also, Mike Stuhff has work I can do for him. I'll be able to earn some much needed money.

Geesus, I wish I'd hear from Carter Camp. I know he's working on my problem.

8-16-91

Dear Bill and Judy,

First, I'll give you an ALS update. (Kinda like Walter Cronkite, huh?)

I've noticed I have much less energy than ever before. It takes me forever to accomplish the simplest of tasks. That is all tasks requiring the most basic motor neuron skills, including and maybe mostly speech. I miss my former ability to carry on a conversation without having to think what I want to say, then modifying the words that are harder to pronounce. I then try in a halting hairlip fashion to articulate the thought. Hardly makes for lightning quick retorts. The word "huh" has taken on the connotation of motherfucker to me. I hate to have the person I'm trying to communicate with get that puzzled look on their face and say, "Huh?" It means I have to begin the process all over. Fucking drag! But it beats no speech at all, which I'm sure is in my near future.

Yesterday, Mike Stuhff and I walked the three block distance from the office to the jail to interview a new client. During the grueling three-block walk, it occurred to me that I might not make it. Pretty scary shit. Same thing, slightly worse, on the way back. Bill, I've walked fifty miles overnight while I was in the infantry that didn't require the effort I expended in that three-block hike yesterday. I'm sure Stuhff noticed, but to his credit he said nothing. I'm very thankful that I made it both ways.

Swallowing is becoming more difficult than before, and

choking more frequent and more violent. Kinda scary when for a couple of minutes you can't draw a breath.

Throughout the remaining course this fucking disease has to run before it kills me, I want only one boon. I want to maintain my dignity. If I get that wish, I'm sure it will be more bearable for me. I'm sure as hell gonna try.

10-16-91

Dear Bill and Judy,

A week ago Monday I went to the hospital here in Vegas and the surgeon put a catheter in my chest. He had some trouble and had to try three times before he got it right. Talk about painful! They push a wire through the muscle in your chest. This wire has a tube attached. Through the muscle, rib cage, and over the collarbone into the large vein leading to the heart. The tube stays in for the course of the treatments which are twice a week for four weeks. So I have two tubes hanging from the left side of my chest about 6″ in length. On the ends are fittings that attach to the machine they hook me up to on Tuesdays and Thursdays. They then remove, a little at a time, all the blood in my body, take the plasma out with a centrifuge, replace the plasma with an albumen solution, and put the blood back in me. The whole process takes about 2–2½ hours and then I go home. So far it seems to have improved my speech some, but little else. Still weak as hell and walking is more and more difficult. As is writing, which I suppose you can tell.

11-16-91

Dear Bill and Judy,

I guess I'm aware from the difficulty I'm having controlling the pen that it won't be too much longer that I'll have the ability to write. So in my usual fashion I'm trying to get it all out before that happens.

Speaking of nearing the end which I guess I was doing, I have some thoughts along that line that I would like to share with you guys. These are a few small thoughts that I've told to no one else and I justify burdening you with them in the name of the biography I'm sure you will write when the time is right. Maybe like van Gogh, some of the things I've been so very involved in will become marketable after the fact, so to speak. I know you'll do it and I'm *eternally* grateful for that. Like you said, no matter what exists after this go-round, I'll be aware of your writing about me and I'll be pleased that you are the only one to do it. Let me thank you in front. Thanks a lot, old pal! But back to the thoughts I'd share for the good of the biography (and my soul, or whatever).

In retrospect, I have some difficulty with my list of things I wish I would have done. I also have difficulty with the list of things I would have done differently if I could do it all over.

Bill, I think you know me better than any living person (or dead person, too). We really got close over the years, I feel. Not that you and I always saw things the same way, but we both saw things way past the bullshit that fools a lot of people. And I'm always grateful to you for providing me the only legacy that I have to pass on, and that's *The Court-martial of Clayton Lonetree, Loud and Clear,* and *Contract Killer.* Without you in my life, these books would never have existed and I'm deeply grateful for that, too.

I have had the rare privilege of being able to do most everything I wanted to do for most of my adult life. That's why I was able to become involved in some of the great cases in the last three decades. The formula is very simple: "work for nothing; try to be a bit bold and innovative." I was willing to work for zip in a lot of them, the cause or proposition made it seem worthwhile, and I tried to be somewhat bold in my conception of what had to be accomplished and usually innovation was the only thing that could work. Not that it always did, but sometimes I got lucky.

Then, too, there were things that just happened. Like the bumper sticker: "shit happens." I was often blessed with being in

the right place, at the right time—case in point, at Wounded
Knee and the citizen's arrest of those two FBI pigs. I consider
that event one of the highest achievements of my life. Maybe
because that one act demonstrated in a highly visible manner
that I was OK, I could be trusted, I was *no rat,* a fact that's hard
to prove in my business. Also it seemed to me a politically correct
move and one of the small incidents that I'm extremely proud of.
I know for sure the FBI (the true enemy) didn't care much for it
and still to this day doesn't. And, of course, anything the FBI
doesn't like, I'm 100% or more in favor of. I guess that about
sums up my feelings about Hoover's Hoodlums. It runs a little
deeper than that, and I'm sure you're aware of my deep rooted
belief that the FBI is organized crime's sixth family and that
there wasn't a whit of difference between J. Edgar and Fat Tony
[Salerno].

But to return to what I would do differently if given the
opportunity. I think I could have been more effective in the civil
rights arena if I would have come up with a way of financing
my activities independent of clients who were almost always
broke and/or lawyers who are always cheap! If I had met you
sooner, maybe that would have solved the problem. I'm sure
I've told you before, one of the things I wanted to do and could
have, given the money was in my pocket, was just show up at
any major case, where I would surely know at least one attorney, and say, "I'm here, I'll work for nothing. I'll pay my own
expenses. What do you want me to do?" I know that would
have worked. Too late now, but it sure would have let me in on
the major cases of the last two or three decades. And with your
help and guidance, a great series of books would have ema-
nated from those cases.

I guess there was something amusing about my hoping that
I had blood cancer. Regardless. I don't. It's ALS, like the odds
said it would be.

An interesting development has arisen in the Bolles case.
The prosecutors, who once again will try to convict Robison

and Dunlap, are demanding that I turn over taped interviews I made more than ten years ago with Robison. These tapes, of course, are privileged, but evidently that doesn't impress the Arizona authorities.

What bothers (amuses?) me is that I thought I had a certain stand-up reputation, but these prosecutors don't believe it. They say if I *don't* turn over the tapes, I could be sent to jail.

That's a threat? I hope they come and get me. What a deal that would be: guy with ALS thrown in the slammer because he won't break the law and "rat" on his friend. I put "rat" in quotation marks because all those tapes contain are Robison's truthful claims of innocence.

12-31-91

Dear Bill and Judy,

Maybe 1992 will be better. I'm making necessary arrangements through my Indian brother, Carter Camp, to take me to the most famous Medicine Man in the country. Wallace Black Elk, who says in his book, *Black Elk,* that he can cure *any* disease. I'm gonna give him a real challenge. Wallace is the grandson of Black Elk, the great Sioux leader and Medicine Man of *Black Elk Speaks* fame. I have more faith in Black Elk than I do in the AMA.

2-10-92

Dear Bill and Judy,

I wish you were here, too, my friend, while I can still speak, and walk a little. I'm not sure how long I'll be able to do either. Seems like I'm going down hill at an accelerated rate now. I fell down in my kitchen yesterday and couldn't get up. I had to crawl to a chair and pull myself up. Not a good sign. The loss of the ability to communicate is the hardest for me to reconcile. But I didn't get a choice. I have to play the hand I got dealt. But I don't have a bitch coming in this lifetime.

I still haven't heard any more from Black Elk, but I will. And if it works, I'll be ecstatic.

2-13-92

Dear Bill and Judy,

Just a short note to say you can see from my enclosure that the State of Arizona is not through with me in connection with the Bolles case. Now it's up to Arizona to go to Nevada District Court and ask Nevada to order me to give the deposition. That's where the fight will be staged. We will go to the press, too, capitalizing on my attorney/client privilege, my debilitating illness and anything else that comes our way. I think we can win, but at least we can demonstrate the lengths the Arizona Attorney General's Office will go to further this vendetta.

I'd rather not go to jail but that could happen. It would be hard to find a better cause than this for my swan song.

Hallelujah! Bill Hoffman tells me that we may have found a publisher for *Contract Killer*. I would love to live long enough to hold the book in my hands.

3-4-92

Dear Bill and Judy,

Today I got a call from Neil Ortenberg, the publisher of Thunder's Mouth Press. He was very nice. He said that he was going to speak to you tomorrow and that he was almost 100% sure that they were going to publish our book. He also said, "It's a wonderful book." He said he would get my address from you and send me some things; he didn't say what, but I have an idea he meant contracts. He asked me to send him my resumé and I said I would. He told me that everyone he'd asked about me had wonderful things to say about me. I guess he means Freed and Kunstler, maybe Mark Lane. That, maybe, is bullshit 101, but he sounded sincere. Nice guy. I told him I was sorry about my speech and he said, "That's OK. Bill told me about your problem." He clearly likes the book and you. We spoke, or rather he spoke and I listened and tried to grunt at the appropriate times, for about ten minutes.

Ortenberg said tomorrow is the day that you will call him at 2 p.m. All my appendages are now crossed and will remain crossed till I hear from you. We're off and running!

3-28-92

Dear Bill and Judy,

I received the contracts by Fed-Ex exactly as you predicted. Mike Stuhff has been in New Mexico with a Navajo case. He returns to Las Vegas tonight and I'll show him the contract tomorrow.

I haven't written much lately due to the fact that I've been having respiratory problems. They (the doctors) tell me it's due to the respiratory muscles weakening from ALS. It figures, all my muscles are really weakening. Walking is very difficult and very tiring. You know about my speech, which is worsening. The only advantage to ALS is that it's painless, at least physically painless. Mentally, not so painless. I seem to be required daily to adjust to something I can no longer do. But adjust I do, at least so far.

I hope you get something going soon with Thunder's Mouth regarding *Vegas P.I.* so that I will be able to work on this book with you, one more time. The SLA, too.

By the time you get this letter Mike Stuhff will have read the contract and you can call him, collect, and ask him what you want. My love to you and your family.

4-3-92

Dear Bill and Judy,

You asked me to update my condition. I hate to do that. No, I really don't hate to do it, but it's just a little depressing for both of us. I did have the doctors fooled this past week or so.

I developed a whole bunch of fluid in my lungs causing three of my doctors to tell Lake III and Terri Lee that this was the final stage of ALS and to be aware that the end was near. One of my doctors, however, called in a prescription for some high powered antibiotics that cost $3.50 *a pill.* But they seem to have cleared out my lungs, clearly demonstrating how little the medical profession knows about ALS. But I feel better now, so I'll try to give you the update.

It'll give you an idea of my condition when I tell you my weight. I now weigh 152 pounds with all my clothes and shoes on. And that reflects how weak I am. I always wanted to be thin, but ALS only attacks muscle tissue so I still have the fat but the muscle is going. You know about my speech. Walking is equally difficult and very tiring. Plus my balance is going to hell, and if I fall down my legs are too weak for me to get up alone. That's happened on a couple of occasions. Kinda scary, but someone came to my assistance right away. I expect a wheelchair is the answer, but so far I've avoided that solution. Now it doesn't seem so radical.

I went to the hospital when my lungs filled up again. I stayed two nights and three days in a semiprivate room, and nothing out of the ordinary was done. Except the bill: it was *$34,000.*

The only good thing about dying is knowing all the doctors and hospitals I'm going to stiff.

I hear from Carter Camp that Black Elk is still in Europe. Geesus, I wish he'd get back.

4-29-92

Dear Bill and Judy,

Terri Lee was supposed to come here today but her baby is sick so she'll come tomorrow. But if she can't come then I'll ask Lake III to drop this letter at the post office. Too many steps for me at the post office. I don't do well with steps, up or down.

And since I've had four falls, two in public places and two in my drive, no broken bones but bruises and very embarrassing, I've become more cautious. The hard part is getting up. I can't do that alone. And I dread strangers helping me to my feet. I'm sure that with my speech and falling down, people are sure that I'm drunk. I wish that was it. I could get over that.

I just saw on TV where the four cops charged with the beating of Rodney King have all been found not guilty despite that highly graphic TV film. Now it's really time to take it to the streets. The best excuse the cops could offer was, "We thought he was on drugs." This is the worst example of our system of justice I've ever seen and it gives LAPD the right to whale on anybody they want to hurt. Since I've been one of those they've wanted to hurt for a long time, I feel strongly about this case. I'm saying the black people should burn something, not Watts but Beverly Hills.

p.s. (Thursday a.m.). Well, I called that. I heard that 9 people were killed and 200 injured. L.A. is in flames. Good for them. Bush is baffled as to what to have Justice do with this.

5-13-92*

Dear Bill and Judy,

I think I'll be able to attend the American Booksellers Association convention in Anaheim the end of this month. Mike Stuhff has agreed to drive me and Lake III. We'd like to stay in the same hotel you and Judy will be in.

I'm really looking forward to this, to seeing *Contract Killer* on display and meeting Neil Ortenberg.

I love you,

Lake

---

*Lake died in the early morning hours of May 15. Lake III, hearing the TV running, rose from bed and found his dad sitting peacefully in his favorite easy chair.

AFTERWORD:
THE GOOD LIVES ON

"The evil men do lives after them," said Mark Antony during his funeral oration for Caesar. "The good is oft interred with their bones."

Shakespeare's words do not apply to Lake. Not only did the good he accomplished live on in the minds of his friends and those he helped, but his work continues to accomplish positive ends.

Lake spent a good portion of his life teaching young Navajos how to protect their rights. Now, each time one of these Native Americans succeeds in foiling the plans of his historic oppressor, the presence of Lake can be sensed in the background. I can almost see him smile.

Lake's prodigious efforts on the Hoffa murder have already produced significant results. The FBI, keeping its investigation not only from the people but from Hoffa's children, has already had to make serious admissions: (1) before Lake, all the feds would say was that Tony Provenzano, a key figure in the union leader's murder, had alibi witnesses that placed him in New Jersey at the time—now the feds admit that, as Lake said, Provenzano was in Detroit on the day of the killing; and (2) now the FBI concedes (it never did before) that the hit on

Hoffa was contracted by Fat Tony Salerno, as Frankos and Lake claimed. The Hoffa murder, thanks to Lake, may soon be solved.

Finally, as this is being written, Jim Robison and Max Dunlap (framed for the Bolles murder) are scheduled to be retried in a few weeks. Thanks to Lake's nonpareil investigation in the 1970s, these men should be acquitted.

If it happens, and it should, I know how Lake would have reacted. He would have laughed out loud and then gone looking for someone else to help.

INDEX